PIMLICO

691

BOLIVIAN DIARY

Ernesto Guevara de la Serna was born in Rosario, Argentina, on 14 June 1928. As a medical student in Buenos Aires and doctor he travelled throughout Latin America. Whilst in Guatemala during 1954 he witnessed the overthrow of the elected government of Jacobo Arbenz in a US-backed operation.

Forced to leave Guatemala, Guevara went to Mexico where he linked up with exiled Cuban revolutionaries seeking to overthrow dictator Fulgencio Batista. In July 1955 he met Fidel Castro, and in November 1956 Guevara was part of the expedition that set out for Cuba to begin the armed struggle in the Sierra Maestra mountains. Originally the troop doctor, he became a Rebel Army *comandante* in July 1957. In December 1958 he led the Rebel Army forces to victory in the battle of Santa Clara, one of the decisive battles of the war.

Following the rebels' victory on 1 January 1959, Guevara served as minister for industry, as the governor of the National Bank of Cuba, and as a roving ambassador to other socialist nations and to the non-aligned movement.

In April 1965 Guevara left Cuba and spent several months in the Congo, returning to Cuba secretly in 1966. In November 1966 he arrived in Bolivia where he established a guerrilla force fighting that country's military dictatorship. Following several months of skirmishes with the Bolivian Army, he was captured on 8 October 1967 and executed the following day.

Lucía Álvarez de Toledo grew up and was educated in Argentina, and was awarded a scholarship at the University of Delhi, where she read philosophy. Having worked as a journalist and broadcaster in her native Argentina, she settled in London in 1968 and established herself as a professional interpreter and translator. Her background, knowledge of Latin America and long-standing interest in the life and works of Ernesto Che Guevara have enabled her to bring a unique understanding to this new edition of the *Bolivian Diary*.

BOLIVIAN DIARY

———

ERNESTO CHE GUEVARA

Translated, introduced and edited by
Lucía Álvarez de Toledo

PIMLICO

Published by Pimlico 2004

2 4 6 8 10 9 7 5 3

First published in Spanish as *Diario del Che en Bolivia* in 1968
Copyright © The Estate of Ernesto Che Guevara 1968, 2000, 2004

Translation, Introduction, Biographical Notes and Chronology
copyright © Lucía Álvarez de Toledo 2004

Lucía Álvarez de Toledo has asserted her right under the Copyright, Designs
and Patents Act 1988 to be identified as the author of this work

First published in Great Britain by Pimlico 2004

Pimlico
Random House, 20 Vauxhall Bridge Road,
London SW1V 2SA

Random House Australia (Pty) Limited
20 Alfred Street, Milsons Point, Sydney,
New South Wales 2061, Australia

Random House New Zealand Limited
18 Poland Road, Glenfield,
Auckland 10, New Zealand

Random House South Africa (Pty) Limited
Endulini, 5A Jubilee Road, Parktown 2193, South Africa

Random House UK Limited Reg. No. 954009
www.randomhouse.co.uk

A CIP catalogue record for this book is available from the British Library

ISBN 1-8441-3829-1

Papers used by Random House UK are natural, recyclable products made from wood
grown in sustainable forests; the manufacturing processes conform
to the environmental regulations of the country of origin

Typeset by SX Composing DTP, Rayleigh, Essex
Printed and bound in Great Britain by
Bookmarque Ltd, Croydon, Surrey

Contents

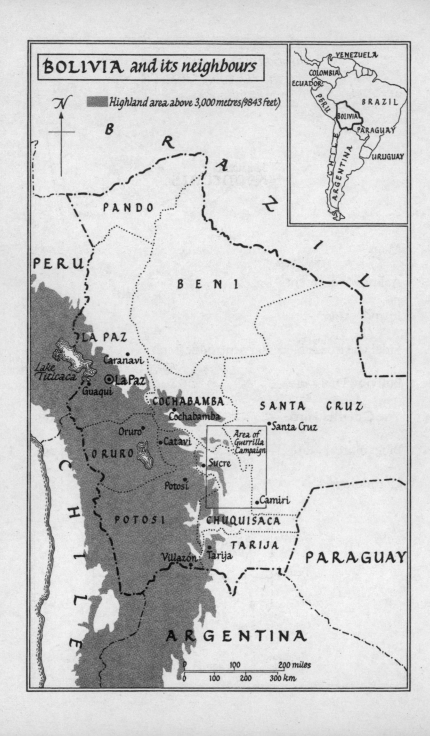

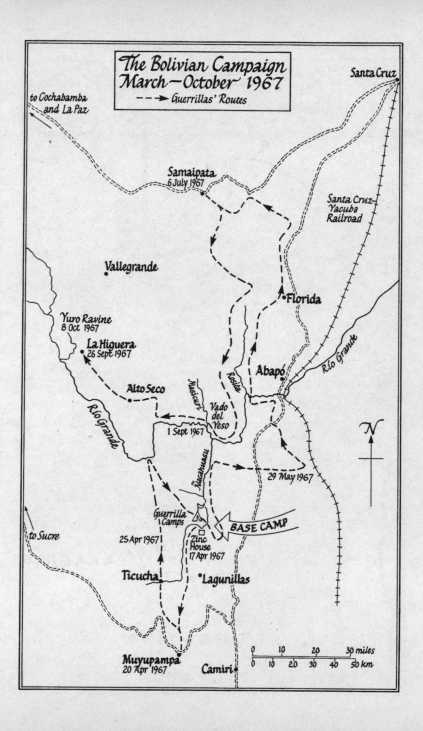

The Bolivian Campaign
March–October 1967

- - - → Guerrillas' Routes

to Cochabamba
and La Paz

Santa Cruz

Samaipata
6 July 1967

Santa Cruz-
Yacuba
Railroad

Vallegrande

Florida

Yuro Ravine
8 Oct 1967

La Higuera
26 Sept 1967

Abapó

Río Grande

Alto Seco

Masicurí

Rosita

Río Grande

Vado
del
Yeso

1 Sept 1967

Ñacahuasú

29 May 1967

N

Guerrilla
Camps

BASE CAMP

to Sucre

25 Apr 1967

Zinc
House
17 Apr 1967

Ticucha

Lagunillas

Muyupampa
20 Apr 1967

Camiri

0   10   20   30 miles
0   10   20   30   40   50 km

Acknowledgements

I wish to thank Stacy Marking and Matthew Reisz for their invaluable editorial advice, and I am grateful to Adys Cupull and Froilán González for their research in Cuba.

The translation of the quote from Pablo Neruda's 'Un Canto Para Simón Bolívar' on p. 91 is taken from Pablo Neruda, *Residence on Earth and Other Poems*, translated by Donald Walsh (New York: New Directions, 2004).

Lucía Álvarez de Toledo

Introduction

How did Che Guevara, a talented, upper-class Argentine, end up in the jungle pursued by the CIA, the US Rangers and the national Army of Bolivia? How did he finish dead on the mud floor of a hut in the remote village of La Higuera?

Che's last campaign was very much of a piece with the rest of his career. He died for the beliefs to which he had devoted his life, so to put the *Bolivian Diary* in context it is illuminating to go back to the very beginning to see how he got there.

He was born Ernesto Guevara de la Serna in the port city of Rosario, Santa Fe, in 1928. He was of Spanish and Irish descent on his father's side – both his paternal grandparents had been born in California – and of pure Spanish descent on his mother's. Both parents were passionate about justice, detested fascism, had discarded their religious upbringing and loved poetry. They were suspicious of money and wary of most methods for obtaining it. In their own way, they were rebels. Many of the attitudes Ernesto exhibited throughout his life – notably his high spirits, self-deprecation and quick, ironical wit – he had learnt from them.

Early on he developed asthma – an affliction that never left him and which many see as a formative influence. (The story goes that the first word he learnt was 'injection'.) As a result, he always experienced other setbacks as challenges.

Years later, in conversation with the Uruguayan writer Eduardo Galeano, his mother would say: 'My son spent his whole life trying to prove to himself that he could do all the things that he could not do.'

Another formative experience was the Spanish Civil War. While conflict raged in Europe, Ernesto's parents became founder members of a committee to help the Republican refugees who arrived in Argentina. The wives and children of combatants arrived first and, when the Republic fell, any men who could escape the Franco regime. Ernesto followed the plight of the Republican Army and later the battles of the Second World War on a map pinned to his bedroom wall.

He soon began to believe in the need for armed struggle. When his friend Alberto Granado was imprisoned for being a member of the Communist Youth Movement, he was asked to mobilise secondary school students in support. Guevara replied that he would not join a march just to be chased by armed police: 'I will only go if I am given a revolver.'

He became a young man in a hurry because of his awareness of how close death could always be. He never allowed his asthma to prevent him from practising sports with his friends and cousins, but when an attack came he would take advantage of the enforced rest to read voraciously. His father had an eclectic library and his mother had taught him French as well as the school syllabus when he was unable to attend classes, so by the end of his teens he had already read works by Marx, Freud, Neruda, Baudelaire, Goethe, Jack London and Robert Louis Stevenson. His father's abridged copy of *Das Kapital* was found to include notes in the margin in Ernesto's tiny handwriting.

As an adult, he was often in danger of suffocation from his asthma and this coloured his whole attitude to life and death. Like the German poet Rainer Maria Rilke, he learnt to think of death as just the dark side of life. Years later, at the end of hostilities in Cuba, Fidel Castro was to remark about his two best men that if Camilo Cienfuegos was courageous, Che was totally fearless and flung himself into danger oblivious of the possibility of death.

During the school holidays of 1950 Ernesto installed a small motor on his bicycle and went on a tour of the northern provinces of Argentina. He travelled more than 4,500 kilometers on his own. In 1951 he enrolled as a male nurse with the Argentine merchant fleet and went on two trips from the southern port of Comodoro Rivadavia to Brazil, Venezuela and Trinidad-Tobago. So he had already seen some of the misery of life in Latin America that was to have such a lasting impact on him. Yet it was the long motorcycle journey he undertook with his friend Granado at the age of twenty-three which truly radicalised him and gave him a sense of being a man of the whole continent.

They left their homes in Córdoba and Buenos Aires, travelled south and crossed over into Chile, where they were forced to abandon their battered motorcycle. Guevara did not mind losing their means of transport; on the contrary, he thought they would see more by having to travel like the local population of an impoverished continent, where the differences between haves and have-nots were (and remain) enormous. From Chile they travelled north to Peru, Colombia and Venezuela. It was during this trip that Guevara studied José Carlos Mariátegui, the first Peruvian writer to blend nationalist and indigenous thought with international Marxism. He also read the poet Pablo Neruda and saw at close quarters the poverty and deprivation that Neruda denounced in his writings. His predilection for Neruda was to last his whole life.

In *The Motorcycle Diaries*, which Che wrote during this trip, he said he was no longer the same man who had left his home in Argentina several months earlier. He now felt he knew what was wrong with his continent. He found it impossible to accept that, by mere accident of birth, a small minority of privileged people should own the soil and means of production while the rest were trespassers in the land where they had been born. In the case of the aboriginal populations this was compounded by the fact that they had been dispossessed twice: first by the Spanish *conquistadores* and then by the *criollos*, the white elite born in Latin American of European ancestry. It was also during this trip that Che made his own the dream of Simón Bolívar: to create a United States of Latin America all the way from the Río Grande to Tierra del Fuego, free from colonialism and offering equality of opportunity to all.

After a brief stay in Miami waiting for a lift home on a plane which carried polo ponies from Argentina to the USA, Guevara returned to Buenos Aires to finish his medical studies, although he had already decided that it was pointless to be a doctor and that it was the *causes* of the poverty and dispossession of the native population that had to be addressed. Soon after he graduated, he left again.

It was 1953. In Bolivia, the year before, a force composed of miners and peasants under the leadership of the Movimiento Nacionalista Revolucionario defeated the professional army. Now the country was in ferment because there had been fundamental reforms: the tin mines, the largest in the world, had been nationalised and the land given back to the peasants. (They had owned it collectively before the arrival of the Spanish *conquistadores* and again briefly after Simón Bolívar had liberated them from the Spanish in the nineteenth century, only to lose it when a Bolivian dictator made it the property of the state.)

Once he had seen what was happening for himself, however, Guevara came to believe that the Bolivian revolution was no such thing. The underpaid miners may have received compensation when the mines were nationalised, but they had promptly spent it on essential food and clothing. Nationalisation, in Che's view, only meant a change in ownership – it did little for the miners materially and nothing at all for them morally. And Bolivia continued to be governed by strongmen who came to power through *coups d'état*. Much of this is probably true. Yet the land reforms, however limited and inadequate, did give poor peasants some sort of stake in the status quo. Perhaps this explains why, unlike their Cuban counterparts, they were notably reluctant to flock to Che's revolutionary banner in 1966.

After Bolivia Che travelled north to Guatemala, where there was a government intent on agrarian reform and a president not prepared to yield to American interests. Guevara could only work at odd jobs, met exiled Cuban revolutionaries, read Marx and sought to participate in the advancement of the Guatemalan revolution. (It was at this early stage that the CIA noticed him and opened a file to record his movements.) President Jacobo Arbenz nationalised some of the disused land of the US-owned United Fruit Company; in response, a force backed by the CIA invaded Guatemala City. Yet Arbenz refused to arm the population, resigned and went into exile. Some of his supporters were massacred. Guevara was forced to take refuge in the Argentine Embassy and eventually left for Mexico. Years later, in Cuba, he was to thank Arbenz for teaching him what *not* to do in a revolutionary situation.

It was now 1955 and Guevara was looking for a movement with which to join forces so he could channel his energies towards the liberation of his America. It was then that he met Fidel Castro, who had arrived in Mexico to organise his armed expedition to liberate Cuba from the CIA-backed dictator Fulgencio Batista. Che was only the third man to sign up after Fidel and his brother Raúl.

Cuba had been the jewel in the Spanish crown – its favourite Latin American colony, the one they were not prepared to let go. And the USA had also attempted to dominate Cuba in the nineteenth century. Consequently, the island had produced several exemplary figures who had fought for its independence: José Martí, the poet-soldier, who gave his life to the cause at the battle of Dos Ríos in 1895; Antonio Maceo and Máximo Gómez, generals who led heroic campaigns against both foreign powers. So the Cuban people already had a tradition of fighting for their country when Fidel Castro and his comrades landed at Las Coloradas in 1956. Perhaps it is partly because of this that a revolutionary uprising succeeded there but failed in Bolivia (and elsewhere).

Ernesto Guevara, nicknamed 'Che' (a colloquial term for Argentine) by his Cuban comrades, joined the expedition to liberate Cuba as its doctor. Initially he was not expected to fight, but circumstances soon changed that. Castro's group landed far from their intended destination and were immediately dispersed. The dictator's modern airforce bombed them mercilessly. Later, Che would describe the crucial moment when he became a soldier: 'On one side I had a rucksack full of medicines, and on the other, an ammunition box. I couldn't carry both, they were too heavy. I took the ammunition. In doing so I made a clear choice.' He would soon demonstrate his capacity to lead men and fight a guerrilla war. Castro made him a *comandante* and gave him his own column, the *Columna Cuatro*, so called to disguise the fact that there were only two. He became a legend through his victory in the decisive battle for Santa Clara that prompted Batista to depart hastily for Miami.

After the triumph of the revolution, Che served as minister for industry, as the governor of the National Bank of Cuba, and as a roving ambassador to other socialist nations and to the non-aligned movement. In 1960 he published *Guerrilla Warfare*, a manual which became a textbook for guerrillas throughout the world and which may well have proved useful to the Rangers who pursued him through the Bolivian jungle.

But the life of a theorist, politician and bureaucrat was never going to be enough for him. He wanted to put his ideas into practice by direct revolutionary action. He wanted to lead rather than expect others to precede him in the fight for the causes he believed in. So he left office and family, gave up his adopted nationality, and went to the Congo.

The Congo had won its independence from Belgium and in 1960 Patrice Lumumba, a left-wing leader, became the country's first prime minister. The Belgians sabotaged the budding nation by engineering the secession of Katanga province. Lumumba asked the Soviet Union for assistance and was promptly assassinated by the CIA. A civil war followed. White mercenaries arrived on the scene. The CIA persuaded exiled Cubans, some veterans of the failed invasion at the Bay of Pigs, to join the struggle in the Congo. Guevara retaliated by going on a tour of African nations to seek support for the Congolese struggle. He then returned to Cuba and trained with a group of men – most of Afro-Cuban origin – so they could go to Africa and fight.

In the event, it proved too late to help the disunited rebel forces which were not psychologically prepared for action. Guevara himself regarded his campaign in the Congo as a disaster. In his preface to the published diary, *The African Dream*, he says:

This is the history of a failure . . . any importance the story might have lies in the fact that it allows the experiences to be extracted for the use of other revolutionary movements. Victory is a great source of positive experiences, but so is defeat, especially if the unusual circumstances surrounding the incident are taken into account: the actors and informants are foreigners who went to risk their lives in an unknown land where people spoke a different language and were linked to them only by ties of proletarian international-ism, so that a method not practised in modern wars of liberation was thereby inaugurated.

When it became clear that his African hosts were not ready

for armed struggle, Che returned secretly to Cuba and trained with a select group of men – many of them veterans of both his renowned *Columna Cuatro* in Cuba and of the Congo campaign – to go to Bolivia in disguise to lead an insurgency against the military government of René Barrientos, another US-approved strongman. Bolivia had the strategic advantage of having boundaries with five countries – Argentina, Chile, Peru, Brazil and Paraguay – that had their own revolutionary movements which seemed ready to join forces with the guerrillas.

Long before the triumph of the Cuban Revolution, Castro had promised Guevara that he would assist him in taking the revolution to the whole continent. In 1962, he had issued the Second Declaration of Havana which invited Latin Americans to overthrow their corrupt governments by means of armed uprising. This put Havana at the heart of the struggle against US imperialism and its client regimes. Now, in 1966, when Che wanted to give practical effect to these commitments, Castro provided the necessary financial and logistic backing for his guerrilla force and invited Bolivians to train alongside the Cuban veterans at installations in Pinar del Río.

Before leaving for Bolivia Che wrote his famous 'Message to the Tricontinental' which was to be read out in his absence at the conference in Havana a few months later. He asked for 'the creation of one, two, three Vietnams' in order to force the imperialists to fight on more than one front, thus helping the people of Vietnam achieve their liberation. He spoke of true proletarian internationalism and said that to die under the flag of any oppressed nation under whose skies one had not been born was an act that contributed to the liberation of one's own country. His closing words became both his legacy and his epitaph:

Our every action is a battle cry against imperialism, and a battle hymn for the people's unity against the great

enemy of mankind: the United States of America.
Wherever death may surprise us, let it be welcome,
provided that this, our battle cry, reaches a receptive
ear, that another hand picks up our weapons, and that
other men are ready to intone our funeral dirge with the
staccato sound of machine guns and new battle cries of
war and victory.

Che left for Bolivia disguised as an Uruguayan business-
man under the assumed name of Adolfo González Mena. His
characterisation was so perfect – thick glasses, a shaved head
and the little remaining hair dyed white, a prosthesis to
change the shape of his teeth – that his little daughter Aleida
did not recognise him when her mother took her to the
secret training camp to bid him farewell.

Eleven months later, Che's guerrilla force had been routed.
Only five of his men managed to escape the trap laid by the
Bolivian Army and their American 'advisers'. He himself
was wounded, captured and then killed. It is interesting to
consider some of the factors which led to the failure of the
campaign. This should also help fill in the background
events happening 'off stage' that Guevara was not in a
position to know about. Isolated in the jungle, he was
unaware that the US Rangers had arrived in large numbers
and were training the Bolivian Army in guerrilla warfare and
(even if the Army denied it) fighting alongside them.
    Che's isolation had several causes. As he describes in the
diary, the Bolivian Communist leader Mario Monje Molina
refused to honour his commitments to the guerrillas.
Although the individual men who had come to the camp
with Monje decided to join Guevara, the loss of a supportive
local mass movement was a severe blow. Nor did the recent
split in the Communist Party help matters. Despite
previous pledges of co-operation from the leaders of both
rival groups, Oscar Zamora washed his hands of Guevara

while Monje went even further and prevented men who had been training in Cuba from joining the guerrilla camp.

In April Che's group become permanently separated from the vanguard led by Joaquín when they attempted to reach Muyupampa and help the visiting French intellectual Régis Debray and the Argentine painter Ciro Bustos leave the area of guerrilla operations. Their capture meant that Debray was unable to establish a European support network and Bustos could not forge further links with organisations in Argentina and other neighbouring countries. They also gave away information about guerrilla aims and activities which proved useful to the authorities.

All this left Guevara further isolated, but the events also embarrassed the Bolivian government and helped harden its attitudes. As soon as Debray was put on trial in Camiri, a media circus descended on the town and the eyes of the world turned on Bolivia, its generals and its legal system – not least the eyes of General de Gaulle, president of France.

Hence the government were desperate to avoid the dangers of another public trial. Once Guevara had been taken prisoner – and despite the fact that there was no capital punishment in Bolivia – three leading generals, Barrientos, Ovando and Torres, met up and decided to execute him. Some claim they were acting on direct orders from Washington and that the exiled Cuban CIA agent Felix Rodríguez was present at La Higuera to ensure they were obeyed. General Onganía, the president of Argentina, should have protested to Bolivia about the treatment meted out to an Argentine national (Guevara had given up his Cuban citizenship); instead he sent the Pentagon a message saying that he was totally in agreement with their decision to liquidate Guevara.

I have always been fascinated by the story of Che Guevara. I remember vividly the stir it caused in Buenos Aires when the newspapers reporting on the Cuban Revolution started mentioning the Argentine doctor who had become a *comandante*. A young man with hardly any military training was leading his troops into one victory after another across the island of Cuba – not many years after he had been declared unfit for service by the Argentine Army.

Ernesto Guevara and I came from similar social backgrounds, and his family home was not far from mine in the Barrio Norte of Buenos Aires. Although he was ten years older than me, our lives were affected by the same political events; we frequented the same venues (I often watched the rugby team he played for in San Isidro), knew the same people and spoke the same language. Argentine Spanish is full of colloquialisms brought by the Italians who were invited to immigrate after the Second World War. Other expressions come from the Portuguese of our Brazilian neighbours of African origin and the Yiddish spoken by Jewish families arriving from Europe during and after the war. By incorporating all these trends into its lyrics, the tango also helped forge a language, *lunfardo*, that is only used and understood by those who grew up in Argentina.

Since most of the people who have written about Che or translated his works were not natives of Buenos Aires, they have often been unaware of these nuances. Yet this diary consists of notes he was writing to himself, as an *aide-mémoire* to form the basis of a later book, like *Guerrilla Warfare, Reminiscences of the Cuban Revolutionary War* and *The African Dream*. As with *The Motorcycle Diaries* and *Once Again on the Road* (both published by his estate after his death), the tone of the *Bolivian Diary* is notably confidential and informal – one sees the person rather than the public persona.

Che writes with an ironic humour typical of a *porteño* (a native of Buenos Aires) that translators have sometimes missed. On occasion he is almost light-hearted. An example is his reference to 'the cavalry' when he is describing the events of 30 July – all they had were a few horses and mules.

When he mentions what they have to eat, he uses
gastronomic terminology such as *'fricassee'* (for a chicken
stew prepared at an abandoned house on 14 May) or
describes a piece of meat stolen by one of the men on 14
September as a *'filete'*; on 19 March rice and beans become
'arroz congrí', a Cuban speciality. In his analysis of the
month of March, when some men remain behind at the
camp, he says he left them there (like dried beans) 'to soak'.
In describing the geography and terrain, Guevara obviously
uses the language spoken by his Bolivian comrades and
occasionally lapses into expressions picked up during his
years in Cuba. I have sought to preserve these qualities in
the text. It is not written in standard formal Spanish and
putting it into elegant English would be a betrayal.

Both Che's methods and his political ideals have always
been controversial and will no doubt remain so. Yet in
travelling around our continent I have often been struck by
his deep significance to many ordinary Latin Americans.

In Cuba some fifteen years ago, I was researching
Santería, a local religion which is an amalgam of
Catholicism and the Yoruba faith African slaves brought
with them. I was talking to an Afro-Cuban who was showing me the altar in his home. To my extreme amazement,
there, amidst the figures of Yemanyá, Ochún and Oxalá, was
Che Guevara. There was no dissuading this old black
peasant: Guevara, according to him, was black and Cuban,
and had joined the pantheon of Santería's gods because of his
sacrifices for his fellow men. Although he could not stand
adulation, this was the sort of accolade I suspect Che would
have relished: transcending the race, social class, background and nationality into which he was born.

I was equally struck by the words of a woman in La
Higuera, the village where the guerrillas were taken as
prisoners in 1967. I was following Che's route from
Ñacahuasu to Vallegrande and stood in the middle of the
dirt track that passes for a road outside the house of the

telegraphist mentioned in Guevara's diary. The woman came out of the house and walked towards me. She turned out to be the daughter of the telegraphist. When I mentioned I had come to see the place where Guevara had died, she said she had been there, aged nineteen, at the time. Then she cast a look around her and said: 'Look at us. Nothing has changed since then. *El Comandante* came too soon. We were ignorant and did not understand him. We abandoned him and he died because of us, when he had come to save us so that we could have a better life, and here we are, just as we were before he came or maybe even worse.'

Lucía Álvarez de Toledo

FIDEL CASTRO

A Necessary Introduction

It was Che's habit, during his time as a guerrilla, to record his daily notes with care in a personal diary. During long marches, over rugged and difficult terrain, in the middle of humid forests, whenever the lines of men, always bent under the weight of their rucksacks, ammunition and weapons, stopped for a moment's rest, or when the column received orders to halt and pitch camp at the end of an exhausting day, one could see Che – as he was affectionately nicknamed by the Cubans right from the beginning – take out a small notebook and, with his minute and almost illegible doctor's handwriting, jot down his notes.

What he was able to save from these notes he would later put to use when he wrote his magnificent historical narratives of the Cuban Revolution, invaluable for their revolutionary, educational and human content.

This time, thanks to that unwavering habit of jotting down the main events of the day, we have detailed, rigorously exact and priceless information about those final heroic months of his life in Bolivia.

He used these notes, which were never intended for publication, as a tool for the constant evaluation of events, situations and men. They were also an outlet through which he expressed his keenly observant and analytical spirit, often blended with an acute sense of humour. They are so soberly drafted that they form a coherent whole flowing from beginning to end.

We should bear in mind that they were written during extremely rare moments of rest, in the midst of a heroic and superhuman physical effort, while he was also fulfilling the exhausting duties of a leader of a guerrilla force, during its difficult initial stages. This struggle unfolded under incredibly hard physical conditions, and his writings reveal to us the sort of man he was, as well as his iron will.

In this diary, as he analysed in detail each day's events, he noted the mistakes, criticisms and recriminations that are inevitable during the development of a revolutionary guerrilla force.

Within a guerrilla force such criticism must be made continually. And it is especially true during the early stages, when the group consists of a small nucleus, facing extremely adverse physical conditions and an enemy force infinitely superior in number. The slightest negligence or the most insignificant error can have fatal consequences. The leader must make fierce demands of his men. At the same time, he needs to use each event or episode, no matter how insignificant it may seem, as a lesson to the combatants and future leaders of the new guerrilla force.

The process of training a guerrilla force makes constant calls on the conscience and honour of every man. Che knew how to touch the most sensitive fibres of his revolutionaries. For example, Marcos was repeatedly admonished by Che, but when he was warned that he could be dishonourably discharged from the guerrilla force, he replied: 'I would rather be shot!' Later he sacrificed his life heroically. This was true of all the men in whom Che had placed his trust, although he had to admonish them for one reason or another. In the course of the struggle each man reacted in a similar way. Che was a brotherly and compassionate leader, but he also knew how to be demanding and, at times, severe. But above all, he was most demanding and severe with himself. He enforced discipline by appealing to the moral conscience of his guerrilla fighters, but also by the tremendous strength of his personal example.

The diary also contains numerous references to Régis Debray, and reflects the great concern Che felt over the arrest and imprisonment of the revolutionary writer. Although he had entrusted Debray with a mission in Europe, in fact Che would have preferred him to stay with the guerrilla force. This is why Che seems uncomfortable and at times even mistrustful of Debray's behaviour.

Che had no way of knowing the odyssey Debray lived through at the hands of the forces of repression, nor of the firm and courageous attitude with which he faced his captors and torturers.

Che did, however, point out the enormous political significance of the trial, and on 3 October – six days before his death – in the midst of bitter and tense events, he wrote: 'An interview with Debray was broadcast, very brave when he was confronted by a student who had been an *agent provocateur*.' That was his last reference to the writer.

Because the diary repeatedly refers to the Cuban Revolution and its relationship with the guerrilla movement, some may interpret our decision to publish it as provocative; they may feel that publication may give the enemies of the Revolution – the Yankee imperialists and their allies, the Latin American oligarchs – an excuse to redouble their plans to blockade, isolate and attack Cuba.

Those who judge the facts should be reminded that Yankee imperialism has never needed an excuse for its misdeeds anywhere in the world. The United States' efforts to crush the Cuban Revolution began as soon as our country passed its first revolutionary law. It is a well-known fact that imperialism is the policeman of world reaction, the systematic promoter of counter-revolution, and the protector of the most backward and inhuman social structures that exist in the world to this day.

Support of a revolutionary movement may be used as an
excuse, but it will never be the real cause of Yankee aggression. To refuse support in order to avoid US provocation is a
ridiculous, ostrich-like policy that is totally alien to the
internationalist nature of the social revolutions of today. To
refuse our support to a revolutionary movement would not
only fail to avoid provoking the US; it would in effect be a
form of support for Yankee imperialism and its policy of
domination and desire to enslave the world.

Cuba is a small country, economically underdeveloped,
as are all the countries that were for centuries dominated
and exploited by colonialism and imperialism. Cuba is only
ninety miles from the coast of the United States and there is
even a Yankee naval base on its territory. We face numerous
obstacles on the road to socio-economic development. Our
country has survived grave dangers since the triumph of the
Revolution. But imperialism will never be able to defeat us
because our consistently revolutionary attitude will not be
swayed by such difficulties.

From a revolutionary point of view, there is no alternative: Che's Bolivian diary must be published. When it was
in René Barrientos's hands, he immediately gave copies to
the CIA, the Pentagon and the US government. Journalists
connected to the CIA were given access to the document in
Bolivia and made photocopies of it – albeit, for the moment,
promising not to publish it.

The Barrientos government and the top military leaders
have ample reasons not to publish the diary. Its pages reveal
the gross incompetence of their army, and the constant
series of defeats they suffered from a handful of determined
guerrillas, who, in a few weeks, seized from them in combat
nearly 200 weapons.

Moreover, Barrientos and his regime have only themselves to blame for the derision of Che's words, which will
last throughout history.

On the other hand, imperialism has its reasons as well:

Che and the extraordinary example he set resonate increasingly throughout the world. His ideas, his image and his name are banners in the struggle against the injustices suffered by the oppressed and the exploited. They arouse the passionate interest of students and intellectuals all over the world.

Even in the United States, progressive students – in ever increasing numbers – as well as the Black Movement have made Che's figure their own. In the most militant civil rights demonstrations, as well as in those against the aggression in Vietnam, Che's image has become a symbol of the struggle. Rarely, if at all, in history has a figure, a name, an example become a universal symbol so rapidly and with such passionate force. This is so because Che, in the most pure and selfless form, embodies the internationalist spirit that is typical of the world today, and will be even more so tomorrow.

Out of a continent oppressed in the past by colonial powers, still exploited and kept underdeveloped today by Yankee imperialism, Che's unique figure emerges to become the universal symbol for revolutionary struggle, even in the cities of the imperialist and colonialist powers themselves.

The Yankee imperialists are afraid of his powerful example and everything that may help to spread it. The diary is the vivid expression of an extraordinary personality. It is a lesson in guerrilla warfare, written in the heat and tension of each day. It is as flammable as gunpowder; real proof that Latin Americans are not powerless against mercenary armies, or in the face of those who enslave their people. That is the diary's intrinsic value, and that is why it has not been published to this day.

Pseudo-revolutionaries, opportunists and charlatans of every sort also have an interest in preventing this diary from being published. These so-called Marxists, Communists and other similar labels have not hesitated to dismiss Che as deluded, an adventurer or, more charitably, an idealist whose death is the swansong of revolutionary armed struggle in Latin America. 'If Che himself,' they exclaim, 'the greatest exponent of these ideas, and an experienced guerrilla fighter, died in the guerrilla struggle, and if his movement failed to liberate Bolivia, it only shows how mistaken he was!' How many of these miserable beings were relieved to hear of Che's death, and did not blush at the thought of their views coinciding with those of imperialism and the most reactionary oligarchs!

His death is their justification – and that of their treacherous leaders, who toyed with the idea of armed struggle, but whose actual purpose – as was seen later – was to destroy the guerrilla force, block revolutionary action, and impose their own despicable and ridiculous political deals, because they were incapable of behaving in any other way. His death is their justification for those who do not have the will to fight and will never take up arms on behalf of the people and their liberation. His death is their justification for those who have made a mockery of revolutionary ideas, draining them of any content or message until they become an opiate for the masses. Those are people who have turned the organisations for popular struggle into instruments of conciliation with domestic and foreign exploiters. They advocate policies that have nothing to do with the genuine interests of the exploited peoples of this continent.

Che envisaged death as a natural and probable part of the process. He deliberately stressed, especially in his final writings, that this eventuality should not slow down the inevitable march of revolution in Latin America. In his message to the Tricontinental, he reiterated that thought: 'Our every action is a battle cry against imperialism . . . Wherever death may surprise us, let it be welcome if our battle cry has reached even one receptive ear, if another hand reaches out to take up our arms . . .'

Che considered himself a soldier of the revolution and never concerned himself with whether he would survive it. Those who believe that the outcome of his struggle in Bolivia signals the failure of his ideas would use the same simplistic argument to deny the validity of the ideas and struggles of all the great revolutionary precursors and thinkers – even the founders of Marxism, who were themselves unable to complete their task, and who did not live to enjoy the fruits of their noble efforts.

In Cuba, the triumph of a revolutionary process that had begun a hundred years earlier could not be halted, in the long run, by Martí's or Maceo's death in combat, followed by Yankee intervention as the War of Independence was coming to an end, frustrating the immediate objectives of their struggle; nor by the death of such brilliant advocates of socialist revolution as Julio Antonio Mella, who was assassinated by the agents of imperialism. And nobody can call into question the just cause or the conduct of those patriots, or the validity of their ideals, which have always inspired Cuban revolutionaries.

From Che's diary you can see how real were the possibilities of success and what powerful catalysts the guerrillas were. At one point, as the signs of weakness and rapid deterioration of the Bolivian government became obvious, he wrote: 'the government is disintegrating rapidly. It is a pity we do not have 100 more men right now.'

From his experience in Cuba, Che knew how often our small guerrilla group had been on the verge of extermination. This could easily have happened, given the imponderables of war. But then, if such a thing had happened, would it give anyone the right to judge our line of conduct wrong, and to use our example to discourage revolution and to inculcate a sense of powerlessness in the people?

Revolutionary processes have often been preceded by adverse episodes! Did we not have the defeat at the Moncada

Barracks only six years prior to the triumph of the people's armed struggle?

For many between 26 July 1953 – the attack on the Moncada Barracks in Santiago de Cuba – and 2 December 1956 – the landing of the *Granma* – there seemed to be no possibility of success for the revolutionary struggle in Cuba against a modern, well-equipped army. The actions of a handful of fighters were perceived as the delusions of idealists and dreamers who were 'deeply mistaken'. The crushing dispersal and defeat of our inexperienced guerrilla force on 5 December 1956 was seen as a complete confirmation of such pessimism and foreboding. But just over two years later that guerrilla unit had regrouped and developed the strength and experience necessary to defeat the very same army.

There will always be a proliferation of excuses, whatever the time and circumstance, not to fight – and that would mean that we could never obtain freedom. Che did not outlive his ideas, but he knew that with the loss of his life they would spread even wider. His pseudo-revolutionary critics, with their political cowardice and eternal failure to act, will certainly outlive the evidence of their own stupidity. It is worth noting, as the diary shows us, that Mario Monje, one of those 'revolutionary' specimens who are becoming so frequent in Latin America, took advantage of his title of secretary of the Communist Party of Bolivia to dispute Che's right to the political and military leadership of the movement. And Monje had also announced his intention of giving up his position within the party. According to him, it was enough to have held the position, and that gave him the right to claim the leadership.

Mario Monje, needless to say, had no experience in guerrilla warfare, nor had he ever been in combat. But the fact that he considered himself a Communist should have rid him of crude and superficial patriotism, as had the true patriots who had fought for Bolivia's first independence. If this is their idea of the internationalist and anti-imperialist struggle on this continent, such 'Communist leaders' have not progressed as far as the aboriginal tribes who were vanquished by the European colonisers at the time of the conquest.

This was the behaviour of the leader of the Communist Party of a country called Bolivia, whose historical capital is called Sucre, in honour of its first liberators, who were both Venezuelan. Monje had the opportunity to count on the co-operation of the political, organisational and military talent of a true and revolutionary giant, whose cause was not circumscribed to the narrow, artificial and even unjust boundaries of Bolivia. However, Monje did nothing but make claims for the leadership in a shameful, ridiculous and unwarranted manner.

Because it does not have an outlet to the sea, Bolivia depends on international solidarity for its own liberation. More than any other country, it needs the revolutionary triumph of its neighbours in order to avoid an atrocious embargo. Because of his own personal prestige, his capacity and his experience, Che was the man who could have accelerated such a process.

Che had established relations with leaders and militants of the Bolivian Communist Party before the split within the party, and had won their promises of help for the revolutionary movement in South America. Some of those militants had worked with Che for many years on a variety of tasks, with the permission of the party. But with the split came a new situation, and many of those who had once worked together with Che ended up in confrontation.

Che did not conceive the struggle in Bolivia as one isolated event, but as part of a revolutionary liberation movement, which would soon extend to other countries of Latin America. His intention was to organise a movement free of sectarianism, to be embraced by anyone who wished to fight for the liberation of Bolivia and all the other peoples of Latin America, the victims of imperialism.

But during the initial preparations of a guerrilla base, Che depended on the co-operation of a group of brave and discreet men, who had remained in Monje's party after the split. It was out of deference to these men that Che invited Monje to be the first to visit his camp, although he felt no sympathy at all for him. Then he invited Moisés Guevara, a political leader of the miners who had left the party to join the organisation led by Oscar Zamora. Moisés Guevara left that group as well because of disagreements with Zamora. Zamora was another Monje, who promised to help Che in the organisation of the guerrilla struggle in Bolivia; but, when it was time for action Zamora backed away and like a coward folded his arms. After Che's death he became one of his most venomous, allegedly 'Marxist-Leninist', critics. Moisés Guevara joined Che without hesitation, as he had offered to do long before Che arrived in Bolivia. He gave Che his support, and heroically laid down his life for the revolutionary cause. So too did the group of Bolivian guerrillas who had remained within Monje's organisation until that moment. Under the leadership of Inti and Coco Peredo, who went on to prove brave and outstanding combatants, they broke away from Monje to back Che without hesitation.

But Monje, unhappy with the outcome, set out to sabotage the movement. While in La Paz, he intercepted the well-trained Communist militants who were about to join the guerrilla force. They were the kind of men who have all the necessary qualities to join the armed struggle, but whose progress is criminally frustrated by their incapable and manipulating leaders.

Che was never personally interested in posts, positions of authority or honours. But he was totally convinced that revolutionary guerrilla struggle – the fundamental form of action for the liberation of the peoples of Latin America, on the basis of the economic, political, and social situation of nearly all Latin American countries – meant that the

military and political leadership must be unified. He
believed that the struggle should be led from the guerrilla
base itself, and not from the comfortable urban premises of
bureaucrats. As a result, he was not prepared to yield to an
inexperienced chauvinist who was so empty-headed and
narrow-minded. He would not surrender the leadership of a
guerrilla force that, at a later stage of its development, would
take the struggle to the wider South American dimension.
Che believed that chauvinism must be challenged. He saw
it as a ridiculous and sterile reactionary sentiment that
could contaminate even the revolutionaries amongst the
different Latin American nations.

'And let us develop genuine proletarian internationalism,' he said in his message to the Tricontinental. 'Let
the flag under which we fight be the sacred cause of the
liberation of humanity, so that to die under the colours of
Vietnam, Venezuela, Guatemala, Laos, Guinea, Colombia,
Bolivia . . . to mention only the current scenes of armed
struggle – will be equally glorious and desirable for a Latin
American, an Asian, an African, and even a European. Every
drop of blood spilled in a land under whose flag one was not
born is experience gathered by the survivor to be applied
later in the struggle for liberation of one's own country. And
every people that liberates itself is a step in the battle for the
liberation of one's people.'

Che believed that his guerrilla force should be made up of
fighters from all over Latin America. He saw that the
struggle in Bolivia could be a training camp for revolutionaries who would serve their apprenticeship in combat.

To help him in this task he wanted with him, together
with the Bolivians, a small group of experienced guerrilla
fighters, nearly all of them his comrades in the Sierra
Maestra during the revolutionary struggle in Cuba. He knew
their capacity, their valour and their spirit of sacrifice. None
of those men hesitated to answer his call. None of them
abandoned him, and none of them surrendered.

In his Bolivian campaign, Che set an example with his proverbial tenacity, ability and stoicism. It can be said that, being fully aware of the importance of the mission he had undertaken, he showed at all times a spirit of responsibility beyond reproach. On those occasions when the guerrilla force made some mistake, or committed some act of carelessness, he was quick to notice and correct it, noting it in his diary.

So many incredibly adverse factors conspired against him. The separation from part of his guerrilla force – a group of valuable men, some sick, some convalescing – should have been for a few days only. But it lasted for several interminable months, when they lost contact because of the difficulties of the terrain, and Che made great efforts to find them. During this period he had unceasing attacks of asthma – he could normally keep it well under control with standard medicines, but in the absence of these, asthma became a terrible enemy. The supplies of medicine that he had laid in beforehand were captured by the enemy and it became a serious problem. Just then, at the end of August [1967], the guerrilla group with whom he had lost contact was liquidated, and events took a disastrous turn. But Che, with his iron will, overcame his physical difficulties and never allowed them to interfere with his capacity for action, or to affect his morale.

He had many contacts with Bolivian peasants, and their character – extremely distrustful and cautious – did not surprise him. He knew their mentality well, because he had met them on many previous occasions, and he knew it would be a long, arduous and patient task to win them over to his cause. He never doubted that, in the end, he would succeed.

If we look carefully into the sequence of events, it is clear that even in September, only weeks before his death, when the number of men on whom Che could count was very small, the guerrilla force still retained its capacity to develop. There were still a few Bolivian members, such as the brothers Inti and Coco Peredo, who were already beginning to show magnificent qualities of leadership.

The ambush at La Higuera – the only successful action by the Army against Che's group – resulted in a situation that even he could not overcome. During that action the Vanguard was killed and several men wounded, in broad daylight, as they were attempting to reach a peasant area with greater political development. This does not appear in the diary, but we know of it from the survivors. Of course it was dangerous to advance by daylight along the track that they had been on for several days. It brought them unavoidably into contact with many people from this new area. It was obvious that the Army would try to intercept them at some point. But Che, who was totally aware of this, decided to run the risk in order to help the Doctor, who was in very bad physical shape.*

The day before the ambush he wrote: 'We arrived at Pujío early, but there were people there who had spotted us the previous day, which means we are preceded by Radio Bemba [word of mouth] . . . Travelling with mules is now dangerous, but I am trying to make it as easy as possible for the Doctor as he is very weak.'

The following day he wrote: 'At 13.00 the Vanguard left to try and get to Jagüey, and to reach a decision about the mules and the Doctor, once they are there.'

So we can see that he was trying to find a solution for his sick comrade, so that they could abandon the road and take all the necessary precautions. But that same afternoon, before they could reach Jagüey, the Vanguard fell in the fatal ambush. Che's Main Force found themselves in an impossible situation.

Days later, encircled in the Yuro ravine, Che fought his last battle.

---

* Doctor Octavio de la Concepción de la Pedraja (Moro), the Cuban guerrilla who was the unit's surgeon as well as a combatant, and who was suffering from severe bouts of lumbago.

We are deeply moved by the achievements of this handful of revolutionaries. The struggle against the hostile nature of the environment in which they operated is itself an insuperable feat of heroism. History shows us that never before has such a small number of men set out on such a gigantic task. This group of men had trust in the immense revolutionary capacity of the peoples of Latin America, and faith that it could be awakened; they had confidence in themselves; and with utter determination they gave themselves to the task.

One day Che said to the guerrilla fighters in Bolivia: 'This type of struggle gives us the opportunity to become revolutionaries, but it also allows us to prove we are men. Those who are unable to reach either of these stages must say so and leave the struggle.'

Those who fought at his side until the end deserved those titles: they were both revolutionaries and men. They symbolise those who, even now, are being called by history to a truly arduous and difficult task: the revolutionary transformation of Latin America.

The enemy in our first war of independence was a decadent colonial power. Today's revolutionaries face the most powerful bastions of the imperialist camp, an enemy highly advanced economically and technically. That enemy not only organised and re-equipped the Army in Bolivia, which once (in 1952) the revolution had destroyed. But in the struggle against the guerrillas, it also provided immediate support with its own weapons and military advisors. Throughout our continent it offers military and technical support to all the forces of repression. When that is not enough, it intervenes directly with its own troops, as it did in Santo Domingo.*

To fight against such an enemy we need the type of

---

* In 1965 the US sent in 23,000 troops to Santo Domingo in support of dictator Leonidas Trujillo.

revolutionaries and men that Che described. To achieve
the liberation of the people of this continent, we need
revolutionaries and men prepared to do what Che's group
have done. We need men with the same readiness to die at
any time: with the same deep conviction of a just cause,
and the same unshakeable faith in the invincible strength
of the people. Only then can we confront a power like that
of the Yankee imperialists, whose military, technical and
economic resources make themselves felt throughout the
world.

The American people themselves are beginning to realise
that the monstrous political superstructure that governs
their country is no longer – and has not been for a long time –
the idyllic bourgeois republic that their founders established
almost 200 years ago. They themselves are increasingly
repelled by the moral barbarism of a system that is
irrational, alienating, dehumanised and brutal. With its
aggressive wars, its political crimes, its racial aberrations, its
mean-spirited hierarchies, the system makes more and more
victims among the American people. The American people
themselves are beginning to see the repugnant waste of
economic, scientific and human resources with its excessive
military apparatus, which is both reactionary and repres-
sive, in the midst of a world three-quarters of which is
underdeveloped and starving.

But only the revolutionary transformation of Latin
America would enable the people of the United States to
settle their own score with that imperialism, just as, by the
same token, the developing struggle of the North American
people against imperialist policies could turn them into a
decisive ally of the revolutionary movement of Latin
America.

This part of the hemisphere must undergo a profound
revolutionary transformation in order to put right the huge
difference and imbalance that have developed since the
beginning of the twentieth century between that powerful

nation (as its social dynamics took it towards imperial summits) – between that industrial nation – and this group of weak and stagnant countries, subject as we are to the yoke of feudal oligarchies and their reactionary armies, in the Balkanised rest of the American continent. In another 20 years the huge present economic, scientific and technical imbalances will have increased horrendously, imposed upon all the peoples of Latin America.

If we travel down that road we will become progressively poorer, weaker, more dependent and enslaved by that very imperialism. This sombre prospect applies equally to all the underdeveloped countries of Africa and Asia.

If even the industrialised and educated nations of Europe (with their Common Market and their scientific supranational institutions) are concerned at the possibility of lagging behind; if Europe fears the prospect of becoming an economic colony of Yankee imperialism, then what does the future have in store for the peoples of Latin America?

Confronted with this real and unquestionable situation, which decisively affects the destiny of our peoples, some liberal or bourgeois reformist, or charlatan pseudo-revolutionary, incapable of action, will try to give an answer that is not revolutionary. If he can take into account all the moral, material and human strengths of this part of the world and launch them forward, so that we can recover from our ever-growing economic and techno-scientific backwardness in an industrialised world to which we make our contributions, then he has earned the right to criticise Che. If he can suggest another formula, a magic road to take our continent forward, a different path from that conceived by Che; if he can sweep away oligarchies, despots, politicians (i.e. servants) to the Yankee monopolies (i.e. masters), and do it with the urgency that circumstances require, then he can raise his hand and challenge Che.

In actual fact, none of them has an honest answer. No one has offered a real hope to the almost 300 million human beings who represent the population of Latin America, and who will be 600 million within 25 years. They are for the most part grievously poor, and yet they have a right to material wealth, to culture and to civilisation. The most appropriate thing would be to remain silent before Che's sacrifice, as well as that of those who fell with him. They died defending their ideas with courage. The deeds of this fistful of men, inspired by the noble ideal of saving a continent, are indeed the highest proof of what will-power, heroism and true greatness can achieve.

Their example will inspire the consciences of the people of Latin America, and will preside over their struggle. Che's heroic cry will reach the receptive ears of the poor and the exploited, for whom he gave his life, and many people will take up arms and win liberation, at last.

Che wrote his last lines on 7 October. The following day at 13.00 hours, in a narrow ravine where he intended to spend the night and then break free, the guerrillas clashed with numerous enemy troops. The few men who were still part of the group that day fought with true heroism until nightfall, from individual positions at the other end of the ravine, and from its higher ridges. They fought heroically against the mass of soldiers who surrounded and attacked them. There were no survivors amongst those who fought closest to Che. Next to him was the Doctor, whose serious state of health has already been pointed out; and then the Peruvian guerrilla whose physical condition was also serious. Everything seems to indicate that, until he was wounded, Che did all he could to protect his comrades, as he tried to withdraw to a safer place. The Doctor was not killed during that clash, but several days later, at a point not far from the Yuro ravine. In that rocky and irregular terrain it was very difficult, and sometimes even impossible, for the guerrillas to see each other. Those who were defending the position at the other entrance to the ravine, a few hundred metres from Che – among them Inti Peredo – resisted the attack until nightfall. They succeeded in evading the enemy and went on to the location previously agreed as the meeting point.

We know that Che fought on while he was wounded, until the barrel of his M-2 rifle was destroyed by a bullet and it was rendered totally useless. The pistol he was carrying had no magazine. These terrible circumstances explain why they were able to capture him alive. The wounds of his legs prevented him from walking, but they were not fatal.

He was taken to the village of La Higuera, where he remained alive for another 24 hours. He refused to say a single word to his captors, and when a drunken officer tried to humiliate him, Che slapped him across the face.

Meeting in La Paz, Barrientos, Ovando and other high-ranking military officers decided in cold blood that Che should be assassinated. The details of the way in which they fulfilled this treacherous agreement, in the village school at La Higuera, are well known. Major Miguel Ayoroa and Colonel Andrés Selnich, Rangers trained by the Yankees, ordered Sergeant Mario Terán to carry out the assassination. When the last-named, totally drunk, entered the room, Che – who had heard the shots that had just wiped out one of the Bolivian guerrillas and a Peruvian – seeing that the executioner vacillated, said to him firmly: 'Shoot! Don't be afraid!' The man turned away and it was necessary for his superior officers, Ayoroa and Selnich, to repeat the order. He then carried it out in a burst of machine-gun fire, aiming from the waist down. There is a version of the story that says Che died several hours after the combat; and that is why the executioners had orders not to aim at the head or chest, so as not to produce mortal wounds. This cruelly prolonged Che's agony. At last a sergeant, who was also drunk, killed him off with a pistol shot to his left side. Such behaviour is in sharp and brutal contrast to the respect Che showed, without a single exception, for the life of the many officers and soldiers of the Bolivian Army, whenever they took a prisoner.

The final hours of his existence at the hands of those despicable enemies must have been very bitter for him: but there was no man better prepared than Che to face up to such an ordeal.

The means by which this diary has come into our hands cannot be divulged for now.* Suffice it to say that it was not done for money. The diary contains all the notes he wrote from 7 November 1966, the day on which he arrived at Ñacahuasu, until 7 October 1967, on the eve of the battle at the Yuro ravine. There are only a few pages missing, which have not yet reached us; but since they do not correspond to days on which important events took place, they do not alter the overall content.

Although there are no doubts of the diary's authenticity, all the photographic copies have been subjected to a rigorous analysis, in order not only to verify their authenticity, but also to check for any possible alterations, no matter how minute. The data was also compared with the diary kept by one of the surviving guerrillas, and both documents coincide in every aspect. The detailed reports of those remaining guerrillas who were witnesses of the events likewise contribute to the verification. We are completely certain that all the photocopies are a true copy of Che's diary.

It was a difficult task to unravel his small and complex

---

* We now know that photocopies were sent to Cuba by Antonio Arguedas Mendieta, a close friend of President René Barrientos who had also been his minister of the interior in 1966–7. It was a number of missing pages that gave Arguedas away, since the CIA seems to have removed some at random just at the time he was making his photocopies. Everything else about him, unfortunately, is shrouded in mystery. Although by his own account Arguedas once worked for the CIA, he later lived in Cuba for seven years before allegedly becoming involved with an ultra-right-wing terrorist organisation back in Bolivia. (The police accused him of several deaths and unexplained bombings in the city of La Paz.) This unusual, almost deranged career trajectory has given rise to much speculation, but it seems highly unlikely that we will ever know the truth about his real ideology and motivation.

handwriting, and this was done with the tireless collaboration of his comrade, Aleida March de Guevara.

The diary will be published more or less simultaneously in France by Editorial François Maspero, in Italy by Casa Editrice Feltrinelli, in the Federal Republic of Germany by Trikont Verlag, in the US by *Ramparts* magazine; and in Spanish in France by Ediciones Ruedo Ibérico, in Chile by Revista Punto Final and in Mexico by Editorial Siglo XXI, as well as in other countries.

¡Hasta la victoria, siempre!

Fidel Castro 1968

BOLIVIAN DIARY

November 1966

Today a new stage begins. It was night when we arrived at the farm. The trip was quite good. After entering, conveniently disguised, via Cochabamba, Pachungo and I made the contacts and travelled on by jeep for two days in two vehicles.

When we approached the farm, we stopped the vehicles and travelled on in only one, in order to avoid arousing the suspicion of the neighbouring landowner, who is muttering that our undertaking may be devoted to the manufacture of cocaine. Oddly enough, it is the ineffable Tumaini who is supposed to be the chemist of the group. When he was driving on to the farm during the second trip, Bigotes, who had just discovered my true identity, almost drove into a gully, abandoning the jeep stuck at the edge of a precipice. We had to walk some 20 kilometres, arriving at the farm, where three workers from the party are staying, around midnight.

Bigotes showed he is ready to co-operate with us, whatever the party does, but he is loyal to Monje, whom he respects and seems to be fond of. According to him, Rodolfo feels the same way and the same goes for Coco, but we must try to get the party to decide to join the struggle. I asked him not to inform the party until the return of Monje – who is travelling to Bulgaria – and to help us, and he agreed to both things.

8 November

We spent the day in the brush, only about 100 metres from

the house, and next to the stream. We were subjected to the attacks of a type of *yaguasa*, very annoying although they do not bite. The types of insects we have seen so far are: *yaguasas*, gnats, *marigüís*, mosquitoes and ticks.

Bigotes retrieved his jeep with the help of Argañaraz and agreed to buy a few things from him, such as pigs and hens.

I thought I would write informing of our mishaps, but I decided to leave it until next week, when we expect the second group to arrive.

9 November

An uneventful day. I went with Tumaini on an exploration of the area and followed the course of the Ñacahuasu* river (which is really a stream), but did not get as far as its source. It runs between narrow banks and the region appears to be deserted. With the right sort of routine we could be here for a long time.

In the afternoon a downpour forced us to leave the brush and into the house. I removed six ticks from my body.

10 November

Pachungo and Pombo went to explore the area with one of the Bolivian comrades, Serafín. They went further than us and found a fork in the stream, a small ravine that seems to be good. When they returned they were lazing around the house and Argañaraz's driver, who was bringing the men who had bought some goods from him, saw them. I was furious and we decided that tomorrow we move to the scrubs where we will set up permanent camp. Tumaini will let himself be seen, since they already know him, and will appear to be one more employee of the farm. This situation is deteriorating rapidly; let us see if we are able at least to bring in our men. With them here I will be more at ease.

---

* Ñacahuasu refers to the river and region, also known as Ñacahuaszu. The author spells it the way the inhabitants of the region pronounce it. A word of Guaraní origin.

11 November

An uneventful day spent at our new encampment, on the other side of the house, where we now sleep.

The insects torment us and we are forced to take cover in our hammocks under the mosquito netting (which only I have).

Tumaini went to visit Argañaraz and bought a few items from him: hens, turkeys. It would seem that we have not yet aroused his suspicion.

12 November

A totally uneventful day. We had made a brief exploration to prepare the ground chosen for the camp when the six from the second group arrive here. The area selected is some 100 metres from the clearing on a mound with a ravine nearby, where caves can be made to store food and other items. By now, the first of the three groups of two into which the men are divided should be beginning to arrive. Towards the end of the coming week they should reach the farm. My hair is growing, although sparsely, and the grey hairs are turning blond and beginning to disappear; my beard is growing. In a couple of months I will be myself again.

13 November

Sunday. Some hunters go by our hideout; men who work for Argañaraz. They are men used to the outdoors, young and single, they would make ideal recruits since they have an intense hatred for their employer. They informed us that eight leagues* along the river there are some houses and that the river has some ravines with water. There is nothing else worth mentioning.

14 November

One week at the camp. Pachungo appears somewhat unable

* One Spanish league is equal to approximately 5.57 kilometres.

to adapt and is sad, but he should recover. Today we started to dig a tunnel to hide all that could compromise us; we will conceal it with intertwined branches and sticks and protect it from the damp as far as possible. The hole, which is one and a half metres deep, has been dug, and we have started on the tunnel.

15 November

We continue working on the tunnel – Pombo and Pachungo in the morning, Tumaini and I in the afternoon. At six when we stopped work, the tunnel was already two metres deep. We intend to finish it tomorrow and put all that might compromise us inside it. During the night rain forced me to leave my hammock, which gets wet because the nylon cover is too small. There was nothing else worth mentioning.

16 November

The tunnel was finished and camouflaged, we only need to conceal the path leading to it; we will take the things to our little hut and tomorrow we will block the entrance with a grille made of sticks and mud. The diagram for this tunnel, known as number I, is in Document No. I. Nothing new otherwise; from tomorrow we can reasonably expect news from La Paz.

17 November

The tunnel has been filled with the items that might compromise those in the house, as well as some tinned food, and it has been adequately camouflaged.

No news whatsoever from La Paz. The men from the house talked to Argañaraz, from whom they bought some items, and he persisted in his wish to participate in the cocaine factory.

18 November

No news from La Paz. Pachungo and Pombo went back to

explore the stream, but they are not convinced that it would be the right site for a camp. On Monday we will explore it with Tumaini. Argañaraz came to repair the road, in order to be able to take stones from the river, and spent quite a while doing that. It seems that he is not suspicious about our presence here. Everything goes on monotonously; the mosquitoes and the ticks are beginning to give us painful sores in our infected bites. At dawn we begin to feel a little cold.

19 November

No news from La Paz. No news here: we spent the day hidden since it is Saturday and therefore the hunters are around.

20 November

At noon Marcos and Rolando arrived. Now we are six. We began by listening immediately to the details of their trip. They took a long time because they only got the notification a week ago. They are the ones who travelled the fastest coming through São Paolo. The remaining four are not expected until next week.

Rodolfo came with them. He made a good impression. Apparently he is more prepared than Bigotes to break off with everything. Papi told him, as well as Coco, of my presence here, thus breaking the rules; apparently it is a case of jealousy of those in authority. I wrote to Manila* with some recommendations (Documents I and II) and to Papi answering his questions. Rodolfo returned at dawn.

21 November

First day of the extended group. It rained a lot and, moving to our new site, we got drenched. We have now settled in. The tent turned out to be a tarpaulin for a truck, which gets

---

* Codename for Cuba.

wet but offers some protection. We have our hammocks with nylon covers. Some more weapons have arrived; Marcos has a Garand, and Rolando will receive an M-1 from the cache. Jorge stayed with us, but in the house; he will direct the efforts to improve the farm. I asked Rodolfo to send us an agronomist that we can trust. We will try to make this last as long as possible.

22 November

Tuma, Jorge and I went on a tour along the river (Ñacahuasu) to inspect the newly discovered stream. Because of the previous day's rain the river was unrecognisable and it required a considerable effort to reach the desired spot: a strip of water that is hidden at the point where it reaches the river; if suitably prepared, we can use it for a permanent camp. We returned after nine o'clock in the evening. Nothing to report from here.

23 November

We established an observation post overlooking the little house of the farm in order to spot any inspection or unwelcome visitors. While two are out exploring, the rest of us are on guard duty for three hours. Pombo and Marcos explored the ground around our camp, up to the stream, which is still flooded.

24 November

Pacho and Rolando left to carry out a recce of the stream, they should be back tomorrow.

At night, two of Argañaraz's men arrived unexpectedly 'on a stroll'. There was nothing unusual going on here but Antonio was out exploring and Tuma, who officially lives in the house, was away. The pretext: they were out hunting. Aliucha's birthday.*

* Birthday of his daughter, Aleida Guevara March.

25 November

From the observation post we were informed that a jeep had arrived with two or three people on board. They were from the campaign against malaria and left immediately after taking some blood samples. Pacho and Rolando arrived very late at night. They found the stream on the map and explored it, besides following the main course of the river until they reached some abandoned fields.

26 November

Because it was Saturday we all remained in our hideout. I asked Jorge to explore the riverbed on horseback to see how far it went; the horse was not there, so he left on foot to borrow one from Don Remberto (20 to 25 kilometres). By nightfall he had not returned. No news from La Paz.

27 November

Jorge was still missing. I gave orders for an all-night watch, but at nine o'clock the first jeep arrived from La Paz. Joaquín and Urbano arrived with Coco and a Bolivian who came to stay: Ernesto, a medical student. Coco left again and came back with Ricardo and Braulio and Miguel and another Bolivian, Inti, who is also staying. Now we are 12 insurgents and Jorge, who acts as the owner; Coco and Rodolfo will be in charge of contacts. Ricardo brought disturbing news: Chino is in Bolivia and wants to send 20 men and come to see me. This is inconvenient because it means the struggle will become international before we have Estanislao on board. We agreed that Chino would go to Santa Cruz and Coco will pick him up there and bring him over. Coco left at dawn with Ricardo, who will take the other jeep to go on to La Paz. Coco must drive past Remberto's to find out about Jorge. During a preliminary chat with Inti, he said that he thought Estanislao will not join the struggle, but he himself seems ready to cut his ties.

28 November

Jorge had still not appeared by morning and Coco had not returned either. They then arrived and all that had happened was that he had stayed at Remberto's. Somewhat irresponsible.

In the afternoon I summoned the Bolivian group to discuss with them the Peruvian offer to send us 20 men, and they all agreed that they should be sent, but after we had seen action.

29 November

We went out to investigate the river and explore the stream where our next camp will be located. Tumaini, Urbano, Inti and I made up the group. The stream is quite safe, but rather murky. We will try to investigate another one that is an hour away from here. Tumaini fell and apparently suffered a fracture of the tarsus. We reached the camp at night, after having measured the depth of the river. Nothing new here. Coco went to Santa Cruz to wait for Chino.

30 November

Marcos, Pacho, Miguel and Pombo went out with orders to explore a stream that is further away; they will be away for two days. It rained a lot. Nothing new at the house.

Analysis of the month

All has gone rather well: my arrival was without incident; half the people are already here, also without incident, although they were delayed; Ricardo's main collaborators are joining the fight, come what may. The general outlook seems good in this remote region, where everything seems to indicate that we will be able to spend as much time as we deem necessary. Our plans are: wait for the arrival of the rest of the men, increase the number of Bolivians to at least 20, and begin to operate. We still need to see what Monje's reaction will be, as well as how [Moisés] Guevara's men will behave.

December 1966

1 December

The day went by uneventfully. Marcos and his comrades returned from a detour that was longer than originally envisaged, wasting time roaming around the hills. At two in the morning I was informed that Coco had arrived with a comrade. I will leave it until morning.

2 December

Chino arrived early and was very effusive. We spent the day talking. The crux of the matter is that he will go to Cuba and inform personally about the situation here. In two months' time five Peruvians will be able to join us – that is, once we have seen action; for the time being only two will come, a radio technician* and a doctor,† who will spend some time with us. Chino asked for weapons and I agreed to give him a BZ, some Mausers and grenades and to purchase one M-1 for them. I also decided to give them assistance so that they can send five Peruvians to establish a conduit to send arms to a region near Puno, on the other side of Lake Titicaca. He told me about his problems in Peru and of an audacious plan to liberate Calixto, which I find a little unrealistic. He thinks that some survivors of the guerrillas are active in the region, although he is not certain, because they were unable to reach the area. The rest of the conversation was circumstantial. He said goodbye with the same enthusiasm and left for La Paz, carrying our photographs. Coco has been instructed to prepare contacts with Sánchez (whom I will

* Lucio Edilberto Galván (Eustaquio), Peruvian radio technician.
† José Cabrera Flores (Doctor or Negro), Bolivian doctor.

see afterwards) and to contact the Head of Information of the Presidency,* who has offered to provide us with information, as he is Inti's brother-in-law. The network is still in its infancy.

3 December

An uneventful day. No exploration as it is Saturday. The three farm workers leave for Lagunillas to run some errands.

4 December

Uneventful. Everybody is quiet as it is Sunday. I give a little talk about the Bolivians who will be arriving and about the war.

5 December

Uneventful. We wanted to go out but it rained throughout the day. We had a false alarm caused by Loro firing a few shots without warning.

6 December

We left to start working on a second cave in the first stream. We are Apolinar, Inti, Urbano, Miguel and me. Miguel is coming to replace Tuma, who has not yet recovered from his fall. Apolinar proposed that he should join the guerrilla force, but he needs to go to La Paz to finalise some personal matters. He was told that he can, but that he should wait for a little while. Around 11.00 we reached the stream; we made a camouflaged path and explored, looking for an appropriate site for the cave, but it is all rock, and the stream, after drying up, continues on its course between clearings of solid rock. We left the exploration until tomorrow. Inti and Urbano left to try and hunt deer because our food supplies are very scarce and they have to last us until Friday.

*Gonzalo López Muñoz, married to a cousin of Inti Peredo and trusted by President Barrientos.

7 December
Miguel and Apolinar located a suitable spot and went to work making the tunnel; the tools are inadequate. Inti and Urbano came back having achieved nothing, but at nightfall they killed a turkey with an M-1; but as food had already been prepared we left it for breakfast tomorrow.

In actual fact today marks the first month of our stay here, but for the sake of convenience I will write down my summary on the last day of each month.

8 December
Inti and I went up to a ridge that overlooks the stream. Miguel and Urbano continued digging the tunnel. In the afternoon Apolinar replaced Miguel. At nightfall Marcos, Pombo and Pacho arrived, the last lagging well behind and very tired. Marcos asked me to remove him from the Vanguard if he did not improve. I marked the path to the cave which appears in diagram II. I left them in charge of the more important tasks during their stay. Miguel will stay with them and we will go back tomorrow.

9 December
We made our return slowly in the morning, arriving around 12.00. Pacho was given orders to remain behind when the group returns. We tried to make contact with camp No. 2, but were not able to do so. There is no other news.

10 December
The day went by uneventfully, except that we had the first batch of bread baked in the house. I discussed several urgent tasks with Jorge and Inti. There was no news from La Paz.

11 December
The day went by uneventfully, but by nightfall Coco turned up with Papi. He was bringing Alejandro and Arturo and a Bolivian, Carlos. The other jeep was left on the road as

usual. They then brought the Doctor, Moro and Benigno and
two Bolivians, both Cambas* from the Caranaví† farm. The
evening went by with the usual comments about the trip
and about the absence of Antonio and Felix, who should
have been here by now. We discussed it with Papi and
decided that he will have to do two more trips to bring
Renán and Tania. We will dispose of the safe houses, and the
depots will be closed down and we will give Sánchez $1,000
to help him. He will keep the van and we will sell one jeep
to Tania and keep the other. We still need to make one
more trip to transport weapons, and I gave the order that
everything should be loaded on to one jeep to avoid switch-
overs that might be detected more easily. Chino left for
Cuba, apparently with great enthusiasm and planning to
return here when he comes back. Coco stayed here to go to
Camiri to get food supplies, and Papi left for La Paz. A
dangerous incident occurred: the Vallegrandino, a hunter,
discovered some footprints we had made, saw the tracks
and found a glove that Pombo had lost. This will result
in a change of plans and we must be very careful. The
Vallegrandino will go with Antonio tomorrow to show him
where he lays his traps to catch tapir. Inti voiced his
reservations to me about the student Carlos, who as soon as
he arrived started an argument about the involvement of
Cubans and had previously said that he would not take up
arms if the party did not participate. Rodolfo had sent him
here as the result of a misunderstanding.

12 December

I spoke to the whole group about their duties, warning them
about the realities of war. I stressed the need for unity of
command and of discipline, and I warned the Bolivians

---

*Cambas: the natives of the eastern region of Bolivia (i.e. Santa Cruz). The description
'Camba' is used in contrast to the native population of the high plateaux, known as
'Kolla' (from the Quechua word *Kollasuyo*), the Bolivian sector of the Inca empire.
†A farm bought by Coco Peredo and owned by the guerrillas, in the area of Caranaví
in the province of Nor Yungas, department of La Paz.

about the responsibility that fell upon them if they broke
away from the party's line to adopt a different one. I made
the appointments, assigning responsibilities as follows:
Joaquín, as military second-in-command; Rolando and Inti,
as group leaders; Alejandro as head of operations; Pombo as
head of services, Inti, finances; Ñato, supplies and arma-
ment; for the moment, Moro, medical services.

Rolando and Braulio left to tell the group to stay put, to
wait for the Vallegrandino to lay down his traps, or to go
exploring with Antonio. They returned in the evening; the
trap is not very far. They got the Vallegrandino drunk and
he left quite happy with a bottle of *singani* inside. Coco
returned from Caranaví, where he bought the necessary
provisions, but he was seen by some people from Lagunillas,
who were surprised by the amount of food.

Marcos arrived later with Pombo. The former had a cut
that split open his superciliar arc and he was given two
stitches.

13 December

Joaquín, Carlos and the Doctor left to meet up with Rolando
and Braulio. Pombo is accompanying them, with the instruc-
tion to return today. I ordered that the path be covered and
that another one be made, coming out of it and leading to the
river. This was so successful that Pombo, Miguel and Pacho
got lost when returning, as they went that way by mistake.

We talked to Apolinar, who will go to his home in Viacha
for a few days. We gave him money for his family and urged
him not to disclose any information. Coco took leave at
nightfall, but three hours later the alarm was sounded
because we heard whistling and noises and a dog barking,
but it turned out to be Coco, who had got lost in the woods.

14 December

A day without incident. The Vallegrandino came past the
house to look at the trap, which he had set yesterday,

contrary to what he had previously said. Antonio was shown the path we had opened in the woods, so he took the Vallegrandino that way, in order to avoid suspicion.

December 15
Nothing new. Precautions were taken to go out (eight men) and to move permanently to camp No. 2.

December 16
Pombo, Urbano, Tuma, Alejandro, Moro, Arturo, Inti and I left for the camp in the morning in order to stay there. We were heavily loaded. It took us three hours.

Rolando stayed with us and Joaquín, Braulio, Carlos and the Doctor went back. Carlos has turned out to be a good walker and a good worker. Moro and Tuma discovered a cave in the river with rather large fish and took 17, which is enough for a good meal; Moro hurt his hand on a catfish. We looked for a site for the secondary cave, since the primary one was finished and all activities were interrupted until morning. Moro himself and Inti wanted to catch a tapir and left to spend the night lying in wait.

17 December
Moro and Inti caught only a turkey hen. We – Tuma, Rolando and I – concentrated on digging the secondary cave, which may be ready by tomorrow. Arturo and Pombo explored a site for the radio and then went on to repair the entrance path, which is in bad shape. During the night it started to rain, and it rained until morning.

18 December
It rained throughout the day but we carried on with the cave, which is not far from the two and a half metres required. We inspected a nearby hill for the installation of the radio. It seems quite right, but the tests will tell.

19 December

Again the day was rainy and not propitious for walking but at 11.00 in the morning, Braulio and Ñato arrived with news that the river could be crossed, although it was deep. When we left, we ran into Marcos and his Vanguard, who are arriving to establish themselves here. He will remain in command and was ordered to send three to five men, depending on the situation. We walked over in a little more than three hours.

At midnight Ricardo and Coco arrived, bringing Antonio and Rubio (they were unable to get transport last Thursday) and Apolinar, who has come to join us permanently. Also, Iván arrived to discuss a whole series of matters.

In fact, it was a sleepless night.

20 December

We proceeded to discuss various points and were putting order into everything when the group from camp No. 2 arrived, led by Alejandro and bringing the news that on the road near the camp there was a dead deer with a string round its leg. Joaquín had gone past an hour earlier and had not made any comment. It was assumed that the Vallegrandino had taken it that far and, for an unknown reason, had dropped it there and run away.

A guard was posted at the rear and two men were sent to catch the hunter if he appeared. Later the news came that the deer had been dead for some time and was infested with worms, and then Joaquín on his return confirmed that he had seen it. Coco and Loro brought the Vallegrandino to show him the little beast and he told us that he thought it was an animal wounded by him several days ago. That was the end of the incident.

It was decided to speed up contacts with the man from Information, whom Coco has done nothing about, and to talk to Megía, who will be the link between Iván and the man from the Information Office. He will be the liaison with Megía, Sánchez, Tania and the man from the party, who has not yet been named. There is the possibility that someone from Villamontes will be appointed, but this has not yet been finalised. We received a telegram from Manila, which states that Monje is arriving from the south.

They have invented a contact system but I do not find it satisfactory because it shows a clear distrust of Monje on the part of his own comrades.

At one in the morning we will be told by La Paz if they have gone to collect Monje.

Iván has the opportunity of doing some business deals, but his badly forged passport prevents him; the next stage is to get him a better one, and he should write to Manila and ask our friends to do it quickly.

Tania will come in the next few days to receive instructions and I will probably send her to Buenos Aires.

Finally, it has been decided that Ricardo, Iván and Coco leave from Camiri by plane and the jeep stays here. When they return they will telephone Lagunillas to say that they are there; Jorge will go at night to ask for news and will collect them if there is something positive. At one o'clock it was impossible to pick up any news from La Paz. At dawn they left for Camiri.

21 December

Loro had not left me the drawings made by the scout, so I have no way of knowing what the road is like between here and Yaki. We left in the morning and made our way without incident. It is a matter of having everything here by the 24th, the day on which we plan to have a party.

We crossed paths with Pacho, Miguel, Benigno and Camba, who were going to carry the equipment. At 17.00 Pacho and Camba returned without the equipment, which they left hidden under brushwood, because it was very heavy. Five men will leave from here tomorrow to bring it over. The cave for the supplies was finished; tomorrow we start the one for the radio.

22 December

We started the cave for the radio operator. At the beginning with great success over loose soil, but we soon ran into tough rock that did not allow us to progress.

They brought the equipment, which is quite heavy, but we have not tested it due to a lack of petrol. Loro announced that he was not sending maps because the scout's report had been verbal, and that he would come tomorrow to give us the information.

23 December

We set out with Pombo and Alejandro to explore the hard ground on the left. We will have to open it up, but my impression is that one can walk along it comfortably. Joaquín arrived with two comrades, informing us that Loro was not coming because a pig had escaped and he had gone to look for it.

So we have nothing on the Lagunillero's exploration.

By the evening the pig arrived, quite a big one, but the drinks are still missing. Loro is incapable of even getting these things, he seems really disorganised.

24 December

The day was devoted to Christmas Eve. There were people who went on two trips and arrived late, but in the end we were all together and we had a good time, with some getting soused. Loro explained that the Lagunillero's trip had not been fruitful and yielded only the minor outcome of some notes, which are very vague.

25 December

Back to work; there were no trips to the first camp. The latter has been named C26, which was proposed by the Bolivian doctor. Marcos, Benigno and Camba went out to explore the hard ground to our right and returned in the afternoon with the news that they had found a sort of barren

plain two hours away from here; tomorrow they will reach
it. Camba had a temperature when they returned. Miguel
and Pacho built some diversionary paths on the left bank
and a path for access to the radio cave. Inti, Antonio, Tuma
and I continued with the cave for the radio, which is difficult
because it is all solid rock. The Rearguard was busy setting
up its camp and looking for an observation post from which
to see both ends of access to the river: the site is very good.

26 December

Inti and Carlos left to explore as far as the point on the map
called Yaki; it is a trip estimated to take two days. Rolando,
Alejandro and Pombo carried on with the cave, which is very
hard. Pacho and I went out to explore the roads built by
Miguel; it is not worthwhile carrying on with the one along
the bank. The access road to the cave is quite good and it is
difficult to find. We killed two snakes today and another one
yesterday; it seems there are many. Tuma, Arturo, Rubio
and Antonio went out to hunt, and Braulio and Ñato went
to stay on guard duty at the other camp. They returned with
the news that Loro had overturned his jeep, and with a note
announcing the arrival of Monje. Marcos, Miguel and
Benigno left to work on the road along the bank, but did not
return all night.

27 December

We went out with Tuma to try and find Marcos. We walked
for two and a half hours until we reached the beginning of a
ravine that came down the left side, to the west; we followed
the tracks, climbing down some rather steep gorges. I
thought we could reach the camp by this route, but the
hours went by and we did not get there. After five in the
afternoon we reached Ñacahuasu, some five kilometres
below camp No. 1, and by seven we reached the camp. We
then discovered that Marcos had spent the previous night
there. I did not send anyone to report where we were because

I assumed that Marcos would have told them about my possible route. We saw the jeep, which was in very poor shape. Loro had gone to Camiri to get some spare parts. According to Ñato, he had fallen asleep at the wheel.

28 December

When we were leaving for the camp, Urbano and Antonio arrived, looking for me. Marcos had continued on with Miguel in order to make a path up to the camp along the bank and had not arrived; Benigno and Pombo went out to find me on the road that we had followed. When I reached the camp I found Marcos and Miguel, who had slept on the bank, being unable to reach the camp. The former complained to me about the way he had been treated. Apparently, the complaint was directed at Joaquín, Alejandro and the Doctor. Inti and Carlos had returned, not having found any inhabited houses – just one that had been abandoned, which presumably is not at the point marked on the map as Yaki.

29 December

With Marcos, Miguel and Alejandro, we climbed the bare hill to gain a better look of the area. It seems to be the beginning of the Pampa del Tigre, which is a range of bare hills of approximately the same height, situated at an altitude of 1,500 metres. The route by the left bank must be abandoned because it bends towards the Ñacahuasu. We went down and reached the camp in one hour and 20 minutes. We sent eight men to get the supplies, but they were unable to bring the whole lot. Rubio and the Doctor replaced Braulio and Ñato. The former made a new path before he came; that path begins at the river through some rocks, and the other one reaches the woods from the opposite side, through some other stones, so that no tracks are left. No work was done on the cave. Loro left for Camiri.

30 December

Despite the rain, which made the river rise, four men went to clear out the remaining things from camp No. 1, which is now empty. There was no news from outside. Six men went to the cave and in two trips put away everything that was meant to be stored there.

It was not possible to finish the oven because the clay was too soft.

31 December

At 7.30 the Doctor arrived with the news that Monje was over there. I went with Inti, Tuma, Urbano and Arturo. The reception was cordial, but tense. The question floated in the air: what are you here for? Monje was accompanied by Pan Divino, the new recruit, and Tania, who had come to receive instructions, and Ricardo, who is to stay.

The conversation with Monje started with generalities, but soon came down to his fundamental position, which can be summarised in three basic conditions:

1. He will resign from the party leadership, but will at least ensure its neutrality, and will recruit cadres for the struggle.
2. The political and military leadership of the struggle rests with him as long as the revolution takes place on Bolivian soil.
3. He handles relations with other South American parties, trying to get them to support liberation movements (as an example he mentioned Douglas Bravo).

I replied that the first point was up to him, as secretary of the party, but that I considered his position to be a great mistake. It was vacillating and compromising and protected the reputation of those whom history would condemn because of their willingness to abandon their principles. Time would prove me right.

As to his third point, I had no objection to his attempting to do that, but it was doomed to failure. To ask Codovila to support Douglas Bravo was tantamount to asking him to condone an insurrection within his own party. Time would also be the judge.

I could not accept the second point under any circumstances. I would be the military leader and would not accept any ambiguity about it. Here the discussion got bogged down and went round in a vicious circle.

We left it that Monje would think it out and talk to the Bolivian comrades. We went to the new camp and there he talked to all of them, putting to them the choice of staying here or supporting the party. They all decided to stay, and that seemed to shock him.

At 12.00 we drank a toast in which he remarked on the historical relevance of the date. I replied, taking advantage of his words to mark the moment as the new 'Grito de Murillo'* of the revolution on this continent, and said that, faced with the fact of the revolution, our lives meant nothing.

Fidel sent the attached messages.

Analysis of the month
The Cuban team is now successfully complete, morale is good and there are only some minor problems. The Bolivians are good, although there are too few of them. Monje's attitude may delay the development, on the one hand, but it may have a positive effect on the other, as it sets me free from any political compromise. The next step, besides waiting for more Bolivians, consists of talking to Moisés Guevara and with the Argentines Mauricio and Jozami (Masetti and the dissident party).

---

* Pedro Domingo Murillo (1757–1810), Bolivian patriot who led the first declaration of independence by a Spanish colony in the Americas. The 'Grito de Murillo' refers to the speech he gave just before he was assassinated: 'Countrymen, I die, but the flame that we have lit nobody can extinguish.'

January 1967

1 January

In the morning, without discussing it with me, Monje informed me that he was leaving and that he would submit his resignation to the leadership of the party on 8 January. According to him, his mission was over. He left looking like a man going to the gallows. My impression is that when he found out from Coco of my decision not to yield on strategic matters, he clung to that point to force the break, since his position is inconsistent.

In the afternoon I met up with everybody and explained Monje's attitude, announcing that we would unite with all those who wanted to make the revolution. And I predicted difficult moments and days of moral anguish for the Bolivians, but that we would try to solve their problems by means of collective discussion or through the group leaders.

I set out the details of Tania's trip to Argentina to meet Mauricio and Jozami and to ask them to come here. With Sánchez, we went over his tasks, and decided to leave Rodolfo, Loyola and Humberto in La Paz for the time being; also Loyola's sister in Camiri, and Calvimonte in Santa Cruz. Mito will travel in the region of Sucre to see where he can base himself. Loyola will be in charge of finances and 80,000 pesos are being sent to her, of which 20,000 will be for a lorry that Calvimonte must acquire. Sánchez will get in touch with Moisés Guevara to arrange a meeting with him. Coco will go to Santa Cruz to meet up with a brother of Carlos and put him in charge of receiving the three arriving from Havana. I wrote to Fidel the message in document CZO No. 2.

2 January

The morning was spent encoding the letter. The others (Sánchez, Coco and Tania) left in the afternoon, once Fidel's speech had ended. He spoke about us in terms that create an even greater obligation, if that were possible.

At the camp we only worked on the cave; the others went to fetch the things from the first camp. Marcos, Miguel and Benigno left to explore the area to the north; Inti and Carlos explored the Ñacahuasu until they ran into some people, presumably at Yaki; Joaquín and the Doctor must explore the river Yaki up to its source or until they run into people. They all have a maximum of five days.

The men came back to the camp with the news that Loro had not returned after leaving Monje.

3 January

We worked on the roof of the cave, but did not manage to finish it; we must do so tomorrow. Two men only went to pick up a load and came back with the news that everybody had left last night. The rest of the comrades worked on a roof for the kitchen – it is now ready.

4 January

Nothing much to report today; the men went to collect supplies. We finished the roof of the radio operator's cave. Target practice was cancelled because of the rain.

5 January

We continue to transport supplies. A few more trips are still required. The cave was finished, together with its accessories (a small cave for the generator). We tested the rifles for the Rearguard and some for the Main Force: all fine, except for Apolinario's. All the scouts are back. Inti and Carlos walked along the Ñacahuasu until they ran into people; they found several houses, among them two medium-sized farms, one with 150 head of cattle whose owner lives in

Lagunillas. There is a small settlement called Iti from where a bridle path leads to Lagunillas. From there they reached Tikucha, which is joined to Vaca Guzmán by a truck route. They returned by a path that leads to the Ikira river, the one we had identified as the Yaki. The point called Yaki is a field near our camp, abandoned by its inhabitants due to cattle disease. Joaquín and the Doctor continued along the Ikira until they came to some impassable rocks, without meeting people, but finding traces of their existence. Marcos, Miguel and Benigno walked along the ridge until they reached an inaccessible point, cut off by a cliff.

We have a new recruit: a small turkey hen caught by Inti.

6 January

In the morning Marcos, Joaquín, Alejandro, Inti and I went to the bare ridge. Once there, I decided that Marcos, with Camba and Pacho, would attempt to reach the Ñacahuasu from the right, avoiding any people. Miguel, Braulio and Aniceto will look for a path along the ridge to try and make a central trail. Joaquín with Benigno and Inti will look for a path to the Frías river, which according to the map runs parallel to the Ñacahuasu, on the other side of the ridge that must be the Pampa del Tigre.

In the afternoon Loro arrived with two mules he had bought for 2,000 pesos, a good buy; the animals are tame and strong. We sent for Braulio and Pacho, so that Loro can leave tomorrow; they were replaced by Carlos and the Doctor.

After class I launched into a tirade about the qualities required of a guerrilla force and the need for greater discipline and I explained that our mission, above all else, is to make up a central group that is an example, made of steel, and in this way I explained the importance of study, which is indispensable for the future. I then brought together those who held responsibilities: Joaquín, Marcos, Alejandro, Inti, Rolando, Pombo, the Doctor, Ñato and Ricardo. I explained why Joaquín had been chosen as second-in-command, due to

mistakes made by Marcos, which he kept repeating; I criticised Joaquín's attitude in the incident with Miguel on New
Year's Day, and I then explained some of the tasks that need
to be carried out in order to improve our organisation. At the
end, Ricardo told me of an incident between him and Iván,
which took place in front of Tania, where they swore at each
other and Ricardo ordered Iván to get off the jeep. These
unpleasant incidents between comrades are damaging our
work.

7 January
The explorers left. The supply team consisted solely of
Alejandro and Ñato, the others working inside the camp. The
generator and all Arturo's things were taken, an additional
little roof was made for the cave, and the source of water was
arranged by building a small bridge across the stream.

8 January
Sunday. The supply team was extended to eight men and
almost everything was brought over. Loro has announced
that he is going to Santa Cruz, which was not scheduled,
apparently in order to find harnesses for the mules. We had
no lessons or any other activities. It was my turn to be
outside, in appalling weather.

9 January
It rained; everything is wet. The flooded river did not allow
us to cross it, so there was no replacement of the guard at the
old camp.
    An otherwise uneventful day.

10 January
We changed the permanent guard at the old camp, Rubio and
Apolinar replacing Carlos and the Doctor. The river is still
flooded although it is going down. Loro went to Santa Cruz
and has not returned.

With the Doctor (Moro), Tuma and Antonio, who is to
stay in charge of the camp, we climbed up to the Pampa del
Tigre, and there I explained to Antonio his tasks for
tomorrow, exploring the possible stream that may be west
of our camp. From there we looked for a junction with
Marcos's old path, which we found with relative ease. At
nightfall, six of the explorers arrived: Miguel, with Braulio
and Aniceto; Joaquín, with Benigno and Inti. Miguel and
Braulio found an exit to the river which cut across the ridge
and ended up at a second river that seems to be the
Ñacahuasu. Joaquín managed to go down the river, which
must be the Frías, and followed it for a while. It seems to be
the same one that the other group followed, which indicates
that our maps are very bad, since both rivers appear
separated by a landmass and flow separately into the Río
Grande. Marcos has not yet returned.

We received a message from Havana informing us that
Chino leaves on the 12th, with the Doctor, the radio
technician and Rhea leaving on the 14th. There was no
mention of our two remaining comrades.

11 January
Antonio left to explore the adjacent stream with Carlos
and Arturo; he returned at night and the only concrete
piece of information he brought was that the stream ends
at the Ñacahuasu, across from the field where we hunt.
Alejandro and Pombo arrived with the news that my
books had got wet: some had disintegrated and the two-
way radios were wet and rusty. Add to this that both radios
are out of order and you get a sad picture of Arturo's
aptitude.

Marcos arrived at night. He had arrived at the
Ñacahuasu far downstream, but had not reached the point
where it meets the river that we think is the Frías. I am not
at all sure about the maps, nor about the identity of this
last waterway.

We began studying Kechua,* taught by Aniceto and Pedro.

Day of the *boro*. Fly larvae were removed from Marcos, Carlos, Pombo, Antonio, Moro and Joaquín.

12 January

The supply team was sent to bring back the last items. Loro has not yet returned. We exercised by climbing the hills around our stream, where we took more than two hours for the sides, but only seven minutes for the centre. This is where we should set up our defence.

Joaquín told me that Marcos was hurt by my referring to his mistakes during the meeting the other day. I must talk to him.

13 January

I spoke with Marcos. His complaint was that I had criticised him in front of the Bolivians. His argument was groundless, but his emotional state deserves attention – the rest is of no consequence.

He referred to some derisory remarks that Alejandro made about him. The subject was discussed with the latter, and it appears that it was not true, just a little idle gossip. Marcos calmed down.

Inti and Moro went out to hunt, but came back empty-handed. We sent out teams to dig a cave in a spot that can be reached by the mules. Nothing could be done, so we decided to build a small earth hut. Alejandro and Pombo made a study of the defence of the entrance and marked the place for the trenches. They will carry on tomorrow.

Rubio and Apolinar came back and Braulio and Pedro went to the old camp. No news of Loro.

14 January

Marcos, with his Vanguard, but without Benigno, went

---

* Kechua or Quechua: the native language of the peoples of the old Inca empire, spoken extensively in Bolivia.

downstream to build the hut; he was supposed to return at night, but because of the rain he came back at midday, before finishing the hut.

Joaquín was leading the group that started on the trenches. Moro, Inti, Urbano and I went out to make a path that would surround our position near the ridge to the right of the stream, but we left in the wrong direction and had to skirt some precipices which were quite dangerous. At midday it started to rain and all activities had to be cancelled. No news of Loro.

15 January
I stayed at the camp, drafting instructions for the city cadres. Because it is Sunday, we worked only half the day. Marcos and the Vanguard worked on the hut, the Rearguard and the Main Force on the trenches. Ricardo, Urbano and Antonio went to improve yesterday's path, but did not succeed because there is a cliff between the hill that leads down to the river and the ridge.

There was no trip to the old camp.

16 January
Work continued on the trenches, but they have not been finished. Marcos almost completed his work, making a rather good little house. The Doctor and Carlos replaced Braulio and Pedro, who came with the news that Loro had turned up and was coming with the mules. But he still did not appear, in spite of the fact that Aniceto went to fetch him.

Alejandro is showing symptoms of malaria.

17 January
A day of little movement; the front-line trenches and the hut were finished.

Loro came to report on his trip. When I asked him why he had gone, he replied that he had assumed we would take it for granted that he would go, and confessed that he went to see a woman he has there. He did bring the harness for the mule, but was not able to make the mule walk through the river.

There is no news of Coco; this is now somewhat alarming.

18 January
It was cloudy at daybreak, so I did not inspect the trenches. Urbano, Ñato, the Doctor (Moro), Inti, Aniceto and Braulio formed the team who went to fetch supplies. Alejandro did not work because he felt ill.

Shortly afterwards it began to rain heavily. Loro arrived while it was pouring down, to report that Argañaraz had spoken to Antonio, letting it be known that he knew what was going on and offering to co-operate with us on the cocaine or whatever it is – showing by 'whatever it is' that he suspects there is something else. I gave instructions to Loro to involve Argañaraz without offering him too much, only payment for what he carries in his jeep, and to threaten him with death if he betrays us. Due to the downpour Loro left immediately to avoid being cut off by the river.

The group with the supplies had not returned by eight, so I gave the others carte blanche with their food ration, which they devoured. A few minutes later Braulio and Ñato arrived, reporting that the flood had surprised them en route, and that they all tried to carry on, but Inti had fallen into the water and lost his rifle and was badly bruised. The rest decided to spend the night there, while these two got here with difficulty.

19 January
The day began routinely, working on the defences and improving the camp. Miguel came down with a high temperature that has all the symptoms of malaria. My body felt strange all day long, but the illness did not break out.

At eight in the morning the four stragglers arrived with a good supply of maize, having spent the night huddled around a fire. We will wait for the river to subside and try to recover the rifle.

At approximately four in the afternoon, when Rubio and Pedro had left to replace the pair on guard duty at the other camp, the Doctor came to inform us that the police had arrived there. A Lieutenant Fernández and four policemen, in civilian clothes, arrived in a rented jeep looking for the cocaine factory. They only inspected the house and noticed some unusual things, such as the carbide brought for our lamps, which had not yet been taken to the cave. They took Loro's gun away from him, but they left him the Mauser and the .22. They went through the motions of taking a .22 from Argañaraz, which they showed to Loro, and left with the warning that they knew everything and that they should be counted in. Loro could claim his gun back at Camiri 'if he makes no fuss and talks to me,' said Lieutenant Fernández. He enquired after the 'Brazilian'. Loro was instructed to distance himself from the Vallegrandino and Argañaraz, who must be the ones who spied on us and squealed. He is to go to Camiri with the excuse of collecting the gun and try to get in touch with Coco (I have my doubts that he is free). They must live in the jungle as much as possible.

20 January

I inspected the positions and gave orders to carry out the defence plan that I explained last night. It is based on the rapid defence of an area next to the river, which depends on a counter-attack by our men from the Vanguard, on paths parallel to the river, leading to the spot where our Rearguard is located.

We intended to carry out some exercises, but the situation in the old camp continues to be compromised, since a gringo appeared, firing an M-2. He claims to be a friend of Argañaraz who has come to spend 10 days at his house. Parties will be sent out to explore and we will move the camp to a site nearer Argañaraz's house. If this blows up, we will make him feel our presence before we leave the area.

Miguel still has a high temperature.

21 January

We staged the mock-battle, which failed in some areas, but which on the whole went well. We need to work on the withdrawal, which was the weakest point of the exercise. Afterwards the teams went out; one with Braulio to make a path parallel to the river towards the west, and another with Rolando to do the same to the east. Pacho went to the bare hill to try one of the two-way radios, and Marcos left with Aniceto to try and find a path that will help us to keep an eye on Argañaraz. Everybody was supposed to return before two, except Marcos. The paths were made, and so were the radio tests, which were successful. Marcos returned early because the rain made visibility impossible. In the midst of the rain Pedro arrived bringing Coco and three new recruits: Benjamín, Eusebio and Walter. The first has arrived from Cuba and goes to the Vanguard because he knows how to use firearms; the other two join the Rearguard. Mario Monje spoke to three men who had got back from Cuba and dissuaded them from joining the guerrillas. Not only did he fail to resign the leadership of the party, but he sent Fidel a letter, attachment D.IV. I received a note from Tania informing us of her departure and of Iván's illness, as well as another note from Iván, which is attachment D.V. At night I asked the whole group to meet and I read them Monje's document, pointing out the inaccuracies in points a) and b), as well as giving them an additional diatribe. Their reaction seemed positive. Of the three new ones, two seem firm and conscientious. The youngest is an Aymara* peasant who looks very healthy.

---

* Aymara: ancient indigenous civilisation whose descendants inhabit the high plateaux of the Andes (La Paz, Oruro and Potosí). It is the majority native language of Bolivia.

22 January

A supply team of 13 men left to fetch supplies, plus Braulio and Walter to relieve Pedro and Rubio. They returned in the afternoon, without having brought the entire load. All is quiet over there. On the way back Rubio had a dramatic fall, although it did not have serious consequences.

I am writing a report to Fidel, Document III, to explain the situation and to test the communication system. I must send it to La Paz with Moisés Guevara, if he turns up for the meeting in Camiri on the 25th.

I am writing instructions for the urban cadres, D.III. Owing to the trip for supplies there were no activities at the camp today. Miguel is better, but now Carlos has a high temperature.

Today we had the tuberculin tests. Two turkeys were caught; a small animal fell into the trap, but severed its foot, so it was able to escape.

23 January

The tasks were distributed, some inside the camp and some for exploration: Inti, Rolando and Arturo went to look for a place in which to hide the Doctor and anyone who might be wounded. Marcos, Urbano and I went to explore the hill in front of us, to find a suitable spot from which we can see Argañaraz's house. We found one and the view is quite good.

Carlos still has a temperature, which is typical of malaria.

24 January

The supply team left with seven men, returning early with the full load, and with some corn. This time it was Joaquín who got wet and lost the Garand, but he recovered it. Loro is back and in hiding, Coco and Antonio are still out; they are due tomorrow or the day after, with Moisés Guevara.

We improved one of the paths, so that we can surround the soldiers in the event of having to defend these positions. In the evening there was a discussion of the exercise we did the other day, and we corrected some of our mistakes.

25 January

Marcos and I went out to explore the path that would lead us to the rear of an enemy attack. It took us almost an hour to get there, but the location is good.

Aniceto and Benjamín went out to test the radio transmitter from the hill above Argañaraz's house, but they got lost and we were not able to communicate, so we will have to repeat the exercise. We started a new cave, for personal belongings. Loro arrived and joined the Vanguard. He spoke with Argañaraz and told him what I had said. Argañaraz admitted that he had sent the Vallegrandino to spy on us, but denied being the police informer. Coco chased the man from the house since Argañaraz had sent him to spy. A message from Manila arrived informing us that everything had been received without a problem, and that Kolle is on his way to meet up with Simón Reyes. Fidel gives warning that he will hear them out and will be hard on them.

26 January

We had hardly started to work on the new cave when the news came that Moisés Guevara had arrived with Loyola. We left for the little house at the intermediate camp and they arrived there at noon.

I stated my conditions to Moisés Guevara: dissolution of the group, no ranks for anyone, as there is no political organisation yet, and all arguments about international or national differences must be avoided. He accepted everything with great humility and, after a cold start, relations with the Bolivians became amicable.

Loyola made a very good impression on me. She is young and soft-spoken, but one can detect a strong will in her. She is about to be expelled from the party's Youth Movement, but they are trying to get her to resign. I gave her the instructions for the cadres and another document. Also, I repaid her the amount so far spent, which totals 70,000 pesos. We are getting short of money.

Dr Pareja will be appointed Head of the Urban Network and Rodolfo will come to join us in two weeks' time.

I sent a letter to Iván (D.VI) with instructions.

I instructed Coco to sell the jeep, but to maintain communication with the farm.

At around 19.00, as night fell, we said goodbye. They will leave tomorrow night and Moisés Guevara will come with the first group between 4 and 14 February. He said he could not come earlier because of communications, and that just now the men are taking time off for the carnival.

More powerful radio transmitters will be arriving.

27 January

A strong team went off to fetch the supplies and they brought almost everything, but there is still a load there. Coco and the visitors left at night; they will stay in Camiri, and Coco will go on to Santa Cruz to arrange the sale of the jeep, so that it will be ready after the 15th.

We continue to dig the cave. An armadillo was caught in the traps. Preparations for the trip are coming to an end. We intend to leave when Coco arrives.

28 January

The supply team cleaned out the old camp. They brought the news that the Vallegrandino had been caught in the cornfield, but managed to escape. Everything seems to indicate that we are reaching the moment when we will have to make a decision about the farm.

The supplies for a 10-day march have been completed and the date has been set: one or two days after Coco arrives on 2 February.

29 January
A day of total idleness except for the cooks, the hunters and the sentries.

Coco arrived in the afternoon. He had not gone to Santa Cruz, but to Camiri instead. He left Loyola to carry on by plane to La Paz, and Moisés to go by bus to Sucre. Sunday is scheduled as the day for contacts.

1 February is set as the date for departure.

30 January
Twelve men formed the supply team and it transported the greatest quantity of food, although there is still a load for five men. The hunters came back empty-handed.

The cave for personal belongings was completed; it has not turned out very well.

31 January
Last day at the camp. The team cleared everything and the guards were withdrawn. Antonio, Ñato, Camba and Arturo remained, with the following instructions: to make contact at least every three days. As long as there are four of them, two will be armed. Sentries will be posted at all times. The new arrivals will be informed on general matters, but must not be told more than is strictly necessary. All personal belongings will be cleared from the camp, and weapons hidden in the woods, covered with a canvas. The money reserves will remain at the camp at all times and always on someone's person. Paths already established will be patrolled, also the nearby streams. In the event of a hasty retreat, two men will go to Arturo's cave: Antonio and Arturo himself; Ñato and Camba will withdraw along the stream and one of them will run to leave a signal for us at a place that we will choose tomorrow. If there are more than four men, a group will guard the supply cave.

I spoke to the troops and gave the final instructions for the march. I also sent Coco his final instructions (D.VII).

Analysis of the month

As I expected, Monje's attitude was evasive at first and then treacherous.

The party is now up in arms against us, and I do not know how far they will go. But this will not stop us and maybe in the long run it will be to our advantage (I am almost certain of this). The most honest and militant people will be with us, even if they have to go through a crisis of conscience that may be quite serious.

Moisés Guevara has so far responded well. We shall see how he and his people behave in the future.

Tania left, but the Argentines have given no signs of life, and neither has she. Now begins the real guerrilla phase and we will test the troops. Time will tell what they are capable of and what are the prospects for the Bolivian revolution.

Of all we had envisaged, the hardest task was the recruitment of Bolivian combatants.

February 1967

The first stage has been completed. The men arrived somewhat tired, but in general they conducted themselves well. Antonio and Ñato came up to agree on the password and bring my rucksack and that of Moro, who is still convalescing from malaria.

A warning system was arranged using messages inside a bottle, under a bush close to the path.

In the Rearguard Joaquín was having problems with his load, and slowed the whole group down.

2 February

A long and arduous day. The Doctor (Moro) slowed down the march, but the pace is generally slow. At four we reached the last spot where there is water, and we set up camp. The Vanguard received the order of going as far as the river (presumably the Frías), but their pace was not good either. It rained during the night.

3 February

It was still raining at dawn, so we delayed our departure until 8.00. When we were starting the march, Aniceto arrived with a rope to help us over the difficult passes, and not long afterwards the rain started again. We reached the stream at 10.00, completely drenched, and decided to stop for the day. The stream cannot be the river Frías; it simply is not on the map.

Tomorrow the Vanguard will leave, with Pacho leading. We will communicate every hour.

4 February

We walked from the morning until four in the afternoon, with a two-hour stop at noon to have some soup. The path follows the Ñacahuasu; it is relatively good, but disastrous for shoes. Some comrades are almost barefoot by now.

The troops are fatigued, but all have responded quite well. I have been relieved of almost 15 pounds and can now walk easily, although the pain in my shoulders is unbearable at times.

We have not found any recent signs of people along the river, but any time now we should arrive at inhabited areas, according to the map.

5 February

Unexpectedly, after walking for five hours in the morning (12 to 14 kilometres), the Vanguard informed us that they had found some animals (they turned out to be a mare and a colt). We stopped and ordered an exploration, to avoid an area that is presumably populated. The question was whether we were at the Iripiti or at the confluence with the Saladillo, which is marked on the map. Pacho came back with the news that there was a large river several times greater than the Ñacahuasu, which was impassable. We went there and found the actual Río Grande, which was flooded besides. There are signs of life, but somewhat old, and the paths that we followed ended in the undergrowth where there were no signs of people having gone by.

We camped at a bad place, close to the Ñacahuasu, to make use of its water. Tomorrow we will explore both sides of the river (east and west) to find out about the area, while another group will try to cross it.

6 February

A day of calm, recovering our strength. Joaquín goes with Walter and the Doctor to explore the Río Grande. Following its course, they walked for eight kilometres without finding a ford, only a stream with salt water. Marcos, accompanied by Aniceto and Loro, was walking against the current and did not reach the Frías. Alejandro, Inti and Pacho tried unsuccessfully to swim across the river. We moved our camp about one kilometre back, looking for a better site. Pombo is rather ill.

Tomorrow we will begin work on a raft to try and cross it.

7 *February*

The raft was built under Marcos's direction. It was too big and difficult to manoeuvre. At 13.30 we began to walk to the site of the crossing and at 14.30 we began to cross. The Vanguard crossed in two stages and, in the third one, half the Main Force came across and my clothes, but not my rucksack. During the following trip to bring across the rest of the Main Force, Rubio miscalculated and the raft was swept downstream by the river. It could not be recovered and came apart. Joaquín started to make a new one, which was ready at nine in the evening, but it was not necessary to cross over at night because it did not rain and the level of the river continued to drop. Of the Main Force, only Tuma, Urbano, Inti, Alejandro and I remained. Tuma and I slept on the ground.

8 *February*

At 6.30 the rest of the Main Force began to cross. At 6.00 the head of the Vanguard left and, when the Main Force arrived, they all left together. The Main Force left at 8.00 when the Rearguard was this side. They were told to hide the raft and carry on. The path became irregular and had to be hacked open using machetes. At 18.00, hungry and thirsty, we arrived at a small stream with a pond and decided to pitch camp. There are many tracks of pigs here.

Braulio, Aniceto and Benigno went to the river some three kilometres away, and came back with the news that they saw prints made by sandals and by animals, one of which had horseshoes. They are all recent.

9 February

When we had walked for more than half an hour, I decided to leave the ascending path and follow on along the stream. Not long afterwards I noticed a cornfield. I sent Inti and Ricardo to explore and then pandemonium broke out. Those coming behind us did not see the signal we had left for them and thought that I was lost. The groups came and went. The Vanguard saw a house and awaited my arrival. Inti and Ricardo encountered some children and went to the house of a young peasant, who had six children and was very friendly and gave them a mass of information. During a second meeting Inti told him that he was the head of the guerrillas and bought two pigs to make *huminta*.*

We stayed in the same spot and ate corn and pork. The punch was ready at dawn, but we left it for tomorrow.

10 February

Pretending to be Inti's assistant, I went to speak to the peasants. I do not think the act was very convincing because of Inti's diffidence.

The peasant is true to type: he is incapable of helping us, but also incapable of seeing the dangers involved and is therefore potentially dangerous. He gave us much information about the peasants, but could not be specific because of a certain insecurity.

The Doctor treated the children; some had worms and another had been kicked by a mare. We then left.

The afternoon and evening were spent preparing *huminta* (it is not very good). At night I made some remarks to all the comrades in a meeting about the next 10 days. To begin with, I intend to walk 10 more days towards the Masicuri, and ensure that all our comrades actually see the soldiers in the flesh. Then we will try to return by the Frías, in order to explore a different route. (The peasant is called Rojas.)

* A dish typical of the region, made with crushed baby corn.

11 February

My old man's birthday:* 67.

We followed a clearly marked trail along the river bank until it became almost impassable. At times it disappeared completely, proving that nobody had been through there in a long time. At noon we reached the point where it just ended, next to a large river, which suddenly made us doubt whether this was the Masicuri or not. We stopped at a stream while Marcos and Miguel went exploring upriver, and Inti with Carlos and Pedro did so downriver, trying to find the mouth. This they did, and confirmed that it is the Masicuri. The first ford is downstream, where they saw peasants in the distance, loading some horses. They have probably seen our footprints, so from now on we will have to take greater precautions. We are one or two leagues from Arenales, according to the peasant's information.
h = 760m.

12 February

We covered the two kilometres walked by the Vanguard rapidly. From that moment on, cutting open the trail went very slowly. At four in the afternoon we fell upon a main road, which seemed to be the one we were looking for. In front of us, across the river, there was a house that we decided to ignore, and to look for one on this side of the river, which should belong to Montaño, whom Rojas had recommended to us. Inti and Loro went there, but found no one at home, although its features seemed to indicate that this was the right house.

At 19.30 we started out on a night march, which served to demonstrate how much we still have to learn. At approximately 22.00, Inti and Loro went back to the house and returned with not very good news: the man was drunk and not very welcoming; he only has corn. He had got drunk at

* Birthday of his father, Ernesto Guevara Lynch.

Caballero's house, on the other side of the river, where there is a ford. We decided to spend the night in a nearby wood. I was dreadfully tired since the *humintas* had disagreed with me, and I had not eaten for a whole day.

13 February

At daybreak a heavy rain began and lasted all morning, flooding the river. The news improved: Montaño, the son of the owner, is about 16 years old. His father was not there, and will be away for a week. He gave us quite a lot of detailed information on the ford, which is about a league from here. A section of the road runs along the left bank, but it is short. On this side there is only a brother of Pérez, an ordinary peasant whose daughter is the fiancée of a member of the Army.

We moved to a new campsite, by the stream and a cornfield – Marcos and Miguel cut a path to the main road. h = 650m. (stormy weather)

14 February

A quiet day, spent at the camp. The boy from the house came three times – once to tell us that some people had crossed the river to fetch some pigs – but that was it. We paid him a little extra for the damage done to the cornfield.

The trail-cutters spent all day hacking, without coming across a house. They estimate that they have prepared some six kilometres, which is half of their task for tomorrow.

A long message from Havana was decoded. Its main point was the news of the meeting with Kolle. Once there, he said that he had not been informed of the continental dimensions of the undertaking, but if that were the case, they would be prepared to co-operate in the plan, of which they asked to discuss the details with me. Kolle himself will come with Simón Rodríguez and Ramírez. I am also informed that Simón has declared his willingness to help us, regardless of what the party decides.

In addition, we are informed that the Frenchman, travelling on his own passport, arrives on the 23rd at La Paz and will be lodging with Pareja or Rhea. A section that we have not been able to decode so far is still pending. We shall see how we tackle this new conciliatory offensive. Other news: Merci turned up without any money, alleging robbery, although we suspect misappropriation and do not rule out something even worse. Lechín intends to ask for money and training.

15 February
Hildita's birthday.*

An uneventful day on the march. At 10.00 in the morning we had reached the point where the trail-cutters had stopped. After that it was a long, slow march. At 17.00 in the afternoon news came that they had come across a cultivated field, and at 18.00 this was confirmed. We sent Inti, Loro and Aniceto to talk to the peasant, who turned out to be Miguel Pérez, brother of Nicolás, a rich peasant. But he is poor and is exploited by his brother, so he was ready to co-operate with us. We didn't have anything to eat because it was so late.

16 February
We walked a few metres to avoid the brother's curiosity and camped on high ground, which looks down on to the river some 50 metres below. It is a good position in that we are shielded from any surprises, but it is a little uncomfortable. We began the task of preparing a considerable quantity of food for the trip across the mountain range to the Rosita river.

In the afternoon a violent and persistent rain began, and it fell right through the night without stop. It interfered with our plans; it made the river flood and left us isolated again.

---

* Birthday of his eldest daughter, Hilda Guevara Gadea (11).

We will lend the peasant 1,000 pesos so that he can buy and fatten some pigs: he has capitalist ambitions.

17 February
The rain continued all morning; 18 hours of rain. Everything is soaked and the river is very high. I sent Marcos, with Miguel and Braulio, to look for a road to reach the Rosita river. He came back in the afternoon having opened a four-kilometre-long trail. He informed us that there is another bare ridge, similar to the one that we call Pampa del Tigre. Inti is not feeling well as a result of stuffing himself.
h = 720m. (abnormal atmospheric conditions)

18 February
Josefina's birthday (33).*

A partial failure. We walked slowly following the pace of the trail-cutters, but by 14.00 they had arrived at the flat ridge where there is no need to hack the path. We were somewhat delayed and at 15.00 we reached a watering place where we camped, intending to cross the ridge tomorrow. Marcos and Tuma went out exploring and came back with very bad news: there are sharp cliffs all down the hill, which makes it impossible to descend. We have no alternative but to turn back.
h = 980m.

19 February
A wasted day. We went back down the hill until we found the stream and attempted to climb along its banks, but it was impossible. I sent Miguel and Aniceto to try and climb up another outcrop to attempt to reach the other side, without result. We spent the day waiting for them and they came back saying that the cliffs were of the same type: impassable. Tomorrow we will attempt to climb the last

---

* Birthday of his wife, Aleida March de la Torre's (33).

ridge beyond the stream, which descends towards the west (the others do so towards the south, and there the hill breaks).

h = 720m.

February 20

A day of slow march and many obstacles. Miguel and Braulio took the old path to reach the small stream by the cornfield, and there they lost their bearings and got back to the stream by nightfall. When we got to the next stream I sent Rolando and Pombo to explore it until they ran into the cliff, but they did not return until three, so we continued through the path that Marcos was opening up, leaving Pedro and Rubio behind to wait for them. We arrived at 16.30 at the stream by the cornfield and camped there. The explorers have not yet returned.

h = 720m.

21 February

Slow walk upstream. Pombo and Rolando returned with the news that the other stream could be crossed, but Marcos explored it and it looked just like the others. At 11.00 we started out, but by 13.30 we encountered some pools of icy water, which we could not wade through. Loro was sent out to explore and took a long time, so I sent Braulio and Joaquín from the Rearguard. Loro came back with the news that the stream widened further up and might be easier to cross, so we decided to carry on without waiting for the results from Joaquín. A 18.00 we camped, when the latter arrived with the news that it was possible to climb the ridge and that there was a suitable path. Inti is unwell, he is full of wind for the second time in one week.

h = 860m.

22 February

The entire day was spent climbing difficult ridges that were

covered in thick undergrowth. After an exhausting day it
was time to camp, without getting to the top. I sent Joaquín
and Pedro to try to do it on their own and they came back at
19.00 with the news that it would require at least three
hours to clear a path. We are at the head of the stream that
runs into the Masicuri, but heading south.

23 February

A black day for me. I made it through will-power alone and
am completely exhausted. Marcos, Braulio and Tuma set
off in the morning to clear the path, while we waited at the
camp. There we decoded a new message, which acknow-
ledges receipt of mine sent to the French post-box. We left
at noon with a sun hot enough to split rocks and not long
after, when we reached the summit, I felt faint and from
that moment I walked on out of sheer determination. The
highest altitude of the area is at 1,420 metres, overlooking
a large region that includes the Río Grande, the mouth of
the Ñacahuasu and part of the Rosita. The topography is
different from what is shown on the map: after a clear
dividing line, it drops abruptly to a kind of tree-topped
plateau, eight to ten kilometres wide, at the end of which
flows the Rosita. Then there is another range of similar
height to this one, and in the distance you can see the
plain.

We decided to descend by a practicable though very steep
route, and follow a stream that leads to the Río Grande, and
from there to the Rosita. It seems that there are no houses
along the river banks, contrary to what is shown on the map.
After an infernal descent, we camped at 900 metres, without
water and as night was falling.

At dawn I heard Marcos telling a comrade to go to hell and
during the day saying it to someone else. I have to talk to
him.

24 February

Ernestico's birthday (2).*

An arduous and wasted day. We made little progress. We had no water because the stream we are following is dry. At noon the trail-cutters were replaced, due to exhaustion. At 14.00 in the afternoon it rained a little, so we filled the canteens; not much later we came across a small pool of water and at 17.00 we camped at a clearing beside the water. Marcos and Urbano continued exploring, and Marcos came back with the news that the river was a couple of kilometres away, but the road beside the stream was very bad because it had turned into a swamp.

h = 680m.

25 February

A black day. We made very little progress and on top of that Marcos, who was with Miguel and Loro, took the wrong route and the morning was wasted. At noon he informed us and asked for relief and a two-way radio communication system. Braulio, Tuma and Pacho went. Two hours later Pacho returned saying that Marcos had sent him back because the reception was poor. At 16.30 I sent Benigno to tell Marcos that, if by 18.00 he had not found the river, he should return. After Benigno left, Pacho called me to say that he and Marcos had had an argument, and that Marcos had given him arbitrary orders and had threatened Pacho with a machete, hitting him in the face with the handle. When Pacho returned and told Marcos that he was not going on, Marcos threatened him again with the machete and shook him, tearing his clothing.

In view of the seriousness of the matter, I called Inti and Rolando, who confirmed that there was bad feeling in the Vanguard because of Marcos's nasty temper, although they also reported on Pacho's insolence.

---

* Birthday of his youngest son, Ernesto Guevara March (2).

26 February

In the morning I asked Marcos and Pacho for an explanation, as a result of which I am convinced that Marcos did insult and maybe ill-treat Pacho, perhaps threatening him with the machete, but not hitting him. However, Pacho is guilty of rudeness in his replies and has an innate tendency towards bravado, of which there have been several incidents recently. I waited until all the men were together to talk to them about the importance of this effort to reach the Rosita, explaining how the sort of privations we were experiencing were an introduction to the suffering that lay ahead for us. I explained that shameful incidents such as the one between the two Cubans were happening as a result of their incapacity to adapt to the circumstances. I criticised Marcos for his attitude and I warned Pacho that another incident like this would bring about his dishonourable discharge from the guerrilla force. Pacho, besides refusing to continue to operate the radio set, came back and said nothing about the incident to me. It is highly probable that he lied to me about being struck by Marcos.

I told the Bolivians that if any of them did not feel up to it, they should not resort to deceit but should tell me and they would be discharged and sent away in peace.

We continued to walk, trying to reach the Río Grande and then follow it. We did so, and were able to follow it for more than one kilometre, but we had to climb up again because there was a cliff by the river that was impassable. Benjamín had fallen behind because of difficulties with his rucksack, and physical exhaustion. When he caught up with us, I ordered him to carry on and he did so. He walked some 50 metres, but lost the trail up and started to look for it from a ledge. When I ordered Urbano to show him the way, Benjamín made a sudden movement and fell into the water. He did not know how to swim. There was a strong current, which dragged him along while he was still able to touch the bottom. We ran to try to help him and, as we were taking our clothes off, he disappeared in a pool of water. Rolando swam towards him and tried to dive underwater, but the current swept him far off-course. Five minutes later we gave up all hope. Benjamín was weak and very unfit, but a boy with an enormous will to prevail against all the odds. The test was stronger than him, his physical attributes were no match for his will, and we have now had our baptism of death on the banks of the Río Grande, in an absurd way. We camped, without reaching the Rosita, at 17.00 in the afternoon. We ate the last ration of beans.

27 February
After another exhausting day walking along the river and climbing up cliffs, we reached the Rosita river. This is bigger than the Ñacahuasu, but smaller than the Masicuri, and its waters are tinged red.

We ate our last reserve ration and found no signs of life nearby, in spite of being so close to populated areas and roads.

h = 600m.

28 February
A day partially devoted to rest. After breakfast (tea) I gave a short talk, analysing Benjamín's death and telling some anecdotes from the Sierra Maestra. The explorers then left. Miguel, Inti and Loro set off upstream along the Rosita, with orders to walk for three and a half hours, which I thought was what it would take to reach the Abapocito river, but this was not so because of the lack of a trail. They did not find any recent signs of life. Joaquín and Pedro climbed the steep banks facing us, but saw nothing and found no trace of a trail. Alejandro and Rubio crossed the river, but did not find a trail, although their search was superficial. Marcos organised the construction of a raft and, as soon as it was ready, we began to cross at the bend of the river into which the Rosita flows. The rucksacks of five men were sent

across, including Miguel's, while Benigno's remained
behind. The opposite happened with the men, and to make
matters worse Benigno left his shoes behind.

The raft could not be recovered. Since the second one was
not finished, we suspended the crossing until tomorrow.

Analysis of the month
*Although I do not have news of what is happening in the
camp, everything is going reasonably well, with the
corresponding exceptions, which in these cases are fatal.*

*From outside, we have no news of the two men who
should have been sent to complete the group; the
Frenchman must already be in La Paz and should arrive at
the camp any day now. I have no news of the Argentines,
nor of Chino. Messages are received well in both directions. The attitude of the party continues to be vacillating
and duplicitous, to say the least, although there is a clari-
fication pending, which could be definitive, when I talk to
the new delegation.*

*The march went quite well, but was ruined by the
accident that cost the life of Benjamín. The men are still
weak and not all the Bolivians will be able to withstand it.
The recent days of hunger have weakened their enthusiasm
and this became more obvious when they were divided.*

*Of the Cubans, two of the less experienced ones, Pacho
and Rubio, have not responded well, but Alejandro has
done so completely. Of the old ones, Marcos is a constant
headache and Ricardo is not totally committed. The others
are doing well.*

The next stage will be combat and certainly decisive.

March 1967

1 March

At 6.00 it started to rain. We postponed the crossing until it stopped, but it poured down and continued to do so until 15.00 in the afternoon, when the river was flooded and we thought it unwise to try and cross.

It is now very high and it does not look as if it will ebb soon. I took myself off to an abandoned hut to stay out of the rain, and camped there. Joaquín stayed where he was. In the evening he informed me that Polo had drunk his tin of milk and Eusebio had both drunk his tin of milk and eaten his tin of sardines. For now, as a punishment, they will not eat whenever the others get their rations of those foods. A bad sign.

2 March

The day dawned rainy and the men were restless – starting with me. The river rose even more. It was decided to leave the camp as soon as the rain should stop and to follow the river along the path that brought us here. We left at noon and stocked up on hearts of palm shoots. We stopped at 16.30 because we had abandoned our path in an attempt to take advantage of an old trail, which we then lost. There's no news of the Vanguard.

3 March

We began enthusiastically, walking well, but as the hours passed the pace slackened and we had to alter our route and walk along the ridge because I feared another accident in the area where Benjamín fell. It took us four hours to cover the same ground that had taken us less than half an hour further down. At 18.00 we reached the bank of the stream, where we camped, but we only had two rations of palm shoots. Miguel and Urbano went further to find some more, and came back at 21.00 in the evening. We ate around 24.00, the palm shoots and the *corojo** (known as *totai* in Bolivia) are saving the day.

h = 600m.

4 March

Miguel and Urbano left in the morning and spent the whole day working with machetes on a trail. They advanced about five kilometres and have seen a plateau that should allow us to make progress, but there is no space for the camp, so we have decided to stay here until the trail is longer. The hunters caught two monkeys, a parrot and a pigeon, which became our meal, with the palm shoots that are abundant beside this stream.

The men's morale is low and our physical condition is deteriorating by the day. I have signs of oedema in my legs.

5 March

Joaquín and Braulio went out in the rain with their machetes to clear the path, but both are weak and did not make much progress. Twelve palm shoots were collected, and some small birds, which enables us to keep our tins for another day, and to make up a reserve of palm shoots for two days.

6 March

A day of intermittent walking, until 17.00 in the afternoon. Miguel, Urbano and Tuma are the trail-cutters. Some progress was made and in the distance we can see some high banks, which appear to be those of the Ñacahuasu. We only

---

*Corojo. American tree of the palm family. Its fruits can be boiled to obtain a greasy substance that is used as vegetable fat.

caught a small parrot, which we gave to the Rearguard.
Today we eat palm shoots with meat. We have three very
frugal meals left.
h = 600m.

7 March
Four months. The men are more discouraged by the day,
seeing the end of provisions, but not the end of the road.
Today we advanced four or five kilometres along the river
bank and at last found a promising trail. Food: three and a
half little birds and the rest of the palm shoots. From
tomorrow just tins, one-third per person, for two days, then
the condensed milk and that's it. We must be two or three
days' march from the Ñacahuasu.
h = 610m.

8 March
A day of little progress, of surprises and tension. At 10.00 we
left the camp without waiting for Rolando, who was out
hunting. After only an hour and a half we met up with the
trail-cutters and the hunters (Urbano, Miguel and Tuma –
the Doctor and Chinchu, respectively), who had many
parrots but had discovered that there was a water inlet and
had stopped. I went to look at the place after ordering them
to pitch camp, and it turned out to be a petrol pumping
station. Inti and Ricardo jumped into the water, they were
pretending to be hunters. They jumped in fully dressed
trying to make it in two stages, but Inti had difficulties and
nearly drowned. Ricardo helped him and at last they came
out on the other side, catching everybody's attention. The
signal to indicate danger never came and in the end they
disappeared. They had begun the crossing at 12.00 and at
15.15 I withdrew without their giving any signs of life. The
whole afternoon went by and they did not appear. The last
sentry duty ended at 21.00 with no new signs from them.
    I was extremely concerned; two valuable comrades had

been exposed, and we did not know what had happened. It
was decided that Alejandro and Rolando, our two best
swimmers, cross tomorrow at daybreak.

We ate better than other days – in spite of the lack of palm
shoots – because of the abundance of parrots and the two
little monkeys that Rolando killed.

9 March

We started preparations for an early crossing, but we had to
build a raft, which took some time. The sentry announced
that he had seen half-naked people on the other side. It was
8.30 and the crossing was postponed. We have made a small
path that leads to a clearing on the other bank, but as we
might be visible there, we will have to leave very early in the
morning to take advantage of the mist from the river.
Around 16.00, after an exasperating watch which for me
lasted from 10.30, the men fetching supplies (Inti and
Chinchu) jumped into the river and came out far below.
They brought pork, bread, rice, sugar, coffee, some tins, half-
ripe corn, etc. We treated ourselves to a little feast of coffee
and bread and I authorised the consumption of a tin of boiled
condensed milk, which we had in reserve, as a sweet. They
said that they had shown themselves once each hour so that
we would see them, but to no avail. Marcos and his men
went by three days ago and it seems that he was up to his
usual tricks, parading the weapons. The engineers at the
petrol plant do not know what distance there is to
Ñacahuasu, but they estimate five days. If it is so, the
provisions will suffice. The pump is part of a pumping plant
that is under construction.

10 March

We started at about 6.30 and walked for about 45 minutes,
when we met up with the trail-cutters. At 8.00 it began to
rain and it went on until 11.00. All told, we walked some
three hours and we camped at 17.00. We can see some hills,

which could be the Ñacahuasu. Braulio went out to explore and returned with the news that there is a path and that the river flows directly west.

h = 600m.

11 March

The day began auspiciously. We walked for over an hour along a perfect trail, but then it suddenly ended. Braulio took his machete and laboriously cut our way through until we reached a small, flat, open clearing. We gave him and Urbano the time to clear a path but just as we were about to follow them, the rising waters prevented us. Quite suddenly the river rose a couple of metres.

We were isolated from the trail-cutters and forced to make our way through the woods. At 13.30 we stopped and I sent Miguel and Tuma to make contact with the Vanguard and convey the order to return, if they had not managed to get to the Ñacahuasu or another suitable spot.

At 18.00 they came back, having run into a steep cliff after walking for about three kilometres. It seems we are near, but the last few days will be very hard if the water does not go down, which looks rather improbable. We walked four to five kilometres.

A disagreeable incident took place because the Rearguard is short of sugar, and there is the suspicion that they were given smaller amounts, or that Braulio had been taking liberties. I must talk to him.

h = 610m.

12 March

We covered the stretch that was cleared yesterday in an hour and 10 minutes. Miguel and Tuma had been the first to leave, and were already exploring to find a way to bypass the steep cliff. The whole day was spent doing this: our only activity was to catch four small birds, which we had as a side-dish to the rice and mussels. We have two meals left.

Miguel stayed on the other side and it seems that he found a
way to the Ñacahuasu. We walked three or four kilometres.

13 March
From 6.30 until 12.00 noon we climbed through some
infernal cliffs, following the trail opened by Miguel – a
heroic task. We thought we had already reached the
Ñacahuasu when we ran into some difficult passes and
advanced very little in five hours. We camped in moderate
rainfall at 17.00. The men are quite tired and again a little
demoralised. There is only one meal left. We walked
approximately six kilometres, but made little progress.

14 March
Almost without realising it, we reached the Ñacahuasu. (I
was – am – as tired as if a rock had fallen on top of me.) The
river is rough and nobody is eager to attempt the crossing.
Rolando volunteered and crossed easily, leaving for the base
at exactly 15.20. I expect him to reach it in two days.

  We ate the last of the food, a *mote** with meat. We are
now dependent on what we hunt. As I write these notes we
have only one little bird, but three shots have been heard.
The Doctor and Inti are the hunters.

  We heard some of Fidel's speech, in which he castigates
the Venezuelan Communists and criticises in harsh terms
the attitude of the USSR towards the puppets of the
Americans.
h = 600m.

15 March
We crossed the river, but only the Main Force, with Rubio
and the Doctor to help us. We wanted to reach the mouth of
the Ñacahuasu, but we have three men who cannot swim,

---

*Threshed and boiled maize, a popular dish in some parts of America. From the
Quechua word *mut'i*.

and a large load. The current dragged us for about one kilometre and we could not cross with the raft as we had intended. Eleven of us remain on this side and tomorrow the Doctor and Rubio will cross back. We caught four hawks, which became our meal – not as bad as you might expect. Everything got wet and the weather continues to be rainy. The men's morale is low; Miguel's feet are swollen and there are others in a similar condition.

h = 580m.

16 March

We decided to eat the horse; our swellings are now alarming. Miguel, Inti, Urbano, Alejandro all showed various symptoms and I am extremely weak. We made a mistake in our calculations because we thought that Joaquín had crossed over, but he had not. The Doctor and Rubio tried to cross to help them, but were swept downstream and we lost sight of them. Joaquín asked for permission for his group to cross and I gave it to him and they too got lost downstream. I sent Pombo and Tuma to find them, but they could not and returned at night. From 17.00 there was an orgy of horse-meat. There will probably be consequences tomorrow. I calculate Rolando should be arriving at the camp today.

Message No. 32 is entirely decoded. It announces the arrival of one Bolivian who is joining up and brings another load of glucantine, an anti-parasitic (leishmania). So far we have no cases of this.

17 March

Once again we have a tragedy, even before our first taste of combat. Joaquín appeared mid-morning; Miguel and Tuma had gone to meet him with some good pieces of meat. Their odyssey had been serious: they were unable to control the raft and it was carried downstream along the Ñacahuasu, until it got caught in a whirlpool and, by their account, was overturned several times. The end result was the loss of

several rucksacks, almost all the bullets, six rifles and one
man: Carlos. He was sucked into the whirlpool together
with Braulio, but suffered a different fate: Braulio reached
the shore and saw Carlos helplessly being dragged off.
Joaquín had already left with all his men, and they did not
see Carlos being swept along. Until now, Carlos was
considered the best of the Bolivians of the Rearguard
because of his seriousness, discipline and enthusiasm.

The weapons we have lost are one Brno, Braulio's, two
M-1s, Carlos's and Pedro's, and three Mausers, Abel's,
Eusebio's and Polo's. Joaquín reported having seen Rubio
and the Doctor on the other bank, and had given them orders
to build a small raft and come across. At about 14.00 they
arrived with their tale of vicissitudes and troubles, both of
them naked, and Rubio barefoot. Their raft disintegrated at
the first whirlpool. They came ashore almost where we had.

Our departure is set for early tomorrow morning, and
Joaquín will leave at noon. I expect to get news tomorrow
during the course of the day. The morale of Joaquín's men
seems to be good.

18 March

We set off early, leaving Joaquín to digest and finish the
preparation of his half of the horsemeat. He had orders to
leave as soon as he felt strong enough.

I had a struggle to keep some of the meat in reserve,
against the wishes of the men who wanted to stuff themselves. By mid-morning Ricardo, Inti and Urbano had lagged
behind and we had to wait for them, contrary to my plan to
rest when we reach the camp from which we had set off. In
any case, we are not making much progress.

At 14.30 Urbano appeared with a small deer, a *urina*,
caught by Ricardo, which gives us a certain amount of
luxury and allows us to keep the horse ribs in reserve. At
16.30 we arrived at what should have been only the
halfway point, but we slept there. Several men are dragging

their feet and getting bad-tempered: Chinchu, Urbano and Alejandro.

19 March

Those of us in front walked well during the morning. We stopped at 11.00, as had been agreed, but again Ricardo and Urbano were slow, and this time so was Alejandro. They arrived at 13.00, but they brought another *urina*, also caught by Ricardo. Joaquín arrived with them. There was an incident caused by an exchange of angry words between Joaquín and Rubio. I had to be harsh with Rubio, although I am not convinced that he is at fault.

I decided to go as far as the stream in any case, but there was a small plane circling above which did not bode well. Also, I was concerned by the lack of news from the base. I thought that it would take longer, but in spite of the men's weariness, we arrived at 17.30. There we were greeted by the Peruvian doctor, Negro, who came with Chino, and the telegraph operator, with the news that Benigno was expecting us, with a meal prepared, and that two of Moisés Guevara's men had deserted. The police had turned up at the farm. Benigno explained that he had set off with food to meet us, and that he had crossed paths with Rolando. He has been here for two days, but had not dared to continue because the Army might advance by the river, and for three days the small plane has been circling. Negro had witnessed the attack on the farm by six men. Neither Antonio nor Coco had been there; the latter had gone to Camiri to meet a new group of Moisés Guevara's men, and Antonio had left immediately afterwards to inform him of the desertion. I received a long report from Marcos (D.VIII) in which he explains his actions in his own way. He had arrived at the farm against my express orders. There were also two reports from Antonio explaining the situation (D.IX and X).

The Frenchman, Chino, his comrades, Pelado and Tania,

and Moisés Guevara with his first group of men, are at the base now.

After eating a lavish meal of rice, beans and venison, Miguel went out to find Joaquín, who had not arrived, and to locate Chinchu, who is delayed once more. He came back with Ricardo, and at daybreak Joaquín appeared and we were all assembled together here.

20 March

We left at 10.00, at a steady pace. Benigno and Negro preceded us with a message for Marcos, ordering him to take charge of the defence and to leave administrative matters to Antonio. Joaquín's group left at leisure, after erasing the tracks leading to the stream. Three of his men are barefoot. At 13.00 when we were making a long stop, Pacho appeared with a message from Marcos. The report was more detailed than the previous one from Benigno, but the situation now appears more complicated. The soldiers had arrived by the path used by the Vallegrandino, 60 of them. They captured a messenger of ours, Salustio, one of Moisés Guevara's men. They had taken a mule and the jeep was lost. No news from Loro, who had been keeping watch at the little house. We decided to reach the Bear Camp, as it is now called, because a bear was killed there. We sent Miguel and Urbano to prepare food for the very hungry men, and we arrived at dusk. At the camp were Danton, Pelado, Chino, as well as Tania and a group of Bolivian men who ferry the supplies and then withdraw. Rolando had been sent to organise the total withdrawal. There is a climate of defeat. Not long afterwards a recently recruited Bolivian doctor arrived with a message for Rolando, informing him that Marcos and Antonio were at the watering place, and to go and meet up with them. I sent word with the same messenger that wars are won with bullets, that they should withdraw immediately to the camp and wait for me there. The general impression is of terrible chaos. They don't know what to do.

I had a preliminary talk with Chino. He is asking for 5,000 dollars a month for ten months, and Havana told him to discuss it with me. He also brought a message, which Arturo could not decode because it is too long. I said that I agreed in principle, on condition that within six months they took up arms. He intends to do so with 15 men under his command, in the area of Ayacucho. We also agreed that I would accept five of his men now and another 15 later. Within a certain period, after training them in combat, I would send them back with their weapons. He must send me a pair of medium-range transmitters (40 miles) and we will work out a code for our own use so that we can be in permanent contact. He seems very enthusiastic.

He also brought a series of reports from Rodolfo, which are now out of date. We learn that Loro has appeared and announced that he has killed a soldier.

21 March

I spent the day chatting and clarifying some points with Chino, the Frenchman, Pelado and Tania. The Frenchman brought news that we had already received from Monje, Kolle, Simón Reyes, etc. He has come intending to stay but I asked him to go back to France – with a stopover in Cuba – to organise a support network in France. This coincides with his desire to get married and have a child by his comrade. I must write letters to Sartre and to B. Russell so that they organise an international fund to assist the Bolivian Liberation Movement. He should also speak to a friend who will organise all the channels to send us assistance, mainly money, medicines and electronics, preferably in the shape of an electrical engineer and equipment.

Pelado is of course ready to put himself at my disposal. I proposed that he becomes a sort of co-ordinator, for the time being getting in touch only with the groups led by Jozami, Gelman and Stamponi, to send me five men so that they can start training. He must give my regards to María Rosa Oliver and to my old man. He will receive 500 pesos to send off and 1,000 for his travels. If they accept, they must start exploring in the north of Argentina and send me a report.

Tania made the contacts and the men came, but according to her, she had to travel in their jeep as far as here. She had intended to stay, but matters have become complicated. Jozami could not stay the first time round, and the second contact was not even made because Tania was here. She refers to Iván with a certain disdain; I do not know what is at the bottom of it. We received Loyola's financial balance sheet up to 9 February (1,500 dollars). She also informed me that she has been removed from the leadership of the party's Youth Organisation.

We receive two reports from Iván: one is of little interest, it contains photos and is about a military school; the other gives information on some points, and it is not very important either.

The main thing is that the written message could not be decoded (D.XIII). We receive a report from Antonio (D.XII) in which he tries to justify his behaviour. We hear a radio broadcast that reports a death – which is later denied – which indicates that Loro was telling the truth.

22 March

At [illegible in the original] we left, abandoning the camp [illegible] with some food, badly stored [illegible]. We reached the downstream area at 12.00. We are a group of 47 men, including visitors and all.

When we arrived Inti pointed out to me a series of ways in which Marcos had been disrespectful. I blew my top and told Marcos that if it was true, he would be expelled from the guerrilla. He replied that he would rather be shot.

We had ordered five men to set an ambush ahead along the river, and sent out a three-man exploration party led by Antonio, with Miguel and Loro. Pacho went as an observer to the bare hill above Argañaraz's house, but did not spot anything. In the evening the exploration party returned and I reprimanded them. Olo reacted very emotionally and denied the charges. The meeting was explosive and untimely, and the result was not good. It is not clear what Marcos said. I sent for Rolando to solve once and for all the problem of the new recruits, their numbers and distribution, since we are now more than 30 people to feed and those in the Main Force went hungry.

23 March

A day of war. Pombo wanted to organise a team to go upstream and retrieve the supplies, but I opposed him until the replacement of Marcos has been resolved. After 8.00 Coco rushed in to report that a section of the Army had fallen into the ambush.

The final result so far is three 60mm mortars, 16 Mausers, two BZs, three Uzis, one .30-calibre machine gun, two radios, boots, etc., seven killed, 14 uninjured prisoners and four wounded. No food supplies could be taken. Their operations plan was captured. It consists of advancing from both ends of the Ñacahuasu to make contact at a central point. We quickly sent men to the other side and I put Marcos, with almost the entire Vanguard, at the end of the path we use for manoeuvres, while the Main Force and part of the Rearguard remain in defensive positions, and Braulio sets an ambush at the end of the second path for manoeuvres. This is how we will spend the night, and we shall see if tomorrow the famous Rangers arrive. A major and a captain, taken prisoner, talked like parrots.

The message that had been sent with Chino was decoded. It mentions Debré's trip, the remittance of $60,000, Chino's requests, and an explanation of why they are not writing to Iván. I also received a communication from Sánchez informing us of the possibilities of setting up Mito at certain points.

24 March

The total booty is as follows: 16 Mausers, three mortars with 64 shells, two BZs, 2,000 Mauser rounds, three Uzis with two magazines each, one .30-calibre machine gun with two cartridge belts. There are seven dead and 14 prisoners, including four wounded. Marcos was sent to explore the area and saw nothing, but the planes were bombing close to our house.

I sent Inti to speak to the prisoners for the last time and to set them free, stripping them of every garment useful to us. The two officers, who were questioned separately, left fully clothed. We told the major that we gave them until the 27th at 12.00 to collect their dead, and we offered them a truce for the whole area of Lagunillas if he stayed around, but he replied that he was retiring from the Army. The captain stated that he had rejoined the Army a year ago, at the request of people from the party and that he had a brother studying in Cuba. He also gave the names of two other officers who were prepared to co-operate. They panicked when the planes started the bombardment, but two of our own men, Raúl and Walter, also panicked; the latter was also weak during the ambush.

Marcos went out to explore, but found nothing in his area. Ñato and Coco went with the rejects to fetch supplies upstream, but they had to return because the men did not want to march. We must discharge them.

25 March

The day went by without anything new. León, Urbano and Arturo were sent to an observation point that overlooks the access to the river on both sides. At 12.00 Marcos was withdrawn from his position in the ambush, and all the others remained concentrated on the main ambush. At 18.30, with almost all present, I made an analysis of our expedition and its significance. I pointed out Marcos's errors, demoting him and appointing Miguel to lead the

Vanguard. At the same time I announced the discharge of Paco, Pepe, Chingolo and Eusebio, letting them know that they will not eat unless they work. Their tobacco ration is suspended and their personal effects will be distributed among those comrades who most need them. I mentioned Kolle's intention to come and discuss what needs to be done with us. At the same time I referred to the expulsion of those who were members of the Communist Youth Organisation who are present here. What matters is deeds. Words that do not coincide with deeds are of no importance. I announced that we would look for a cow, and resume our studies.

I spoke with Pedro and the Doctor and told them that they were almost fully graduated as guerrilla fighters, and I talked to Apolinar in order to encourage him. I criticised Walter for being slack during the expedition, for his attitude in combat, and for the fear of the planes that he showed. He did not react well. I went over some details with Chino and Pelado and I gave the Frenchman a long verbal report on the situation. During the meeting the group was given the name of National Liberation Army of Bolivia – Ejército de Liberación Nacional de Bolivia. A report of the meeting will be drafted.

26 March
Inti left early with Antonio, Raúl and Pedro to find a cow in the area of Tikucha, but they encountered troops some three hours from here. They turned back, apparently without being seen. They reported that the soldiers had a sentry in a clearing, and another in a house with a shining roof, from which they saw eight men leaving. They are in the area of the river we referred to as Yaki. I spoke with Marcos and sent him to the Rearguard. I don't think his behaviour will improve much.

We organised a small supply trip and the usual sentries; from the observation post overlooking Argañaraz's house 30–40 soldiers were seen and a helicopter landed.

27 March
The news exploded today, monopolising all the airwaves and resulting in a multitude of communiqués, including a press conference by Barrientos. The official report includes one more dead than we do, and says that they were wounded and then shot. It gives our losses as 15 dead and four prisoners, two of whom are foreigners. It also states that a foreigner killed himself, and gives the composition of the guerrilla unit. It is obvious that the deserters or the prisoner talked. The only thing is that I don't know how much they said, or how they said it. Everything seems to indicate that Tania has been identified, as a result of which we lose two years of good and patient work. The departure of the visitors will now be very difficult. I got the impression that Danton was not amused when I told him. We shall see later on.

Benigno, Loro and Julio left to look for the road to Pirirenda. They have two or three days, and their orders are to arrive at Pirirenda without being seen, and then go on an expedition to Gutiérrez. The reconnaissance plane dropped some parachutes, which our lookouts said had fallen in the hunting field. Antonio and two others were sent to investigate and try to take prisoners, but there was nothing.

At night we held a meeting of the General Staff during which we set the plans for the next days: to send a supply team to our little house to collect corn, then another one to shop in Gutiérrez, and finally a little diversionary attack on passing vehicles, which is to be in the wooded areas between Pincal and Lagunillas.

We drafted Communiqué No. 1 and we will try to get it to the press in Camiri (D.XVII).

28 March
The radio broadcasts continue to be saturated with news of the guerrillas. We are surrounded by 2,000 men in a radius of 120 kilometres and the circle is tightening, complemented by napalm bombings, and are said to have 10–15 casualties.

I sent Braulio, with nine men, to try and find some corn. They returned at night with a catalogue of crazy reports:

1) Coco, who had gone on ahead to warn us, had disappeared.
2) At 16.00 they reached the farm and found that the cave had been searched. So they spread out to start gathering the scattered things, when seven men from the Red Cross appeared, two doctors and several unarmed military men. They are taken prisoner and told that the truce has expired, but they are allowed to carry on.
3) A truck full of soldiers arrives and, instead of firing at them, tell them to withdraw.
4) The soldiers withdraw in an orderly fashion and our men lead the medics to where the rotting corpses lie. Unable to carry them, the medics say that they will come back tomorrow to burn them. Our men confiscate two horses belonging to Argañaraz and return, leaving Antonio, Rubio and Aniceto at the point where the animals could no longer continue. When they were setting out to find Coco, he appeared; apparently he had fallen asleep.

Still no news of Benigno.

The Frenchman emphasised rather too vehemently how useful he could be outside.

29 March

Day of little action, but of extraordinary events in the news. The Army is supplying a vast amount of information, which, if true, can be of great value to us. Radio Havana has already reported the news. The government announced that it will support Venezuela when it presents the case of Cuba before the Organisation of American States. Among the news items there is one that worries me: the one that says there was an encounter at the Tiraboy ravine in which two guerrillas were killed. Through that ravine you get to

Pirirenda, the area that Benigno was supposed to explore. He should have been back today and he has not returned. His orders were not to go through the ravine, but in the last few days my orders have been disobeyed repeatedly.

Moisés Guevara is making slow progress in his work. He was given dynamite, but was not able to set it off all day. A horse was killed and generous helpings of meat eaten, in spite of the fact that it ought to last us for four days. We will try to bring the other one here, although it seems difficult. Judging by the birds of prey, the bodies have not yet been burned. As soon as the cave is ready we can move from this camp, which is now getting uncomfortable and too well known. I informed Alejandro that he would remain here with the Doctor and Joaquín (probably at Bear Camp). Rolando is also really exhausted.

I talked to Urbano and Tuma; the latter could not even understand the source of my criticisms.

30 March

Everything is quiet again: by mid-morning Benigno and his comrades appeared. They had in fact gone through the Tiraboy ravine, but had only found the tracks of two people. They arrived at their destination, but were seen by the peasants and returned. The report states that it takes up to four hours to reach Pirirenda and that, apparently, there is no danger. The Air Force machine-gunned the little house constantly.

I sent Antonio with two men to explore upriver and the report is that the soldiers are stationary, although there are signs of movement along the river. They have dug trenches.

The missing mare arrived at camp, so that in the worst case we have enough meat for four days. Tomorrow we will rest, and the day after tomorrow the Vanguard will start out for the next two operations: to take Gutiérrez, and to lay an ambush on the Argañaraz–Lagunillas road.

31 March

A day without any noteworthy events. Moisés Guevara announced the completion of the cave for tomorrow. Inti and Ricardo reported that the soldiers had retaken our little farm, after an attack with artillery (mortar), aircraft, etc. This obstructs our plans to go to Pirirenda for supplies. However, I gave orders to Manuel to advance with his men towards the little house. If it is empty, to take it and send two men to let me know, so that we can move the day after tomorrow. If it has been taken, and we cannot launch a surprise attack, they are due to return and explore the possibility of outflanking Argañaraz's house to lay an ambush between El Pincal and Lagunillas. The radio continues with its exaggerations, and the communiqués follow the unofficial reports of fighting. They have set our position with absolute precision between the Yaki and the Ñacahuasu, and I fear that they will try to encircle us. I spoke to Benigno about his mistake in not coming to find us, and I explained the situation with Marcos, who reacted well.

At night I spoke with Loro and Aniceto. The conversation went very badly. Loro went so far as to say that we were falling apart, and when I pressed him, he left it to Marcos and Benigno. Aniceto was partially in solidarity with Loro, but he then confessed to Coco that they had been accomplices in the theft of some tins, and to Inti that he was not in agreement with Loro's statements about Benigno or about Pombo, nor about the 'general breakdown of the guerrilla forces', more or less.

Analysis of the month

The month was brimming with events, but the general picture has the following characteristics:

Stage of consolidation and purification of the guerrilla forces: fully accomplished.

Slow stage of development with the incorporation of some Cuban elements, who do not seem bad, and Moisés

Guevara's men, who on the whole are of poor quality (two deserters, one 'talking' prisoner, three thrown out and two feeble ones).

Stage of beginning the struggle, characterised by a precise and spectacular blow, but marked by gross indecision before and after the event (Marcos's withdrawal and Braulio's action).

Stage of beginning an enemy counter-offensive, characterised up to now by: a) a tendency to establish controls to isolate us; b) a clamouring at national and international level; c) total ineffectiveness so far; d) mobilisation of peasants.

It is evident that we will have to take to the road earlier than planned, leaving behind a group 'to soak' and with the dead weight of four possible informers. The situation is not good, but a new stage begins now that will test the guerrilla forces but, once surpassed, will be greatly beneficial.

The composition:

Vanguard: Head – Miguel, Benigno, Pacho, Loro, Aniceto, Camba, Coco, Darío, Julio, Pablo, Raúl.

Rearguard: Head – Joaquín, second-in-command Braulio, Rubio, Marcos, Pedro, the Doctor, Polo, Walter, Victor (Pepe, Paco, Eusebio, Chingolo).

Main Force: Myself, Alejandro, Rolando, Inti, Pombo, Ñato, Tuma, Urbano, Moro, Negro, Ricardo, Arturo, Eustaquio, Moisés Guevara, Willy, Luis, Antonio, León (Tania, Pelado, Danton, Chino – visitors), (Serapio – refugee).

April 1967

1 April

The Vanguard left at 7.00, considerably delayed. Camba is missing, as he did not get back from his expedition with Ñato, hiding the weapons in the cave at Bear Camp. At 10.00 Tuma arrived from the lookout to say that he had seen three or four soldiers in the hunting field. We took up positions, and Walter from the lookout post said that he had seen three soldiers with a mule or donkey and that they were setting up something. He showed me, but I did not see anything. At 16.00 I withdrew, deciding that in any case it was no longer necessary to remain since they would not attack, but I think it was an optical illusion of Walter's.

I decided that we should evacuate everything tomorrow without fail and that Rolando will take command of the Rearguard while Joaquín is away. Ñato and Camba arrived at 21.00, having put everything away, except some food for those who were staying. They are: Joaquín, Alejandro, Moro, Serapio, Eustaquio and Polo. The three Cubans stay under protest. The other mare was killed in order to leave some *charqui** for the six. At 23.00 Antonio arrived with the news that everything had gone without incident. He brought a sack of maize.

At 4.00 Rolando left, handicapped by the four weaklings (Chingolo, Eusebio, Paco and Pepe). Pepe asked for a weapon and said he would stay. Camba went with him.

At 5.00 Coco arrived with a new message saying that they had killed a cow and were expecting us. I said the meeting

*Sun-dried salted meat.

point should be the day after tomorrow at midday, where the stream flows into the forest below the farm.

2 April

The incredible amount of things we have accumulated meant that we spent the whole day storing them in their respective caves, completing the task at 17.00. Four men were kept on guard duty, but the day went by in absolute calm; no planes flew over the area. The radio reports spoke of 'tightening the circle' and said that the guerrillas were preparing to defend the gully at Ñacahuasu. They also reported that Don Remberto is in jail, and how he had sold the farm to Coco.

In view of the time, we decided not to leave today, but to do so at three in the morning and gain a day by going straight along the Ñacahuasu, in spite of the fact that our meeting place is in the other direction. I talked to Moro and explained that I had not included him in the group of outstanding men because of his weakness over food, and his tendency to exasperate the comrades with his jokes. We talked about these subjects for a while.

3 April

The plan was carried out without hindrance: we left at 3.30 and walked slowly until we passed the bend where we took the shortcut at 6.30. We reached the edge of the farm at 8.30. When we passed the site of the ambush, we saw that only perfectly clean skeletons of the seven corpses remained – the birds of prey had taken their responsibility seriously. I sent two men (Urbano and Ñato) to make contact with Rolando, and in the afternoon we went to the Tiraboy ravine where we slept, stuffed with beef and corn.

I talked to Danton and Carlos and gave them three options: to continue on with us, to leave on their own, or, when we take Gutiérrez, to try their luck as best they could. They chose the third option. We will try our luck tomorrow.

4 April

Almost total failure. At 14.30 we reached a point where we saw the tracks of soldiers, as well as one of the paratrooper's berets. There were remnants too of individual food rations made in the USA. I decided to take the first house by assault of [*illegible in the original*] and we did so at 18.30. Guaraní* farmhands came out and told us that the Army, approximately 150 men, had withdrawn yesterday, and the owner of the house had also left yesterday to take his cattle away. We ordered that a meal of pork and yucca be prepared, while we took the second house of [*illegible*]. Loro, Coco, Aniceto and later Inti went to this second house accompanied by another peasant.

The couple was not there, but when they returned, the young farmhand had disappeared in the confusion. In the end we were able to discover that a company from the second regiment, the Bolívar, had been there and had left that morning. They had orders to climb down the Tiraboy ravine, but they chose a different route and that is why we did not clash with them. There are no soldiers in Gutiérrez, but they will be returning tomorrow, so it is not wise to stay.

In the first house we found items belonging to the military, such as plates, canteens, even bullets and equipment, and we appropriated it all. After eating well but not excessively, the Rearguard left at 3.00, and the Main Force at 3.30. The Vanguard was supposed to leave when they had eaten their last rations. We got lost and came out below the ambush, causing confusion that lasted until morning.

5 April

A day short of events, but with some tension. At 10.00 we were all together, and a little later Miguel's group left with their rucksacks to occupy the head of the ravine. They had

---

* Guaraní: ancient indigenous civilisation whose descendants inhabit the area from the Amazon to the Río de la Plata. The population of Paraguay is mainly Guaraní in origin.

orders to send the three men from the Rearguard who were on guard duty to the same spot to collect their rucksacks. To speed up the operation, I ordered Urbano, Ñato and León to replace the three men from the Rearguard. At 15.30 I stopped with the Main Force to set up an ambush to confront any troops that might climb down the ravine, since the Vanguard and the Rearguard will be defending both entrances at the mouth of the stream. At 14.00 I sent Tuma with three men to see what was going on, and at 17.00 he came back, not having seen anything. We moved to the previous campsite and I repeated the order. At 18.15 Rolando arrived, bringing the three rucksacks between them, as the other three had not met up with them. Braulio gave a report that throws into serious doubt Marcos's actual readiness for combat.

I had intended to start downriver at dawn, but soldiers were seen bathing only 300 metres from our position. We decided to cross the river, being careful to leave no tracks, and walk along the other path to our stream.

6 April

Day of great tension. We crossed the Ñacahuasu at 4.00, then waited for daybreak to set out. Miguel began to explore, but had to return twice because of mistakes that brought us too near to the soldiers. At 8.00 Rolando reported that some 10 soldiers were facing the ravine we had just left. We left slowly, and at 11.00 we were out of danger, up on a ridge. Rolando brought the news that more than 100 soldiers had taken up positions in the ravine.

At night, when we had not yet reached the stream, we heard the voices of cowherds in the river. We approached them and captured four peasants, who had some of Argañaraz's cows with them. They had a safe conduct from the Army to collect 12 head of cattle, some of which had already gone by, so they were unable to pick them up. We kept two cows for ourselves, and took them along the river to our stream. The four civilians are the contractor and his son, a peasant from Chuquisaca, and another one from Camiri, who was very well disposed. We gave him our document and he promised to circulate it.

We held them for a while, then let them go, with the request that they say nothing, which they promised.

We spent the night eating.

7 April

We went into deep water, taking the surviving cow, which was slaughtered to make *charqui*. Rolando remained on ambush by the river, with orders to shoot, if anything came into sight. Nothing showed up all day. Benigno and Camba followed the path that should take us to Pirirenda and reported that they had heard something like the motor of a sawmill at a canyon near our stream.

I sent Urbano and Julio with a message for Joaquín. They did not return all day.

8 April

A relatively uneventful day. Benigno left and returned without completing his work, and says that he won't finish it tomorrow, either. Miguel left to look for the canyon that Benigno saw from above, and did not return. Urbano and Julio came back with Polo. The soldiers have taken the camp and are sending out reconnaissance patrols through the hills. They passed by the elevator* on the way down. Joaquín gives his report on this and other problems in the attached document (D.XIX).

We had three cows and their calves, but one pair escaped, so we have four animals left. We will make *charqui* with one or two of them, using the salt we have left.

---

*A pathway built by the guerrillas up a dry waterfall, leading to one of the supply caves.

9 April

Polo, Luis and Wyly left with the mission to deliver a note to Joaquín. To help them return, they are to position themselves in a hidden area upstream, chosen by Ñato and Moisés Guevara. According to Ñato, there are some good areas about an hour from our present position, although a little near the stream. Miguel arrived. According to his exploration, the ravine leads to Pirirenda and it takes up a day's marching with rucksacks. Consequently I gave orders to suspend the route that Benigno is making, which would require at least another day's work.

10 April

Dawn and morning passed without any events as we were preparing to leave the stream, having erased all our traces; we planned to cross by Miguel's ravine to Pirirenda-Gutiérrez. Negro arrived mid-morning, very agitated, reporting that there were 15 soldiers coming downriver. Inti went to warn Rolando at the site of the ambush. There was nothing to do but wait, and that is what we did. I sent Tuma out so that he could be ready to bring the information to me. Soon the first report arrived, with bad news: Rubio, Jesús Suárez Gayol, had been fatally wounded. He was brought to our camp, but arrived dead, with a bullet through his head. This is how it happened: the ambush was composed of eight men from the Rearguard – plus a reinforcement of three men from the Vanguard, distributed on both banks of the river. When Inti had gone to warn them of the arrival of the 15 soldiers, he went past Rubio's position and noticed that he was in a very bad spot, because he could be seen clearly from the river. The soldiers advanced, taking few precautions, looking for tracks along the river banks. Along one of these tracks they ran into Braulio or Pedro, before falling into the ambush. The shooting lasted a few seconds, leaving on the ground one dead and three of their men wounded, as well as six prisoners. Later a sub-lieutenant also fell and four of their men escaped. Next to one of the wounded lay Rubio, who was dying. His Garand was jammed and by his side there was a grenade, with the pin almost loosened, but which had not exploded. It was not possible to interrogate the prisoner because of his serious condition, and not much later he died, as did the sub-lieutenant who commanded them.

From the interrogation of the prisoners the following picture emerges: these 15 men belong to the company that was upriver at Ñacahuasu. They had crossed the canyon, collected the skeletons and then taken the camp. According to the soldiers, they had not found anything, although the radio broadcasts talk about photos and documents found there. The company consists of 100 men, of whom 15 were sent to accompany a group of journalists to our camp, and then went out to explore, to return at 17.00. The main forces are at El Pincal. In Lagunillas there are around 30 of theirs, and it is assumed that the group that went past Tiraboy has withdrawn to Gutiérrez. They told us about the odyssey of their group, getting lost in the woods without water, so that a rescue mission had had to be sent for them. I calculated that the ones who had escaped would arrive later, so I decided to leave the ambush in place. Rolando has brought it forward around 500 metres, and we can now rely on the help of all the Vanguard. At first I gave orders to withdraw, but then it seemed logical to leave it like this. Around 17.00 the news came that the Army was advancing, with many men. All we can do is wait. I sent Pombo to bring me a clear idea of the situation. Isolated shots were heard for a while, and Pombo came back saying that soldiers again fell into the ambush. There are several dead, and a major taken prisoner.

This time this is how things happened: they advanced, fanning out along the river, taking few precautions, so the surprise was total. There are seven dead, five wounded and a total of 22 prisoners. The balance is as follows: (total) (cannot be included for lack of data).

11 April

In the morning we began transferring all the equipment, and we buried Rubio in a shallow grave, given the lack of materials. Inti was left with the Rearguard to accompany the prisoners and set them free, as well as to look for any scattered weapons. The only result of the search was two new prisoners, with their respective Garands. Two copies of Communiqué No. 1 were given to the major, who undertook to hand them over to the press. The total casualties are as follows: 10 dead, among them two lieutenants; 30 prisoners, a major and some sub-lieutenants, the rest are soldiers: six are wounded, one during the first battle and the rest in the second.

They are under the command of the Fourth Division, but with some elements from other regiments mixed in. There are Rangers, paratroopers and soldiers based in the area, who are almost children.

Not until the afternoon did we finish transporting all our stuff. We located a cave to stash all the equipment in, although we did not arrange it properly. At the last stage the cows took fright and ran away, leaving us with only a single calf.

Early, as we were arriving at the new camp, we ran into Joaquín and Alejandro, who were coming down with all their men. From their account it seems that the reported sighting of soldiers was only a figment of Eustaquio's imagination, which makes our transfer here a waste of effort.

The radio announced a 'new and bloody clash' and talks of nine Army dead, and four of ours 'confirmed' dead.

A Chilean journalist gave a detailed report of our camp and discovered a photo of me, without a beard and with a pipe. We must investigate further how this was obtained. There is no evidence that the upper cave has been located, although some indications would point to this.

12 April

At 6.30 I gathered all the combatants, minus the four rejects, in a simple ceremony to remember Rubio, and to mention that the first blood shed was Cuban. I tackled a trend I had noticed in the Vanguard, to despise the Cubans, which was brought to a head yesterday by Camba, who said that he trusted the Cubans less every day, after an incident with Ricardo. I called upon them to unite, as it was the only way we could develop our army, which is increasing its firing power and gaining experience in combat, but does not increase in numbers. On the contrary, it has decreased in recent days.

After storing all the stuff we had captured in a cave well prepared by Ñato, we left at 14.00, at a slow pace. So slow that we almost did not advance. We had to stop for the night at a watering place, not long after starting off.

The Army now admits to 11 dead. Either they have found another corpse or one of the wounded died. I started a short study course of Debray's book.

Part of a message was decoded, but is does not seem important.

13 April

We split the group into two in order to walk faster, in spite of which wc made slow progress. We reached the camp at 16.00 while the last ones arrived at 18.30. Miguel had arrived during the morning: the caves have not been spotted and nothing is missing; the benches, the stoves, the oven and the seedbeds are intact.

Aniceto and Raúl went exploring, but did not do well, so tomorrow they will have to go out again, to reach the Ikira river.

The North Americans announce that sending Special Advisors to Bolivia was part of a previous plan, and has nothing to do with the guerrillas. We may be witnessing the first stage of a new Vietnam.

14 April

Monotonous day. We brought some things from the shelter for the sick, which gives us food for five days. We fetched tins of milk from the upper cave and found that there are 23 inexplicably missing. Moro left 48 tins and nobody seems to have had the time to take them. Milk is one of our greatest corrupters. We took one mortar and one machine gun from the special cave to reinforce the position until Joaquín comes. It is not clear how the operation should be conducted, but it seems to me that the whole group should go out and operate in the Muyupampa area, and then withdraw to the north. If it is possible, Danton and Carlos could be put on their way to Sucre-Cochabamba, depending on the circumstances. Communiqué No. 2 is drafted for the Bolivian people and Report No. 4 for Manila, which the Frenchman should deliver.

15 April

Joaquín arrived with the whole Rearguard and we decided to leave tomorrow. He reported that there had been flights over the area, and that they were firing artillery into the woods. The day went without incident. The task of arming the group was completed and the .30 machine gun was assigned to the Rearguard (Marcos), with the rejects as assistants.

At night I informed them all about the march, and gave a severe warning about the problem of tins of milk disappearing.

Part of a long message from Cuba was decoded. In brief, it states that Lechín knows about me and will write a declaration of support. He will re-enter the country clandestinely in 20 days' time.

I wrote a note to Fidel (No. 4) informing him of recent events. It is coded and in invisible ink.

16 April

The Vanguard left at 6.15 and the Main Force at 7.15, walking well as far as the Ikira river, but Tania and Alejandro lagged behind. When their temperature was taken, Tania's was above 39 and Alejandro's 38. Besides, the delay prevented us from keeping to our schedule. We left the two of them, plus Negro and Serapio, one kilometre upriver from the Ikira and continued on to a hamlet called Bella Vista or, more precisely, a spot where four peasants sold us potatoes, a pig and some corn. They are poor peasants and very frightened at our presence here. We spent the night cooking and eating and did not move, waiting until the early hours to go on to Tikucha to avoid being seen, because we are now so conspicuous.

17 April

The news kept changing and so did our decisions. Tikucha is a waste of time. According to the peasants, there is a direct route to Muyupampa (Vaca Guzmán), which is shorter and which allows vehicles to cross over the last section. We decided to go direct to Muyupampa, after much hesitation on my part. I sent word for the stragglers, so that they stayed with Joaquín, and I gave him orders to make their presence known in the area, which will prevent excessive movement of the military. He is to wait for us for three days, at the end of which he should stay in the area, but without getting into frontal combat, and wait for our return.

At night it was known that one of the sons of a peasant had run away and could have gone to give the alarm, but we decided to leave anyway to try and get the Frenchman and Carlos out once and for all. Moisés joined the group of stragglers. He has had to stay behind because of an acute attack on his gall bladder.

This is a sketch of our situation:

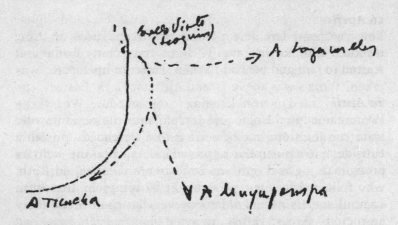

If we return by the same route, we risk clashing with the
Army on the alert at Lagunillas, or with a column coming
from Tikucha, but we must do it, to avoid being cut off from
the Rearguard.

We left at 22.00, walking with breaks up to 4.30 when we
stopped to sleep a little. We advanced some 10 kilometres.
Of all the peasants we have encountered, there is one,
Simón, who shows a willingness to co-operate, although he
is scared, and another one, Vides, who could be dangerous.
He is the 'rich' one of the area. We must also take into
consideration the disappearance of the son of Carlos Rodas,
who could be an informer (due to the influence of Vides,
who is the economic boss of the area).

18 April

We walked until dawn, dozing for the last hour of the night,
and feeling the cold considerably. In the morning the
Vanguard went to explore and found the house of some
Guaraní, who gave very little information. Our sentries
stopped a rider, who turned out to be one of Carlos Rodas's
sons (a different one) on his way to Yakunday, and we took
him prisoner. We advanced slowly and at 3.00 we were able
to reach Matagal, the house of A. Padilla, the poor brother of

another man who lives one league from there, and whose house we passed by. The man was scared and did everything he could to make us leave. Then, to make matters worse, it started to rain and we had to take shelter in his house.

19 April

We remained in the place all day, stopping the peasants who were coming from both directions, so we ended up with a considerable assortment of prisoners. At 13.00 the sentries brought us a Greek gift: an English journalist called Roth, who followed in our trail, brought by some children from Lagunillas. His papers were in order, but there were some suspicious things: in his passport the word 'student' had been crossed out and replaced by 'journalist' as his profession (in fact he says that he is a photographer). He has a visa for Puerto Rico, and he later confessed to having been a Spanish tutor for the students from the Peace Corps, when he was asked about a card from the organiser in Buenos Aires. He said he had been into the camp and had been shown Braulio's diary, in which he describes his experiences and travels. It is the same old story. Lack of discipline and lack of responsibility throughout. From reports made by the young boys who had guided the journalist, we learned that the very night we arrived here, they knew in Lagunillas, thanks to an informant. We pressed Rodas's son, and he confessed that his brother and one of the Vides farmhands had gone to collect the reward, which is between 500 and 1,000 pesos. We confiscated his horse as a reprisal, and told him about the peasants we have detained.

The Frenchman asked if he could put the problem of their leaving to the Englishman, and ask him to help as proof of his good faith; Carlos accepted with reluctance, and I washed my hands of them. We arrived at 21.00 at [*illegible*] and continued on to Muyupampa, where according to reports from the peasants all was quiet. The Englishman accepted Inti's conditions, including a short account that I

had written, and at 23.45, after shaking hands with those
departing, the march to take the village began. Pombo and I,
Tuma and Urbano stayed behind. The cold was intense and
we lit a small fire. At 1.00 Ñato arrived to tell us that the
village was in a state of alert, with some 20 Army troops
stationed there, as well as self-defence patrols. One of these,
with two M-38s and two revolvers, surprised our Vanguard,
but surrendered without a fight. Our men asked for
instructions and I told them to withdraw, seeing how late it
was, letting the English journalist go, while the Frenchman
and Carlos decide what is best for them. At 4.00 we started
on the road back, without having achieved our objective, but
Carlos decided to stay with us and the Frenchman followed
him, this time reluctantly.

20 April
We arrived at Nemesio Caraballo's house at about 7.00. We
had run into him during the night, and he offered us coffee.
The man had gone, leaving the house locked, with only some
frightened servants remaining behind. We prepared our meal
there, buying corn and *jocos* (pumpkins) from the hired
hands. At about 13.00 a van with a white flag arrived
containing the sub-prefect, the doctor and the priest from
Muyupampa, who is German. Inti spoke to them. They came
on a peace mission, but it was to be a national peace, for
which they offered themselves as intermediaries. Inti offered
peace for Muyupampa, on the basis of a list of goods they
were to bring us before 18.30 – something which they did not
undertake to do because, according to them, the Army is in
control of the village. They asked for the deadline to be
extended until 6.00 in the morning, which we did not grant.

As a gesture of goodwill they brought two cartons of
cigarettes – and the news that the three who had tried to
leave had been captured in Muyupampa, and two of them
were compromised because they had false papers. It looks
bad for Carlos, but Danton should be able to get away.

At 17.30 three AT-6 planes flew over and carried out a little bombing over the very house where we were cooking. One of the bombs fell only 15 metres away and Ricardo was slightly wounded by a piece of shrapnel. This was the Army's response. We must make our intentions known in order to achieve the total demoralisation of the soldiers, who, judging by their envoys, are scared shitless.

We left at 22.30 with two horses, the confiscated one and the one belonging to the journalist. We walked towards Tikucha until 1.30, when we stopped to sleep.

21 April

We walked a little up to the house of Roso Carrasco, who looked after us very well and sold us what we needed. At night we walked up to the Muyupampa–Monteagudo crossing of the road, to a place called Taperillas. The idea was to stay by a watering place and explore the site in order to set an ambush. There was an additional reason, and that was the news the radio gave of the death of three mercenaries: a Frenchman, an Englishman and an Argentine. We must discover if it is true and make reprisals in order to give them a special punishment.

Before having dinner we went past the house of old Rodas, the stepfather of Vargas, the man who was killed at Ñacahuasu. We gave him an explanation that seemed to satisfy him. The Vanguard misunderstood us, and carried on walking along the road, waking up some dogs that barked loudly.

22 April

The mistakes began in the morning: Rolando, Miguel and Antonio went to explore and to lay an ambush. We then retreated into the woods, but we surprised a man in a van from YPFB* who was studying our tracks, while a peasant

*Yacimientos Petrolíferos Fiscales de Bolivia, the national oil company of Bolivia.

informed him of our presence here during the night, so we
decided to take everyone prisoner. This upset our plans. We
now decided to lie in ambush during the day and capture any
supply trucks that went by, and to ambush the Army if they
came. A truck with some supplies and abundant bananas
was captured, as well as numerous peasants, but some who
came because they noticed our tracks were allowed through,
as well as some vans from YPFB. It was the temptation of
capturing more supply trucks, which kept not materialising,
that delayed us.

It was my intention to load the YPFB van with all the
food and, with the Vanguard, advance to the crossroads
for Tikucha, four kilometres away. At nightfall the plane
started circling above our position, and the dogs from the
neighbouring houses barked more insistently. At 20.00 we
were ready to leave, in spite of the evidence that our
presence had been detected, when a short battle started, and
then voices were heard calling on us to surrender. We were
all taken by surprise and had no idea of what was going on.
Fortunately, our belongings and the goods were already in
the van. A short while later we got organised. Only Loro was
missing, but everything seemed to indicate that nothing had
happened to him, since the clash had been with Ricardo,
who had surprised the soldiers' guide when they reached the
top of the ridge, intending to surround us. It is possible that
the guide was hit.

We left with the van and all the horses available, six in
total, taking turns to go on foot and on horseback, ending
with all on board the van and six from the Vanguard forming
the cavalry. We reached Tikucha at 3.30 and El Mesón, the
property of the priest, at 6.30, after getting stuck in a
pothole.

The balance of the action is negative: on the one hand,
there was a lack of discipline and foresight, and the loss of
one man (although I hope only temporarily). On the other,
we paid for supplies we did not receive, and finally we lost a

packet of dollars, which I dropped out of Pombo's bag. These are the results of the action, and that without taking into account that we were outwitted by a group that must have been small. We have a long way to go before we become a fighting force, although morale is quite high.

23 April

A day of rest was declared and it went by without incident. At midday the AT-6 aircraft flew over the area. The sentries were reinforced, but nothing happened. At night I gave instructions for tomorrow. Benigno and Aniceto are to go to look for Joaquín: four days; Coco and Camba will explore the path to the Río Grande, and will prepare it so that it is passable: four days; we will stay close to the cornfield, to see if the Army comes while we are awaiting the reincorporation of Joaquín. His instructions are to bring everybody here, and to leave behind only any of the rejects that might be ill.

The mystery of what happened to Danton, Pelado and the English journalist continues; there is censorship of the press and they have already announced another clash in which between three and five prisoners were taken.

24 April

The explorers left. We positioned ourselves one kilometre upstream on a small ridge. We can see as far as the house of the last peasant, some 500 metres before the priest's farm (we found marijuana in the fields). The peasant reappeared and was snooping around: in the afternoon an AT-6 strafed the little house twice. Pacho disappeared mysteriously – he was ill and he stayed behind; Antonio showed him the way and Pacho set out in our direction. It should have taken him five hours, but he never arrived. We will look for him tomorrow.

25 April

A black day. At about 10.00 in the morning Pombo returned

from the lookout, saying that 30 soldiers were advancing towards the little house. Antonio remained at the lookout. While we were preparing, he arrived with news that there were 60 men getting ready to advance. The lookout proved ineffective in terms of giving us advance warning. We decided to lay an improvised ambush on the access path to the camp. At full speed we selected a short stretch that borders the stream, with visibility of 50 metres. I positioned myself there with Urbano and Miguel, with the automatic rifle: the Doctor, Arturo and Raúl occupied positions on the right, to prevent any possibility of retreat or advance along that side. Rolando, Pombo, Antonio, Ricardo, Julio, Pablito, Darío, Willi, Luis and León occupied the lateral position on the other side of the stream, to cover their flank completely. Inti remained at the riverbed to attack anyone who sought refuge there. Ñato and Eustaquio went to the lookout with orders to withdraw to the rear when the shooting began. Chino remained behind, guarding the camp. My meagre forces had been reduced by three men. Pacho was lost, and Tuma and Luis were out looking for him.

Not long after, the vanguard of the Army appeared. To our surprise it included three German shepherd dogs and a guide. The animals were restless, but I did not think they had detected us. However, they continued to advance, so I fired at the first dog, and missed. When I was about to fire at the guide, my M-2 jammed. Miguel killed the other dog, as far as I could see, but this could not be confirmed. Nobody else entered the ambush. Intermittent fire broke out along the Army's flank. When there was a pause I sent Urbano to order the withdrawal, but he came back saying that Rolando had been wounded. He was bleeding to death, and they brought his body back not long afterwards. He died as they began to give him plasma. A bullet had split open his thighbone as well as the entire nerve and vascular system. He bled to death before we could do anything.

We have lost the best man in the guerrilla force, one of its pillars. He was a comrade of mine from the time when he was still almost a child, and came as a messenger for Column No. 4, then throughout the invasion, and now in this new revolutionary venture. All I can say about his obscure and unheralded death, that it was for a hypothetical future for all that may come out of this, is: 'Thy little brave captain's corpse has stretched to immensity its metallic form.'*

The rest of the day was spent in slow withdrawal, gathering all our things and the body of Rolando (San Luis). Pacho joined us later. He had taken the wrong trail and caught up with Coco, returning during the night. At 15.00 we buried the body under a thin layer of earth. At 16.00 Benigno and Aniceto arrived, saying that they had fallen into an Army ambush (more precisely, a little skirmish). They lost their rucksacks, but were unharmed. This had occurred, according to Benigno's calculations, just before they reached Ñacahuasu.

Our two natural outlets are now blocked off and we will have to 'head to the mountains'. The exit along the Río Grande is not adequate, both because it is predictable and because it would lead us away from Joaquín, whom we have not heard from at all. At night we reached the crossroads, one leading to Ñacahuasu and one to the Río Grande, and there we slept. We will wait here for Coco and Camba in order to reunite our small force.

The balance sheet of the operation is extremely negative. First of all there is Rolando's death. But not only that: the Army's losses were two at most, plus the dog, but that is because our positions were either not adequately planned or prepared, and because those doing the shooting could not see the enemy. Finally, our lookout system was very poor, and this prevented us from making preparations with enough time.

*From 'Un Canto Para Simón Bolívar' by Pablo Neruda.

A helicopter landed twice at the priest's house, possibly to remove the wounded. Planes bombed our previous positions, which indicates that they have not advanced at all.

26 April

We walked a few metres and I ordered Miguel to look for a place to camp, while we sent someone to find Coco and Camba, but at noon he appeared with both of them. According to them, they had cleared enough track for a four-hour walk carrying loads, and it is possible to try and climb the ridge. Nevertheless, I sent Benigno and Urbano to explore the possibility of climbing the canyon of the stream that flows into the Ñacahuasu, but they returned at sundown saying that it does not look good. We decided to go on along the path opened by Coco, and try to find another one that leads to the Ikira.

We have a mascot: Lolo, a baby deer. We shall see if it survives.

27 April

Coco's four hours turned out to be two and a half. We thought we had arrived at a place that appears on the map as Masico, where there are many bitter orange trees. Urbano and Benigno carried on opening the path and prepared the ground for one more hour. At night it is intensely cold.

Bolivian radio stations are broadcasting official statements from the Army detailing the death of one civilian guide, the dog trainer and the dog, Rayo. They give us two losses: one, allegedly Cuban, nicknamed Rubio, and one Bolivian. They confirmed that Danton is held near Camiri. The others must also be alive with him.

h = 950m.

28 April

We walked slowly until 15.00. The stream had dried up by

then and went off in a different direction, so we stopped. It was too late to explore, so we went back to the camp by the water. We have food for scarcely four days. Tomorrow we will try to reach the Ñacahuasu from the Ikira and we will have to cut through the mountains.

29 April
We tried to explore some other clearings. With negative results. At this point, at least, we are in an unbroken canyon. Coco believes he saw a canyon that intersects this one, but he did not explore it; we will do so tomorrow with all the men.

With considerable delay we finished decoding Message No. 35. It contains a paragraph asking me to agree to add my name to an appeal in support of Vietnam, headed by Bertrand Russell.

30 April
We began the assault on the hill. The alleged canyon ends up at some steep cliffs, but we found a crevice over which we could climb. Night surprised us near the top and there we slept, not feeling too much cold.

Lolo died, a victim of Urbano's impulsiveness. He threw a rifle at its head.

Radio Havana broadcasts news from some Chilean reporters who state that the guerrillas are strong enough to threaten cities, and that we recently took two military lorries full of supplies. The magazine *Siempre* interviewed Barrientos, who, among other things, admitted that Yankee military advisors are involved and that the guerrillas are the result of social conditions in Bolivia.

Analysis of the month
Things are developing normally, although we have to regret two severe losses: Rubio and Rolando; the death of the latter is a serious setback, since I was thinking of putting

him in charge of an eventual second front. We have seen action four more times. All four had positive results on the whole, and one of them – the one in which Rubio died – was very good.

On the other hand, the isolation continues to be total. Sickness has undermined the health of some comrades, forcing us to divide our forces, which has greatly reduced our effectiveness. We still have not been able to make contact with Joaquín. The peasant base still has not developed, although it would seem that through a campaign of terror we could neutralise the majority of them. Their support will come later. We have not had a single recruit, and, apart from the deaths, we have suffered the loss of Loro, who disappeared after the action at Taperillas.

Of the points noted in relation to military strategy, we can stress:

a) the Army's control measures have not been effective until now and they inconvenience us, but we are able to move, given their lack of mobility and their weakness. Also, after the last skirmish with the dogs and their trainer, we can assume that they will be far more careful before entering the woods;

b) the clamour continues, but now it is from both sides and, after the publication of my article in Havana, there can be no doubt of my presence here.

It seems certain that the North Americans will intervene heavily here and are already sending helicopters and even Green Berets, it seems, although they have not been seen around here;

c) the Army (at least one company, maybe two) have improved their tactics. They surprised us at Taperillas and were not demoralised at El Mesón;

d) peasant mobilisation is non-existent, except as informants, which causes some trouble, but as they are not quick or efficient, it will be possible to nullify them.

The status of Chino has changed; he will be a combatant until a second or third front is formed. Danton and Carlos fell victims to their own haste – desperation almost – to leave, and I lacked the energy to prevent them doing so, so that communications with Cuba are cut off (Danton) and the plan of action for Argentina is lost (Carlos).

To summarise: a month in which everything has evolved normally, taking into consideration the necessary developments in guerrilla warfare. Morale of all combatants is good because they have passed their first test as guerrilla fighters.

May 1967

We celebrated the date by opening up the path, but we walked only a little: we have not yet reached the point where the waters divide.

Almeida spoke in Havana, lauding me and the famous Bolivian guerrillas. The speech was rather long, but good. We have enough decent food for three days. Today Ñato killed a little bird with his slingshot: we are entering the era of the bird.

2 May

A day of slow advance, and confusion about our geographic position. We walked in effect for two hours, owing to the difficulty of clearing a path. From a height, I could distinguish a point near the Ñacahuasu which indicates that we are quite far north, but there is no sign of the Ikira. I ordered Miguel and Benigno to clear a path all day, in order to try to reach the Ikira or, at least, reach water, since we have none. There is food for five days, but it is very scant.

Radio Havana carries on with its information offensive about Bolivia, but exaggerating the news.

h = reached 1,760m., we slept at 1,730

3 May

After a day of continuous path-clearing, which resulted in a trail good for more than two hours' march, we reached a stream with quite a lot of water, which seems to flow to the north. Tomorrow we will explore it, to see if it changes direction. We will also continue to clear a path. We have

scant food, enough for two days only. We are at a height of
1,080 metres, 200 above the level of the Ñacahuasu. The
noise of an engine can be heard in the distance, but we
cannot tell from which direction.

4 May

During the morning we continued to clear the path, while
Coco and Aniceto explored the stream. They returned at
about 13.00 confirming that the stream turned to the east
and south, so perhaps it is the Ikira. I gave orders that the
trail-cutters be called, and that we should continue downstream. We started at 13.30 and stopped at 17.30, certain by
now that the general direction was east-north-east, so it
cannot be the Ikira, unless it changes direction. The trail-
cutters informed that they had not found water, and that
there are only ridges to be seen. It was decided to carry on,
as we are under the impression that we are going towards
the Río Grande. We only caught one bird, a *cacaré*, which
was split up between the trail-cutters, in view of its
diminutive size. We have scarcely enough food for two days.

The radio gave the news of the capture of Loro, wounded
in the leg. His statements so far have been good. Everything
seems to indicate that it was not in the house that he was
wounded, but somewhere else, presumably while trying to
escape.

h = 980m.

5 May

We marched effectively for five hours, some 12–14 kilometres, reaching a camp prepared by Inti and Benigno. We
are therefore at the Congrí stream, which does not appear on
the map, much further north than we thought. This raises
several questions: where is the Ikira? Was it perhaps where
Benigno and Aniceto were taken by surprise? The attackers:
could they have been Joaquín's men? For the moment we are
planning to go to the Bear Camp, where there should be

enough food left for two days' breakfast, and from there on to the old camp. Two large birds and one *cacaré* were killed today, so we saved our food and have enough in reserve for two days: powdered soup in packets and tinned meat. Inti, Coco and the Doctor set up a hide for hunting.

It was reported today that Debray will be tried by a military court in Camiri, as the alleged head or organiser of the guerrillas, his mother is arriving tomorrow and there is a lot of fuss about the affair. Nothing about Loro.
h = 840m.

6 May

The calculations about the arrival at Bear Camp turned out to be wrong, since the distance to the little house was greater than we thought, and the path was blocked, so we had to clear it. We arrived at the little house at 16.30, having reached heights of 1,400, with the men too weak to march. We ate the penultimate ration, which was very poor. We only caught a partridge, which we gave to Benigno, who had been clearing the path, and to the two men who were right behind him during the march.

News reports are concentrated on the Debray case.
h = 1,100m.

7 May

We arrived at Bear Camp early and there were eight tins of milk left for us, which made a nourishing breakfast. A few things were taken from the nearby cave – amongst them, a Mauser for Ñato, who will be our bazooka operator, with five anti-tank missiles. He is not well, after an attack of vomiting. As soon as we arrived at the camp, Benigno, Urbano, León, Aniceto and Pablito went out to explore the little farm. We ate the last soup packets and meat tins, but we have a supply of lard that was in the cave. We detected some footprints, and there is minor damage, which indicates that the soldiers were here. At daybreak the explorers returned empty-handed: the soldiers are at the farm and they have cut down the maize. (It is six months since the official initiation of the guerrillas and my arrival.)

h = 880m.

8 May

Early in the morning I insisted that the caves should be repaired, and that the other tin of lard be brought down to start filling the bottles, since this is all we have left to eat now. At about 10.30 isolated shots were heard from the ambush. Two unarmed soldiers were coming up the Ñacahuasu, and Pacho, who thought they were an advance column, wounded them both, one in the leg and the other superficially in the stomach. They were told that they had been shot at because they had not stopped when ordered to but of course they had not heard anything. The ambush was badly co-ordinated and Pacho's attitude was not good; he was too nervous. To improve the situation we sent Antonio with a few others to the right side. The soldiers said that they were stationed near the Ikira, but in fact they were lying. At 12.00 two soldiers were captured, running at full speed downstream along the Ñacahuasu. They said they were moving so quickly because they had gone out hunting and, when they returned to the Ikira, they discovered that their company had disappeared and were trying to find it. They were also lying; in fact, they are camping in the hunting field, and went off to find food on our farm because the supply helicopter had not come. From the first pair we took loads of toasted and raw maize and four tins of onions, plus sugar and coffee, which solved our food problems for the day, together with the lard, which we ate in large quantities. Some in fact fell ill.

Later on our sentries informed us of soldiers on patrol, who repeatedly went as far as the river bend and back. Everyone grew tense when 27 soldiers appeared. They had seen something odd, and the group commanded by Second

Lieutenant Laredo advanced: he himself opened fire and fell dead on the spot, together with two other recruits. Night was falling and our men advanced to capture six soldiers; the rest withdrew.

The total result is: three dead and 10 prisoners, two of them wounded, seven M-1s and four Mausers, personal kit, ammunition and some food, which, eaten with lard, mitigated our hunger. We slept there.

9 May

We got up at 4.00 (I did not sleep) and released the soldiers, after giving them a talk. We took their boots and exchanged clothes with them. The ones who lied were sent off in their underpants. They left for the little farm, taking the wounded man with them. At 6.30 we completed our withdrawal towards the monkeys' stream along the path to the caves, where we stored our booty. All we have left for nourishment is lard. I felt faint and had to sleep for a couple of hours to be able to carry on, slowly and haltingly. That is how we advanced as a whole. We ate lard soup at the first watering place. The men are weak and some already have oedema. At night the Army issued a statement about the action, naming the dead and wounded, but not their prisoners. They announced great battles, with heavy losses on our side.

10 May

We continued to advance slowly. When we arrived at the camp where Rubio's grave is situated, we found the *charqui* and tallow that we had left there, in a bad condition. We picked it all up. There were no signs of soldiers. We crossed the Ñacahuasu cautiously and started on the way to Pirirenda by the ravine explored by Miguel, although the path has not been totally cleared. We stopped at 17.00 and ate the *charqui* and tallow.

11 May

The Vanguard left first; I stayed behind listening to the news. Not long afterwards Urbano arrived, saying that Benigno had killed a *pecarí* (a wild pig) and requesting authorisation to make a fire and skin it. We decided to stay behind and eat the pig while Benigno, Urbano and Miguel continued to open a path towards the lagoon. At 14.00 we started on our way, camping at 18.00. Miguel and the others went on ahead.

I must speak seriously with Benigno and Urbano. The former ate a tin of food on the day of the battle and denied it, and Urbano ate some of the *charqui* we had left at the camp where Rubio is.

The news came that Colonel Rocha, head of the Fourth Division, which operates in the region, is being replaced. h = 1,050m.

12 May

We walked slowly, Urbano and Benigno opening up the trail. At 15.00 we saw the lagoon, some five kilometres away, and not long afterwards we found an old track. An hour later we came into a huge field of maize with pumpkins, but there is no water. We prepared roasted *jocos* with lard and we shredded the corn. We also toasted some cobs. The explorers arrived with the news that they had ended up in the house of Chicho, the one that Lieutenant Henry Laredo mentions in his diary as a good friend. He was not at home, but there were four farmhands and a servant woman; when her husband came to collect her, we detained him. We cooked a large pig with rice and fritters as well as pumpkin. Pombo, Arturo, Willi and Darío guarded the rucksacks. Unfortunately we have not located any water near the house.

We withdrew at 5.30, slowly because almost everybody was ill. The owner of the house had not returned, so we left him a note detailing damages and expenses, and the

farmhands and the servant were paid 10 pesos each for their work.
h = 950m.

13 May
A day of belching, farting, vomiting and diarrhoea – a veritable organ concert. We remained completely inactive, trying to digest the pig. We have two tins of water. I was really ill until I vomited and felt better. At night we ate fried corn and roasted pumpkin, as well as the leftovers of the banquet – those who were fit enough to do so. All the radio stations kept giving the news that a Cuban landing had been forestalled in Venezuela* and that Leoni's government produced two of the men, with their name and rank. I don't know them, but everything seems to indicate that something went wrong.

14 May
Early, and with little energy, we left for the Pirirenda lagoon, taking the trail that Benigno and Camba found while exploring. Before leaving, I gathered everyone and launched on a diatribe on the problems we had faced: mainly that of food. I criticised Benigno for having eaten a can of food and having denied it, Urbano for eating a piece of *charqui* behind our backs, and Aniceto for his willingness to co-operate in anything to do with food and his reluctance when it has to do with anything else. During the meeting we heard the sound of approaching trucks. In a nearby hiding place we stored some 50 *jocos* and 200 pounds of husked corn in case of need.

When we were far from the road, picking beans, explosions were heard nearby, and a little later we saw the Air Force 'ferociously bombing us', only it was some two or three kilometres from our positions. We continued to climb

---

*Venezuelan and Cuban guerrillas attempted to land and were routed by Venezuelan troops on 8 May.

up a hillock and reached the lagoon, while the Army carried on firing. At nightfall we approached a house recently abandoned by its inhabitants. It was well stocked and had water. We ate a delicious chicken fricassee and stayed until 4.00.

15 May
An uneventful day.

16 May
As we began to walk I had severe colic pains, with vomiting and diarrhoea. I was given Demerol, which stopped it, and I lost consciousness and had to be carried in a hammock. When I woke up I felt much relieved, but I was covered in my own shit, like a newborn baby. I was lent a pair of trousers, but without washing, I stink of shit from a league away. We spent the whole day there, while I dozed. Coco and Ñato went exploring and found a path due north. At night we followed it while there was moonlight and then rested. We received Message No. 36, from which we can infer our utter isolation.

17 May
We continued the march until 13.00 when we arrived at a sawmill that showed signs of having been abandoned some three days ago. We found sugar, corn, lard, flour and canned water, apparently brought from a great distance. We camped here, and explored the roads leaving the camp, which end in the jungle. Raúl has an abscess on his knee. He is in great pain and unable to walk. He was given a powerful antibiotic and tomorrow it will be lanced. We walked some 15 kilometres. h = 920m.

18 May
Roberto and Juan Martín.*

---

*Birthday of his brothers, Roberto and Juan Martín Guevara de la Serna.

We waited all day in ambush, in case the workers or the Army came; nothing happened. Miguel left with Pablito and found water some two hours from the camp, along an intersecting path. Raúl's abscess was lanced, and 50cc. of purulent fluid was extracted; he received general treatment against infection and can scarcely take a step. I extract my first tooth of this campaign, the sacrificial lamb: Camba. It went well. We ate the bread we had baked in a little oven, and in the evening an appalling stew that gave me serious stomach pains.

19 May
The Vanguard left early to take up their ambush positions at the crossroads. We left later, and replaced the part of the Vanguard that was returning to fetch Raúl, to take him to the crossing; the rest of the Main Force group followed to the watering place to leave the rucksacks, then fetch Raúl, who is slowly improving. Antonio went on a short exploration downstream and found a camp abandoned by the soldiers, where there are remnants of dried rations. The Ñacahuasu cannot be far from here and I calculate that we must come out below the stream of the Congrí. It rained all night, which surprised the experts. We have food for 10 days and there is pumpkin and maize in the vicinity.
h = 780m.

20 May
Camilo.*
   Day without movement. In the morning the Main Force lay in ambush, and in the afternoon the Vanguard. They are led by Pombo, as always, who thinks that the position chosen by Miguel is a bad one. The latter explored downstream and found the Ñacahuasu is a two-hour march away, walking without a rucksack. A shot was clearly heard, but

* Birthday of his eldest son, Camilo Guevara March.

we do not know who fired it. On the banks of the Ñacahuasu there are signs of another Army camp, this one for a couple of platoons. There was an incident with Luis, who was grumbling, and as punishment he was not sent out to the ambush. He seems to have reacted well.

At a press conference Barrientos refused to grant Debray press status and announced that he will ask Congress for the return of the death penalty. Almost all the journalists, including the foreign ones, asked him about Debray. Barrientos defended himself with an incredible lack of intelligence. He is the most incompetent man you could ask for.

21 May

Sunday. No movement. We continued with the ambush, rotating the men 10 at a time, at midday. Raúl is improving slowly. A second lancing drained another 40cc. of liquid pus. He no longer has a temperature, but he is in pain and cannot walk. At night we ate a sumptuous meal: stew, flour, crushed *charqui* and pumpkin sprinkled with *mote*.

22 May

As was to be expected, at midday Guzmán Robles, the foreman of the sawmill, appeared with a driver and his son, in a rickety jeep. At first it looked like an advance patrol of the Army, investigating what was going on, but gradually he opened up and agreed to go to Gutiérrez tonight, leaving his son as hostage. He is to return tomorrow. The Vanguard will spend the night at the ambush, and tomorrow we will wait until 15.00. Later, we may have to withdraw because the situation might be too dangerous. I am under the impression that the man will not betray us, but we do not know whether he can make these purchases without arousing suspicion. We paid him for all that was consumed at the mill. He gave us reports on the situation in Tatarenda, Limón and Ipitá, where there are no troops, except for a lieutenant in Ipitá. He is only saying what he has heard about Tatarenda since he has not been there.

23 May
Day of tension. The foreman did not appear all day. Although there was no movement, we decided to withdraw at night with the hostage, a big 17-year-old lad. We walked for an hour along the trail by moonlight, and slept en route. We left with 10 days' worth of food.

24 May
In two hours we reached the Ñacahuasu, which was clear. We left about four hours later, downstream of the Congrí. We walked slowly, putting up with Ricardo's slow pace, and today Moro's as well. We arrived at the camp we had used on the first day of our first expedition. We did not leave any tracks and neither were there any recent ones. The radio gave the news that the habeas corpus petition for Debray has been turned down. I estimate that we are one or two hours from the Saladillo. When we reach the summit we will decide what to do.

25 May
We reached the Saladillo in an hour and a half, leaving no tracks. We then walked for about two hours upstream to the source of the water. There we ate and at 15.30, after walking for another couple of hours, we camped at 1,100 metres, without reaching the top of the ridge. We still have, according to the lad, a couple of leagues to go before his grandfather's plot, or, according to Benigno, a whole day's march up to Vargas's house, on the Río Grande. We will decide tomorrow.

26 May
After two hours on the march, and after passing the summit at 1,200 metres, we reached the land that belongs to the

boy's great-uncle. Two farmhands were working and had to be apprehended, as they had been coming in our direction; they turned out to be brothers-in-law of the old man, who is married to one of their sisters. Their ages: 16 and 20. They told us that the boy's father had made the purchases, but had been detained and had confessed everything. There are 30 soldiers in Ipitá patrolling the village. We ate fried pork with a pumpkin and lard stew. Since there is no water in the area, it has to be brought in cans from Ipitá. At night we left for the land that the men own eight kilometres away, four towards Ipitá itself and four to the west. We arrived at dawn. h = 1,100m.

27 May

A day of idleness and some despair. Of the marvels the boys had promised, there was only some old sugarcane, and the mill was useless. As was to be expected, the owner of the land, an old man, came at midday with his cart, bringing water for the pigs. He noticed something strange on the approach to the area, where the Rearguard lay in ambush, so they apprehended him, together with a farmhand. They were held until 18.00, when we released them, together with the younger of the brothers, ordering them to remain in the area until Monday and not to say anything. We walked for two hours, and slept in a cornfield, lying in the direction that will take us to Caraguatarenda.

28 May

Sunday. We got up early and started to march; in an hour and a half we were on the edge of the land at Caraguatarenda. Benigno and Coco were sent to explore, but they were spotted by a peasant and had to apprehend him. Not long afterwards we had a whole colony of prisoners, showing no signs of fear, until an old woman and her children started to scream when ordered to halt. Neither Pacho nor Pablo dared to stop her and she fled towards the village. We captured it

at 14.00, posting sentries at both ends of the village. Not
long afterwards a jeep from YPFB arrived. In total two jeeps
and two trucks arrived, half private ones and half belonging
to YPFB. We had something to eat, drank coffee and, after
many arguments, left towards Ipitacito. There we broke into
a store and picked up 500 pesos worth of goods, leaving the
money in the care of two peasants with a very legalistic
document that we drafted. We continued on our pilgrimage
and reached Itay. We were very well received at a house
where the schoolteacher, who is also the owner of the store,
happened to be, so we were able to check the prices with her.
In the exchange I think they recognised me; they had some
cheese and bread, which they offered to us with coffee, but I
sensed a false note in their reception. We went on towards
Espino, travelling on the rail track to Santa Cruz, but the
truck – a Ford which had had the front-wheel-drive removed
– got stuck, and morning found us three leagues from
Espino. The vehicle's engine finally gave up the ghost, two
leagues from Espino. The Vanguard took the settlement, and
the jeep had to make four trips to bring us all over.
h = 880m.

29 May

The settlement at Espino is relatively new, since the old one
was flattened by the floods in 1958. It is a Guaraní community whose members are very shy and do not speak, or
pretend not to speak, any Spanish. There were people from
the oil company working nearby, so we took over another
truck that could accommodate us all. But the opportunity
was ruined when Ricardo ran it into the mud and we could
not dig it out. There was absolute quiet. It was as if we were
in a world apart. Coco was in charge of getting information
about the roads, but what he found out was deficient and
contradictory. As we were about to leave on a somewhat
dangerous journey, which would take us towards the Río
Grande, it transpired at the last minute that this

information was wrong, and that we must go to Muchiri, where there is water. As a result of all these organisational problems we left at 3.30, the Vanguard with the jeep (six of them, seven with Coco) and the rest on foot.

The radio gave the news that Loro has escaped. He was held in Camiri.

30 May

During the day we reached the railroad tracks, and found that the road marked, which was to take us to Muchiri, did not exist. Looking around, some 500 metres from the crossing, we found a straight road used by the petrol company, and the Vanguard followed it in the jeep. When Antonio was leaving, a young man with a shotgun and a dog appeared along the tracks and, when ordered to halt, he ran away. Faced with this news, I left Antonio lying in ambush at the entrance to the road while we moved away some 500 metres. At 11.45 Miguel appeared with the news that he had walked 12 kilometres east without finding either houses or water, only a road that went north. I gave orders for him to explore that road with three men, for 10 kilometres to the north, and to be back before nightfall. At 15.00, while I was sleeping placidly, I was woken up by gunfire coming from the direction of the ambush. The news came quickly: the Army had advanced and fallen into the trap. Three dead and one wounded seems to be the outcome. Those involved were: Antonio, Arturo, Ñato, Luis, Willy and Raúl; the last was weak. We withdrew on foot, walking the 12 kilometres to the crossing without running into Miguel. We found out that the jeep had broken down for lack of water. Some three kilometres later we ran into it: we all urinated into the radiator and added one canteen of water and managed to reach our destination, where Julio and Pablo were waiting for us.

By 2.00 everybody was round a fire in which we cooked three turkeys and fried the pork meat. We kept one animal to test the watering places, just in case.

We are descending from 750 metres; we are now at 650 metres.

31 May

The jeep bravely carried on, with its urine and the occasional canteen of water. Two things happened that altered our pace: the road north came to an end, so that Miguel had to stop the march; and someone from the security group detained the peasant Gregorio Vargas, on a side-road, as he was coming on his bicycle to set some traps, which is his job. The man's attitude was not totally clear, but he gave us valuable information about the watering places. There was one behind us, and I sent a group to find water and to cook. As they reached it, with him as guide, they saw two Army trucks and hastily set an ambush. It appears that they hit two men. Ñato, when the first blank bullet of his anti-tank grenade failed, inserted a real bullet and the thing exploded in his face, without harming him personally, but destroying the barrel. We continued to withdraw without harassment by the Air Force, and walked some 15 kilometres before finding the second watering place after dark. The jeep sounded its death-rattle for lack of petrol and overheating. We spent the night eating. The Army issued a statement acknowledging their dead from yesterday: one second lieutenant and one soldier. They attributed several fatalities to us, 'seen with their own eyes'. For tomorrow, I intend to cross the railway line and head for the mountains.

h = 620m.

Analysis of the month

The negative point is the impossibility of making contact with Joaquín, in spite of our pilgrimage through the mountains. There are indications that he has gone north.

From the military point of view, there were three new battles and we inflicted losses on the Army, and suffered none ourselves. Also, our forays into Pirirenda and Caraguatarenda point to our success. Their military dogs have been declared incompetent and have been withdrawn from circulation.

The main features are:

1) Total lack of contact with Manila, La Paz and with Joaquín, which reduces us to the 25 men of this group.

2) Total lack of peasant recruitment, although they are beginning to be less afraid of us and we are winning their admiration. This is a slow task that requires patience.

3) The party, through Kolle, is offering to co-operate, it would seem without reservations.

4) The clamour over the Debray case has raised our profile more than 10 victorious battles.

5) The guerrilla force is gradually acquiring a strong morale, which, properly handled, is a guarantee of success.

6) The Army continues to fail to organise, and their tactics are not improving substantially.

News of the month: the capture and escape of Loro, who should now join us, or go to La Paz to make contact.

The Army has announced the detention of all the peasants who co-operated with us in the region of Masicuri. A stage is now beginning when pressure on the peasants will come from both sides, although with different qualities: our triumph will bring about the necessary qualitative change in them to take the leap into development.

June 1967

1 June

I sent the Vanguard to post themselves on the road and to explore as far as the oil company's crossing some three kilometres away. The Air Force has started to fly over the area. According to radio reports, the bad weather has made operations difficult, but they will now resume. They put out a strange report about one dead and two wounded; we cannot tell if they are the ones we know or some new ones. After eating, at 17.00 we left towards the railway tracks. We advanced seven or eight kilometres without incident; we walked one and a half kilometres along the tracks and took an abandoned lane, which should lead us to a farm seven kilometres away. However, as everybody was tired we slept halfway there. We heard only one shot during the entire march.

h = 800m.

2 June

We walked the seven kilometres described by Gregorio and reached the farm. There we caught a good strong pig and killed it, but at that point the cowherd Braulio Robles, his son and two farmhands appeared. One turned out to be the stepson of the owner, Symuní. We used their horses to carry the quartered pig for the next three kilometres and we held the four men there, while we hid Gregorio, since his disappearance was known. When we were almost at the centre, an army truck drove by with two young soldiers and some water cans, easy pickings, but it was a day of revelry and pork. We spent the night cooking and at 3.30 we let the four peasants go, after paying them 10 pesos each for the day. Gregorio left at 4.30, having waited for the food and new instructions and received 100 pesos. The water of the stream is sour.

h = 800m.

3 June
We left at 6.30, taking the left side of the stream, and walked until 12.00, when we sent Benigno and Ricardo to explore the road. They found a good spot for an ambush. At 13.00 we took up our positions, Ricardo and I each with a group in the middle, Pombo at one end, and Miguel with the whole Vanguard at an ideal spot. At 14.30 a truck carrying pigs went by and we let it pass. At 16.20 a van with empty bottles, and at 17.00 an Army truck. It was the same one we saw yesterday, with two young soldiers wrapped up in blankets in the rear of the vehicle. I did not have the heart to shoot them, and my brain did not react fast enough to stop them, so we let it go by. At 18.00 we lifted the ambush and continued down the road until we found the stream again. As soon as we arrived four trucks passed by in a row, and then three more, but without troops, it seems.

4 June
We continued walking along the bank of the stream, intending to set another ambush if we found suitable conditions. However, we came across a path leading west and took it. It then followed a dry riverbed and turned south. At 14.45 we stopped to make coffee and oatmeal next to a small pool of muddy water, but it took so long that we camped there. During the night the *surazo** howled and it rained throughout the night.

---

*A cold wind from Antarctica, which blows between 21 June and 21 September.

5 June

We left the path and continued cutting our way through the wood under the constant roar of the wind. We walked until 17.00, in effect two and a quarter hours, clearing the jungle slopes that seem like the Sierra Maestra. The camp fire turned into the great God of the day. We fasted all day and kept the salty water in our canteens for breakfast tomorrow. h = 250m.

6 June

After a meagre breakfast, Miguel, Benigno and Pablito left to clear a path and to explore. At approximately 14.00 Pablo came back saying that they had reached abandoned farmland with cattle in it. We all got on our way and, following the course of the stream, we crossed the farm and ended up at the Río Grande. From there we sent men out to explore with the purpose of occupying a house, if there was one nearby and isolated. This was done, and the first information showed that we were three kilometres from Puerto Camacho, where there were some 50 soldiers. It is connected by a trail. We spent the night cooking pork and *locro*.* We did not achieve the results expected so we left, tired and in daylight.

7 June

We walked unhurriedly, avoiding old pasture fields, until the guide, one of the sons of the owner, said that this was the last one. We continued along the sandy bank until we found more farmland, which he had not mentioned, where there were *jocos*, sugarcane, bananas and some beans. We camped there. The boy who is our guide began to complain of severe stomach pains. There is no way of knowing if they are real. h = 560m.

---

*Meat, potatoes, rice and regional products are used to prepare this typical dish of the region. The name comes from the Quecha word *roghro*.

8 June

We moved the camp some 300 metres to avoid having to watch the bank and the farm at the same time. Later, however, we discovered that the owner had never cut open a path, but always arrived by punt. Benigno, Pablo, Urbano and León went to try cutting a path across the cliff, but they returned in the afternoon with the news that it was impossible. I had to caution Urbano again about his griping. We decided to build a raft near the cliff tomorrow.

The radio broadcast news of the state of siege, and threats from the miners, but it all came to nothing.

9 June

We walked for two hours until we reached the cliff. Ñato was there making a raft with great determination, but it took too long and was not a success. We have not tested it yet. I sent Miguel to try and find another exit, but he failed. Benigno caught a large fish, a *dorado*.
h = 590m.

10 June

The raft, as was to be expected, could only carry three rucksacks and scarcely that . . . the swimmers jumped in and could do nothing because of the cold. I decided to send for a punt from the prisoner's house and Coco went with Pacho, Aniceto and Ñato. Not long afterwards we heard mortar fire and Ñato came back with the news that they had clashed with the Army. They are on the other side of the river. It all seems to indicate that our men walked without taking precautions and were spotted. The soldiers started to fire as usual, and Pombo and Coco began shooting without rhyme or reason, alerting them. We decided to stay put and start an exit path tomorrow. The situation is somewhat uncomfortable because, if they decide to mount a serious attack, under the best circumstances, we would have to cut our way through wooded cliffs, without water.

11 June

A totally calm day. The ambush remained in position but
the Army did not advance. A small plane flew over the area
for only a few minutes. Maybe they are waiting for us at the
Rosita. The path over the ridge almost reached the top of the
hill. We will leave tomorrow in any case. We have food for
five or six days.

12 June

We thought that we would reach the Rosita, or at least the
Río Grande, so we set out. When we got to a small watering
place we saw how difficult it was, so we remained there
waiting for news. At 15.00 we received a report that there
was a larger watering place, but it was impossible to climb
down. We decided to stay there. The weather deteriorated,
and the *surazo* treated us to a night of cold and rain. The
radio gave some interesting news: the newspaper *Presencia*
reports one dead and one wounded for the Army after
Saturday's clash; this is very good and almost certainly
true, so we are keeping up our pace of clashes with
casualties. Another communiqué announced three dead,
among them Inti, one of the guerrilla leaders. They also
gave the count for foreign guerrillas: 17 Cubans, 14
Brazilians, four Argentines, three Peruvians. The Cubans
and Peruvians correspond with reality. I would like to
know how they got that news.

h = 900m.

13 June

We only walked for an hour, to the next watering place,
since the trail-cutters did not reach the Rosita or the Río
Grande. It is very cold. We may get there tomorrow. We
have food for scarcely five days.

The political upheaval in the country is interesting – the
fabulous number of pacts and counter-pacts that are in

the air. Rarely has the possibility of guerrilla action serving as a catalyst been so promising.
h = 840m.

14 June
Celita (4?).*

We spent the day at the cold watering place, by the fire, waiting for news of Miguel and Urbano who were opening up a path. The time set to start moving was 15.00, but Urbano arrived later to inform us that they had reached a stream, and that they could see fences, so they believed we could reach the Río Grande. We stayed put, eating the last of the stew. All we have left now is a ration of peanuts and three of *mote*.

I am 39 today. The day when my future as a guerrilla will have to be reconsidered is inexorably approaching. As for now, I am still 'all in one piece'.
h = 840m.

15 June
We walked for a little under three hours to reach the banks of the Río Grande. We recognised the spot, which according to my calculations is two hours from the Rosita. Nicolás, the peasant, says it is three kilometres. We gave him 150 pesos and the opportunity to leave, and he went off like a rocket. We stayed at the spot we had arrived at. Aniceto explored the area and believes it is possible to cross the river. We ate peanut soup and some boiled palm shoots, sautéed in lard. All we have left is *mote* for three days.
h = 610m.

16 June
We had walked one kilometre when we spotted men from the Vanguard on the opposite bank of the river. Pacho had

---

*Birthday of his daughter, Celia Guevara March (4).

crossed the river and explored, and found the ford. We crossed in freezing water up to the waist, with quite a current, but without incident. An hour later we reached the Rosita, where there are some old footprints, looking like Army ones. We found that the Rosita has more water in it than we thought, but there is no trace of the path marked on the map. We walked for an hour in the icy water, and decided to camp to take advantage of the palm shoots and to try to find a beehive that Miguel saw during a previous exploration. We did not find the beehive and only ate *mote* and palm shoots with lard. We have food for tomorrow and the day after tomorrow (*mote*). We walked some three kilometres along the Rosita and another three along the Río Grande.

h = 610m.

17 June

We walked some 15 kilometres along the Rosita, in five and a half hours. On the way we crossed four streams, in spite of the fact that the map has only one: the Abapocito. We have found a multitude of recent tracks. Ricardo killed a rodent, a *hochi*, and with this and the *mote* we got through the day. We have enough *mote* for tomorrow, but presumably we will find a house.

18 June

Many of us burned our bridges, eating all our *mote* for breakfast. At 11.00, after a two-and-a-half-hour march, we fell upon a farm with corn, yucca, sugarcane and a mill to grind it, *jocos* and rice. We prepared a meal without protein and sent Benigno and Pablito to explore. Two hours later Pablo came back with the news that he had run into a peasant whose farm is 500 metres from this one. Other peasants were on their way here and all were taken prisoner when they arrived. At night we moved our camp and slept at the farm that belongs to the boys, just at the end of the road

from Abapó, some seven leagues from here. Their houses are some 10–15 kilometres above the point where the Mosquera and the Oscura rivers fork, on the latter.
h = 680m.

19 June

We walked slowly for some 12 kilometres to reach the hamlet, which consists of three houses and as many families. Two kilometres further down there is a family, the Gálvez, just on the fork of the Mosquera and the Oscura. You have to hunt down the inhabitants to talk to them, as they are like little animals. In general we were well received, but Calixto, who was appointed mayor by a military committee that passed through here about a month ago, appeared reserved and reluctant to sell us a few little things. As night fell three pig sellers arrived carrying a revolver and a Mauser rifle – they had not been stopped by the Vanguard sentries. Inti interrogated them, but did not take their weapons, and Antonio, who was on sentry duty, watched very carelessly. Calixto assured us that they are dealers from Postrer Valle and that he knows them.

There is another river that flows into the Rosita from the left and is called Suspiro; nobody lives along it.
h = 680m.

20 June

In the morning Paulino, one of the boys from the farm below, informed us that the three men were not pig dealers: one was a lieutenant and the other two were not from the pig trade. He got this information from Calixto's daughter, who is his girlfriend. Inti went with several men and gave them until 9.00 for the officer to come out, otherwise they would all be shot. The officer came out immediately, crying. He is a police sub-lieutenant and he was sent with an armed policeman and the teacher of Postrer Valle, who came as a volunteer. They were sent by the colonel who is stationed at the village with 60 men. His mission was to include a long journey, for which they gave him four days, including points along the Oscura. We considered killing them, but then I decided to send them back with a severe warning about the rules of warfare. Questioning how they could have got through, I established that Aniceto left his post to call Julio, and that was the time when they went through. Also, Aniceto and Luis were found asleep during sentry duty. They were punished with seven days as cooking assistants, and one day without pork, be it roasted or fried, and the stew that is being dished out to infinity.

The prisoners will be stripped of all their belongings.

21 June
The Old Girl.*

After two days of an orgy of dental extractions, in which I acquired fame as Fernando Tooth-Extractor, alias Chaco, I closed my surgery. We left in the afternoon, walking for over an hour. For the first time in this war, I set out riding a mule. The three detainees were taken for an hour down the path along the Mosquera and then stripped of all their belongings, including their watches and sandals. We thought of taking Calixto, the mayor, as a guide, along with Paulino, but he was sick or pretended to be and we left him behind with a severe warning, which will probably be useless. Paulino has undertaken to get my message to Cochabamba. He will be given a letter for Inti's wife, a coded message for Manila, and the four communiqués. The fourth one details the composition of our guerrilla force and clears up the lie of Inti's death, it is [illegible]. We shall see if we can now establish contact with the city. Paulino pretended to be coming along as our prisoner.
h = 750m.

---

*Birthday of his mother, Celia de la Serna, who died in 1965, while he was in Africa.

22 June

We walked for three hours, leaving behind the river Oscura or Morocos to reach a watering place in a spot called Pasiones. We consulted the map and everything indicated that we were not less than six leagues from Florida or Piray, the first spot where there are houses, where a brother-in-law of Paulino lives. But he does not know the way. We considered going on to take advantage of the moon, but it is not worth it, in view of the distance.

h = 950m.

23 June

We only advanced an hour's worth of our route, as we lost the trail, and it took us all morning and part of the afternoon to find it. We took the rest of the day to clear it for tomorrow. The Eve of Saint John* was not as cold as it is supposed to be.

My asthma is seriously threatening me and there is very little medicine in reserve.

h =1,050m.

24 June

We walked a total of some 12 kilometres, four hours in fact. There were sections where the trail was good and was visible, others where we had to improvise it. We climbed down an incredible cliff following the trail of some drovers who were herding their cattle. We camped by a trickle of water on the slopes of the Durán hill. The radio broadcasts news of a struggle in the mines.† My asthma attacks are on the increase.

h = 1,200m.

---

*The Eve of Saint John: a traditional holiday in the region, reputed to be the coldest night of the year.

†The military junta Barrientos-Ovando had reduced the salaries of the workers of the Bolivian Mining Corporation by 45 per cent. The clandestine Mining Workers' Federation summoned a meeting during which the workers of the Catavi mine voted to give a day's salary, as well as a consignment of medicines, to the guerrillas. Simón Reyes presided. On 24 June at dawn, after the celebrations for the feast of Saint John, the Army opened fire on the miners' housing at the Siglo XX mine, the largest tin mine in Bolivia. It went down in history as the Massacre of Saint John.

25 June

We followed the trail made by the cattle herders, without catching up with them. By mid-morning we reached a burning field and a plane flew over the area. We never discovered for certain what the relationship was between these two facts, but we carried on and at 16.00 we reached Piray, where Paulino's sister lives. There are three houses here. One of them is abandoned, another one empty and Paulino's sister was in the third one, with four children but not with her husband, who has gone to Florida with Paniagua, the owner of the empty house. Everything seemed normal. One kilometre away lives the daughter of Paniagua and that was the house we chose to camp in. We bought a calf and slaughtered it immediately. I sent Coco with Julio, Camba and León to Florida to buy a few things but they discovered that the Army is there: some 50 men and more are expected, making a total of about 120–130. The owner of the house is an old man called Fenelón Coca.

The Argentine radio gave the news of 87 victims, whereas the Bolivians do not reveal the number of casualties at the Siglo XX mine. My asthma continues to increase and now it stops me getting any sleep.

h = 780m.

26 June

A black day for me. Everything seemed to be going quietly and I had sent five men to replace those who were manning the ambush on the road to Florida, when we heard some shots. We went quickly on horseback and came across a strange sight: in the midst of total silence, the corpses of four young soldiers lay on the sand by the river. We could not take their weapons because we did not know where the enemy was positioned. It was 17.00 and we decided to wait for nightfall to collect them. Miguel sent word that he could hear the noise of branches breaking over on the left; Antonio and Pacho went over to look, but I gave the order not to fire unless they saw something. Almost immediately we heard gunfire, which became generalised on both sides. I gave the order to withdraw, since under such conditions we were at a disadvantage. The withdrawal was delayed and we got word of two men wounded: Pombo in the leg and Tuma in the stomach. We took them quickly into the house to operate on them with whatever there was. Pombo's wound is superficial and only his lack of mobility will represent a headache. Tuma's wound had destroyed his liver and he had intestinal perforations. He died during the operation. With him I have lost an inseparable comrade of all these years. He was loyal to the very end, and from now on I will feel his absence almost like the loss of a son. After he fell he asked that his watch be given to me, and as they did not do so, while they were treating him, he took it off and gave it to Arturo. That gesture shows his wish that it be given to his son, whom he never met, just as I have done in the past with the watches of other fallen comrades. I will wear it throughout the war. We loaded the body on to a mule and will take it far from here for burial.

Two new spies were taken prisoner: a lieutenant and a policeman from the National Police Force. They were cautioned and set free, in only their underpants, due to a misinterpretation of my order that they be stripped of anything useful to us. We left with nine horses.

27 June
After fulfilling the painful task of burying Tuma as best we could, we carried on, arriving by daylight at Tejería. At 14.00 the Vanguard left on a 15-kilometre journey and we left at 14.30. The journey was long for the final group, because night fell and they had to wait for the moon, arriving at 2.30 at the house in Paliza, which is where the guides come from.

We returned the two animals to the owner of the house in Tejería, who is the nephew of the old Paniagua woman, so that they can return them to her.

h = 850m.

28 June

We found a guide who, for 40 pesos, offered to take us to the crossing leading to Don Lucas's house. But we stayed at a crossing that came before it and had its own watering place. We left late, but the last ones took for ever and I missed the news. We walked an average of one kilometre an hour. According to the different versions, the Army, or an independent radio station, mention three dead and two wounded in an encounter with guerrillas in the area of Mosquera. They must be referring to our combat, but we could see, almost certainly, four corpses, unless one of them managed to pretend perfectly to be dead.

The house belonged to a certain Zea. It was not inhabited, but he had several cows whose calves we fenced in. h = 1,150m.

29 June

I had a serious conversation with Moro and Ricardo because of the delay. Mainly with Ricardo. They left with rucksacks and on horseback. Since Ñato is in charge of all the animals, he carried his own, as well as Pombo's and mine on a mule. Pombo arrived with relative ease on a lowland mare. We put him up comfortably in the house that belongs to Don Lucas, who lives on the summit, at 1,800 metres. He was there with two daughters, one of whom suffers from goitre. There are two other houses. One of them belongs to a seasonal worker and is almost empty, and the other is well stocked. The night was rainy and cold. Reports say that Barchelón is a half-day's walk away, but according to the peasants who came along the path, it is in very bad condition. The owner of the house does not agree and assures us that it can easily be cleared. The peasants had come to see the man in the other house and we detained them as we thought they were suspicious.

During the march I had a conversation with our group, which now consists of 24 men. I added Chino to the roll of men of example. I explained the significance of our losses, as well as the personal loss that the death of Tuma means to me, as I considered him as a son. I criticised the lack of self-discipline and the slowness of the march, and I promised to provide some further guidelines so that we do not repeat in future ambushes what has happened: needless loss of life due to failure to comply with the rules.

30 June

Old Lucas gave us some information about his neighbours, from which we can deduce that the Army has already been here making preparations. One of his neighbours, Andulfo Díaz, is the Secretary-General of the Peasant Union for the area, and on record as pro-Barrientos. Another one is an old chatterbox, who was allowed to leave because he is paralysed. And the other is a coward, according to his colleagues, who might well talk to spare himself any complications. The old man promised to accompany us and to help us clear a path to Barchelón. The two peasants will follow. We spent the day resting since it was rainy and unsettled.

On the political level, the most important event is Ovando's official declaration that I am here. He also said that the Army was having to face perfectly trained guerrillas, among them Vietcong officers who had defeated the best North American regiments. He based his words on Debray's statements, who, it appears, said more than he needed, although we have no way of knowing what implications this might have, nor the circumstances under which he spoke. There are rumours that Loro was assassinated. They attributed to me the inspiration for the miners' planned insurrection, to coincide with the one at Ñacahuasu. Things are hotting up. Before long I will stop being 'Fernando the Tooth-Extractor'.

We received a message from Cuba, explaining the lack of development by the guerrilla organisation in Peru, where they have almost no weapons or men, but have spent a

fortune. There is talk of an alleged guerrilla organisation
between Paz Estenssoro, a Colonel Seoane and a certain
Rubén Julio, a very rich man of the Revolutionary National
Movement in the Pando area. They might be from
Guayamerín. It is [*illegible*].

Analysis of the month

*The negative points are the complete failure to make
contact with Joaquín and our gradual loss of men; each one
of them signifies a serious defeat, even if the Army does not
know it. We have fought two minor battles this month,
causing the Army four deaths and three wounded, according to their own information.*

The most important characteristics are:

*1) The almost total lack of contacts continues, which
reduces us to the 24 men we now are, with Pombo wounded
and our mobility reduced.*

*2) The lack of peasant recruitment continues to be felt.
It is a vicious circle: to achieve such recruitment we need to
be in action permanently in a populated area and for that
we need more men.*

*3) The legend of the guerrillas sweeps on like a tide: we
are now invincible supermen.*

*4) The lack of contact extends to the party, although we
have made an attempt through Paulino that may still come
to something.*

*5) Debray continues to be in the news, but now they are
linking him to me, as I am now seen as the leader of this
movement. We shall see the result of this step by the
government, and whether it is positive or negative for us.*

*6) The morale of the guerrillas continues to be strong
and their will to fight grows. All the Cubans set an example
in combat and only two or three of the Bolivians are weak.*

*7) The Army continues to amount to nothing militarily,
but they are working on the peasants, and this we must not
ignore because it turns every member of a community into*

an informer, be it through fear or by lying to them about our aims.

8) The massacre in the mines greatly clarifies the outlook for us. If our proclamation is broadcast, it will play a part in the enlightenment of people.

Our most urgent task it to re-establish contact with La Paz, re-equip ourselves with military and medical supplies, and recruit 50–100 men from the city, even if the number of active combatants is no more than 10–25 men.

July 1967

1 July

Although the day had not cleared completely, we set out for Barchelón – Barcelona on the map. Old Lucas gave us a hand repairing the path, but in spite of that, it remained quite steep and slippery. The Vanguard left in the morning and we set off at noon, spending all afternoon going up and down the ravine. We had to stop to sleep in the first farm and were separated from the Vanguard, who carried on. There were three children called Yépez, who were extremely shy.

Barrientos gave a press conference during which he admitted that I am here, but predicted that I would be wiped out in a few days. He said his usual series of nonsense, calling us rats and serpents, and repeated his intention of punishing Debray.

We detained a peasant called Andrés Coca, whom we ran into along the trail. We also took the other two with us, Roque and his son Pedro.

h = 1,550m.

2 July

In the morning we joined the Vanguard. They had camped on the hill, in the house of Don Nicomedes Arteaga. There is an orange grove there, and they sold us cigars. The main house is down below, on the Piojera river, and there we went and ate a lavish meal. The Piojera river runs through a narrow canyon and one can only follow it on foot towards Angostura: the way out is towards La Junta, another point on the same river, but it cuts through the hill, which is quite high. It is important because it is a crossroads. This place is at an altitude of only 950 metres and is much more temperate. Here the ticks give way to gnats. The settlement consists of Arteaga's house and those of his sons. They have a small coffee plantation, where people from the area come to work for a share of the crop. There are some six farmhands from the region of San Juan.

Pombo's leg is not healing with sufficient speed, probably due to the endless trips on horseback, but he has not had any complications, nor need we fear them now.

3 July
We spent all day there, trying to give Pombo's leg more time to rest. Our purchases are being charged at high prices and this means that the peasants balance their fear with self-interest and provide us with what we need. I took some photos, which roused everybody's interest. We will see how to develop, enlarge and get them back here: three problems. A plane flew over in the afternoon, and in the evening there was talk of the possibility of nocturnal bombings, so no one wanted to sleep indoors. We stopped them and explained that there was no danger. My asthma continues to plague me.

4 July
We walked the two leagues to La Junta (the junction) at a slow pace, arriving at 15.30. A peasant called Manuel Carrillo lives there, and he was terrified at our arrival. We ate sumptuously, as has been our custom recently, and slept in an abandoned shack. My asthma was severely punishing and for the first time prevented me from sleeping.

Two days ago seven soldiers went by, coming from El Filo and going towards Bermejo.
h = 1,000m.

5 July
The whole area the families with their belongings fled to

escape the Army's reprisals. We mingled with oxen, pigs, hens and people as far as Lagunillas, leaving the Piojera river and following its tributary, the Lagunillas, for one kilometre. Our guide was an unhappy-looking peasant called Ramón. His family suffers from the proverbial fear that permeates this area. We slept beside the road. Along the way we ran into a man from Sandoval Morón, who lives in San Luis and seems to be much more alert.

6 July

We left early for Peña Colorada, crossing a populated area where the people greeted us in terror. At dusk we reached Alto de Palermo, 1,600 metres, and started to descend to a point where there is a little grocery store, where we bought things just in case. It was dark when we reached the road, where there is only a little house owned by an old widow. The Vanguard was not very inspired when they took it, due to indecision. The plan was to take a vehicle coming from Samaipata, find out how things were there, and make our way there with the driver of the vehicle, occupy the DIC,* acquire some items at the chemist's, raid the hospital, buy some tins and sweets and then return.

We changed the plan because there were no vehicles coming from Samaipata, and we heard that vehicles were no longer being stopped there, which meant that the barrier had been raised. Those commissioned for the action were Ricardo, Coco, Pacho, Aniceto, Julio and Chino. They stopped a truck coming from Santa Cruz, without problems, but then another one coming behind stopped in solidarity and had to be detained. A tug-of-war then started with a lady who did not want to let her daughter get off. A third truck stopped to see what was going on, and the road was blocked as a result, so a fourth one had to stop in view of the general chaos. Matters were sorted out and the four vehicles were

*Department of Criminal Investigation, the secret police of Bolivia.

left parked on the side of the road. One of the drivers was to
say that they were taking a rest, if asked. Our men left on a
truck, arrived at Samaipata, captured two policemen and
then Lieutenant Vacaflor, the head of the post. The sergeant
was made to give the password, and our men took the post
in a lightning action, capturing its 10 soldiers after a brief
exchange of fire when one of the soldiers resisted. They
captured five Mausers, one BZ-30, and then drove the
prisoners a kilometre from Samaipata and left them there
naked. From the point of view of supplies, the action was a
failure. Chino allowed himself to be overruled by Pacho and
Julio, and nothing useful was acquired. As for medicines,
they got none of the ones I need, although they did get some
of the more indispensable ones for the guerrillas. The action
took place in front of the whole village and a crowd of
travellers, so the story will spread like wildfire. At 2.00 we
were already walking back with the booty.

7 July
We marched without rest until we reached a cane-field
where last time a man had received us well, one league
from Ramón's house. Fear continues to dominate the
people. The man sold us a pig and was amiable, but warned
us that there were 200 men in Los Ajos and that his brother
had just returned from San Juan saying that there were
100 soldiers there. He should have had some teeth
extracted, but preferred not to. My asthma attacks are
getting worse.

8 July
We walked with caution from the house beside the cane-
field to the Piojera river, but it was all clear there. There
were no rumours of soldiers, and the people coming from
San Juan said that there were no soldiers there. It seems that
it was a ruse by the man to get us to leave. We walked some
two leagues along the river to El Piray, and from there

another league to the cave, where we arrived at nightfall. We are near El Filo.

I injected myself several times so that I could carry on, and ended up having to use eye-drops containing 1/900 adrenaline. If Paulino has not carried out his mission, we will have to return to Ñacahuasu to get medicines for my asthma.

The Army gave news of the skirmish, admitting to one dead, which must have been the result of the exchange of fire; Ricardo, Coco and Pacho took the little military post.

9 July
As we started off, we lost the track and spent the morning looking for it. At midday we followed a difficult path, which took us to the greatest height we have reached so far, some 1,840 metres. Not long afterwards we reached a shack where we stopped for the night. We are uncertain about the route to El Filo. The radio gave the news of a 14-point agreement between the workers at Catavi and Siglo XX and the Empresa Comibol [mining company]. It is a total defeat for the workers.

10 July
We left late because a horse was missing. It turned up later. We reached our highest altitude yet, 1,900 metres, on a seldom-used route. At 15.30 we arrived at a shack, where we decided to spend the night. The unpleasant surprise is that there are no more paths. We sent out a party to explore some unused ones, but they all lead nowhere. Ahead of us we can see some farmland, which could be El Filo.

The radio gave the news of a clash with guerrillas in the area of El Dorado, which does not appear on the map and is between Samaipata and the Río Grande: they admit to one wounded and attribute two dead men to us.

On the other hand, the statements made by Debray and Pelado are not good; above all, they have admitted to the intercontinental aims of the guerrillas, something they should not have done.

11 July

Coming back, on a rainy and foggy day, we lost every path, becoming totally separated from the Vanguard. They climbed down by reopening an old path. We slaughtered a calf.

12 July

We spent all day waiting for news of Miguel, but only at dusk did Julio arrive with the news that they had climbed down to a stream that runs south. We stayed in the same place. My asthma hit me badly.

The radio now brings news that seems accurate in its most important point. They talk about combat on the Ikira, with one dead on our side, whose body they have taken to Lagunillas. Their euphoria about the corpse indicates that there may be an element of truth in the report.

13 July

In the morning we climbed down a steep hill, which had turned slippery in bad weather. We met up with Miguel at 11.30. He had sent Camba and Pacho to explore a path that leads away from the one following the course of the stream. They returned an hour later, with news that there were farms and houses, and that they had found an abandoned one. We went there, and then, following the course of a small stream, we arrived at the first house, where we spent the night. The owner of the house arrived later and told us that a woman, the local magistrate's mother, had seen us and would have told the soldiers who are at the settlement at El Filo, a league from here. We kept watch all night.

14 July

After a night of continuous drizzle, it went on raining all

day, but we left at 12.00, taking two guides with us. They
were Pablo, the mayor's brother-in-law, and Aurelio
Mancilla, the man from the first house. The women were
left behind, weeping. We reached a fork in the road, one path
leading to Florida and Moroco and the other to Pampa. The
guides proposed taking the one to Pampa, from where we
could take a narrow path recently opened up, to the
Mosquera. We accepted, but after we had walked some 500
metres, a soldier and a peasant appeared with a load of flour
on a horse, and a message for the sub-lieutenant at El Filo
from his colleague at Pampa, where there are 30 soldiers. We
decided to change direction and took the path to Florida,
camping not much later.

The PRA and the PSB* withdrew from the Revolutionary
Front, and the peasants have given warning to Barrientos
against an alliance with the Falange.† The government is
disintegrating rapidly. It is a pity we do not have 100 more
men right now.

15 July
We walked very little because of the bad condition of the
road, abandoned years ago. On the advice of Aurelio, we
slaughtered a cow belonging to the local magistrate and ate
sumptuously. My asthma has let up a little.

Barrientos announced Operation Cintia, to wipe us out
within a few hours.

16 July
We started to walk very slowly because clearing a path was
such a strenuous task. The animals suffered a lot because
of the awful condition of the road. By the end of the day we
had reached a canyon where the horses cannot continue
without risk, if they are loaded. Miguel and four men

---

* PRA: Partido Revolucionario Auténtico, led by Walter Guevara Arce. PSB: Partido
Socialista de Bolivia.
† Falange Socialista Boliviana (FSB), a right-wing party.

from the Vanguard went on ahead and slept separately.

. There was no news worth mentioning on the radio. We passed a height of 1,600 metres near the Durán hill, which was on our left.

17 July

We continued to walk slowly, since stretches of the trail had disappeared. We hoped to arrive at an orange grove which the guide had mentioned, but when we got there we found that the plants were dried and shrivelled. There was a backwater, which we took advantage of to set up camp. We did not make more than three hours of actual progress. My asthma is much better. It looks as if we will get back to the path we used to reach Piray. We are near the Durán.
h = 1,560m.

18 July

We had walked for an hour when the guide lost the trail and said that he did not know how to carry on. In the end we found an old track and, while we cleared it, Miguel followed it, cutting his way through, and reached the crossroads leading to the Piray. When we reached a little stream where we camped, we released the three peasants and the young soldier, after giving them a serious warning. Coco left with Pablito and Pacho to find out if Paulino had left anything in the hole; they should get back by tomorrow night, if all our calculations are correct. The young soldier says he is going to desert.
h = 1,300m.

19 July

We made the short trip to the old camp and stayed there. We reinforced the sentries and waited for Coco, who arrived later, at 18.00, saying that nothing had changed there. The rifle is in its place and there is no sign of Paulino. Instead, the soldiers have left many tracks as they passed. They had also left tracks on our section of the path.

The political news is of a huge crisis, and nobody knows how it will end. For a start, the agricultural unions of Cochabamba have formed a political party of 'Christian inspiration', which supports Barrientos, who is asking 'to be allowed to govern for four years': it is almost a plea. Siles Salinas threatens the opposition, saying that if we succeed it will cost everyone his head. He is calling for national unity, declaring that the country is now on a war footing. He seems to be pleading on the one hand, and sounds like a demagogue on the other: maybe he is preparing for a takeover.

20 July

We walked cautiously until we reached the first two little houses, where we met one of the Paniagua boys and Paulino's son-in-law. They knew nothing about him, except that the Army was after him for having been our guide. The foot-marks correspond to a group of 100 men who went by a week after us, and went on to Florida. It seems the Army suffered three dead and two wounded in the ambush. Coco was sent with Camba and León to explore Florida, and to buy whatever he could find there. He returned at 4.00 with some provisions and a certain Melgar, the owner of two of our horses, who offered his services and brought detailed but apparently reliable information from which we can glean the following: four days after our departure Tuma's corpse was found, gnawed by animals; the Army only advanced the day after the clash, after the naked lieutenant appeared. The action at Samaipata is known in every detail, plus embellishments, and the Army's failure is the subject of derision to the peasants; they found Tuma's pipe as well as some of his belongings scattered around. A major called Soperna seems to be half-sympathetic, perhaps an admirer of ours; the Army reached Coca's house, where Tuma died, and from there went on to Tejería, and then returned to Florida. Coco wanted to use the man to send a letter, but I thought it more prudent to test him first, by sending him to purchase medicines. Melgar told us about a group, including a woman, which is on its way here. He learned it from a letter sent by the magistrate of Río Grande to the local one here. As the latter lives on the way to Florida, we sent Inti, Coco and Julio to interview him. He denied having news of another group, but confirmed the information given by Melgar, along general lines. We spent a miserable night because of the rain. The radio broadcast news of the identification of the dead guerrilla as Moisés Guevara. But, at a press conference, Ovando was rather cautious and said that identification was the responsibility of the Ministry of the Interior. It is possible that the alleged identification is a farce, or the whole thing an invention.

h = 68om.

21 July

We spent a calm day. We spoke to old Coca who had sold us a cow that was not his and later said that he had not been paid. He emphatically denied the fact, but we put him on notice to pay.

In the evening we went to Tejería and bought a large pig and some *chankaka*.* The people there greeted Inti, Benigno and Aniceto, who are the ones who went, with friendliness.

22 July

We started off early, carrying heavy loads on shoulders and on the animals with the intention of misleading everyone about the reality of our presence here. We left the path that leads to Moroco and took the one for the lagoon, one or two kilometres to the south. Unfortunately we did not know the rest of the way and had to send explorers ahead of us. In the meantime, Mancilla and the Paniagua boy appeared beside the lagoon, herding cattle. They were warned that they

---

*Traditional Bolivian candy made from sugarcane juice boiled and dried and cut into small pieces of different shapes.

should say nothing, but matters are very different now. We walked for a couple of hours, and slept beside a stream, which has a path following its course south-east, and another less clear one to the south.

The radio brought the news that the wife of Pelado Bustos confirmed that he saw me here, but she says that he came with different intentions.

h = 640m.

23 July

We stayed on in the same camp, while we sent out explorers to the two possible paths. One of them leads to the Río Seco, to the point where the Piray flows in and the sand has not absorbed the waters – that is, between the place we set the ambush and Florida. The other path leads to a shack some two to three hours away and, according to Miguel who explored it, it is possible to reach the Rosita. Tomorrow we will take that path, which could be one of Melgar's, according to the accounts he gave Coco and Julio.

24 July

We walked for some three hours, following the path that had been cleared which took us over 1,000 metres high. We camped at 940 metres, on the bank of a stream. Here all tracks come to an end, and tomorrow we must devote the day to finding the best way out. There are a number of cultivated plots here, which suggests a relationship with Florida – it could be the place called Canalones. We are trying to decode a long message from Manila. Raúl spoke at the officers' graduation ceremony at the Máximo Gómez School Academy. Among other things, he refuted the Czechs' criticism of my article on the many Vietnams. My friends are calling me the new Bakunin and lamenting the blood already shed and the blood that will be shed in the case of three or four Vietnams.

25 July

We spent the day resting, sending out three pairs to explore different points. Coco, Benigno and Miguel were in charge of this. Coco and Benigno both emerged at the same place, which is where one can take the path to Moroco. Miguel had information that the stream definitely flows into the Rosita and that one can walk along it, clearing the path with machetes.

There are reports of two actions, one at Taperas and another at San Juan del Potrero. They cannot have been carried out simultaneously by the same group, which raises two questions: whether the events actually took place, and how accurate the reports are.

26 July

Benigno, Camba and Urbano were sent to clear a path along the stream, avoiding Moroco. The rest of the personnel remained at the camp and the Main Force set an ambush at the back. No incidents.

The news of the action at San Juan del Potrero was broadcast by foreign radio stations in great detail, reporting the capture of 15 soldiers and one colonel, who were stripped of everything and set free – which is now our technique. That is on the other side of the Cochabamba–Santa Cruz road. In the evening I gave a little talk about the meaning of 26 July* – a rebellion against the oligarchies and against revolutionary dogmas. Fidel made a brief mention of Bolivia.

27 July

We had everything ready to go and the men at the ambush had orders to leave – whatever happened – at 11.00, when

---

*26 July is the anniversary of the failed attack on the Moncada Barracks led by Fidel Castro in 1953 in Santiago de Cuba. The date became the name of the movement that launched the Cuban Revolution which triumphed in 1959, again under the leadership of Fidel Castro.

Willy arrived, a few minutes before that, reporting the presence of the Army. Willy, Ricardo, Inti, Chino, León, Eustaquio, together with Antonio, Arturo and Chapaco, went into combat. It went as follows: eight soldiers appeared at the summit; they walked to the south, following an old path, and then returned. They fired some mortar rounds and made signals, waving a rag. At some point we heard a call to a certain Melgar, who could well be the one from Florida. After a little rest, the eight soldiers started towards the ambush. Only four fell into it, since the rest were lagging behind. There are three dead and probably a fourth, who in any case is wounded. We withdrew without taking their weapons or equipment because it would have been too difficult. We went downstream. When we came to the mouth of another little canyon we set a new ambush. The horses went on as far as the path goes.

My asthma was hard on me, and the few sedatives are running out.

h = 800m.

28 July

Coco, Pacho, Raúl and Aniceto were sent to cover the mouth of the river that we believe is the Suspiro. We walked very little, opening a path through a fairly narrow canyon. We camped, separated from the Vanguard because Miguel advanced too far for the horses. They were sinking into the sand, or suffering because of the stones.

h = 760m.

29 July

We went on walking through a canyon that slopes down towards the south, with good hiding places at the sides, and in an area with enough water. At approximately 16.00 we ran into Pablito who reported that we were at the mouth of the Suspiro. No incidents. For a moment I thought the canyon could not be the Suspiro, because it runs towards the south, but on the last stretch it turns west and flows into the Rosita.

At approximately 16.30 the Rearguard arrived and I decided to continue on, to leave behind the mouth of the river. But I could not risk demanding the effort needed to go beyond Paulino's farm, so we camped on the edge of the path, an hour's march from the mouth of the Suspiro. In the evening I asked Chino to say a few words about the independence of his country, on 28 July, and afterwards I explained why this camp is badly situated, giving orders to rise at five and leave to take Paulino's farm.

Radio Havana spoke of an ambush in which some Army regulars fell and were rescued by helicopter, but we could not hear it properly.

30 July

My asthma played up and I spent the night awake. At 4.30, when Moro was making coffee, he told us that he saw a torch moving across the river. Miguel, who was awake because he was changing guards, went with Moro to halt those who were approaching. From the cooking area I heard the following dialogue: 'Who goes there?' 'Trinidad Detachment.' The shooting started then and there. Miguel brought back an M-1 immediately, as well as a cartridge belt taken from a wounded soldier, with the news that there were 21 men on the road to Abapó, and that at Moroco there were 150. We inflicted more casualties on them, although in the general confusion we could not discover how many. It took us a long time to load the horses, and Negro got lost, carrying a hatchet and mortar that we had taken from the enemy. It was already about 6.00 and we lost more time, because some of the loads slipped off. The end result was that, during the last crossings, we were under fire from the young soldiers, who had regained their courage. Paulino's sister was at her farm and greeted us very calmly, and informed us that all the men in Moroco had been arrested and were in La Paz.

I hurried up the men and went across the river canyon with Pombo, still under fire; we reached the point where the path ends and we could reorganise the resistance. I sent Miguel with Coco and Julio to take up the forward position, while I spurred on the cavalry. Covering the retreat were seven men from the Vanguard, four from the Rearguard, with Ricardo who had been delayed, to reinforce the defence. Benigno, with Darío, Pablo and Camba, was on the right bank; the rest were coming up from the left. I had just given the order to rest, at the first suitable position, when Camba appeared with the news that Ricardo and Aniceto had fallen crossing the river. I sent Urbano with Ñato and León and two horses to look for Miguel and Julio, leaving Coco at the head, on sentry duty. They went through without my instructions, and not long afterwards Camba appeared again with the news that, together with Miguel and Julio, they had been taken by surprise by the soldiers, who had advanced further. They had withdrawn and were awaiting instructions. I sent Camba back with Eustaquio, and only Inti, Pombo, Chino and I remained. At 13.00 I sent for Miguel, leaving Julio on advance sentry duty, and I withdrew with the group of men and the horses. As I was reaching Coco's position the news came that all the survivors had showed up: Raúl was dead, and Ricardo and Pacho wounded. This is how it happened: Ricardo and Aniceto were imprudently crossing the clearing when Ricardo was wounded. Antonio organised a line of fire, and between Arturo, Aniceto and Pacho they rescued him, but Pacho was wounded and Raúl was killed by a bullet through the mouth. They withdrew with difficulty, dragging the two wounded men, with little help from Willy and Chapaco, especially the latter. Then they rejoined Urbano and his group with the horses and Benigno with his men, leaving the other flank unguarded, enabling the soldiers to advance and surprise Miguel. After a painful march through the forest, they came to the river and were reunited with us. Pacho came on horseback, but Ricardo could not mount and had to be carried in a hammock. I sent Miguel with Pablito, Darío, Coco and Aniceto to guard the mouth of the first stream on the right bank, while we saw to the wounded. Pacho had a superficial wound which had penetrated his buttocks and the skin of his testicles, but Ricardo was seriously wounded and our last plasma had been lost with Willy's rucksack. At 22.00 Ricardo died, and we buried him near the river in a well-hidden spot so that the soldiers would not find him.

31 July
At 4.00 we started along the river and, after crossing by a shortcut, went on downriver without leaving any tracks. We arrived in the morning at the stream where Miguel was ambushed. He had not heard the order and had left footprints. We advanced some four kilometres upriver and then turned into the forest, erasing our tracks and camping near a tributary of the stream. At night I explained our mistakes in the action: 1) bad location of the camp; 2) bad timing, which enabled them to shoot at us; 3) excessive confidence, as a result of which Ricardo and then Raúl fell during the rescue; 4) failure of determination to save all the equipment. We lost 11 rucksacks with medicines, binoculars and some potentially damaging materials, such as the tape recorder used to copy the messages from Manila, Debray's book with my annotations and a book by Trotsky, without taking into account the political capital that the government can derive from this capture, and the confidence it will give the soldiers. We calculate that they have some two dead and up to five wounded, but the news is contradictory: a bulletin from the Army admits to four dead and four wounded on the 28th, and another bulletin from Chile gives six wounded and three dead on the 30th. The Army then reported the capture of a body and says that their sub-lieutenant is out of danger. Of our dead, Raúl hardly counts, in view of his introspection; he was not very

combative and not very hard-working, but one could see that he was always interested in political problems, although he never asked any questions. Ricardo was the least disciplined of the Cuban group, and the least decisive when it came to our daily sacrifices, but he was an extraordinary combatant and an old comrade of adventures, from the days of Segundo's first failure, in the Congo and now here. It is another serious loss because of his quality. We are 22, two of whom are wounded, Pacho and Pombo, and me, with my asthma going full steam ahead.

Analysis of the month
The negative points of the previous month remain, i.e. the impossibility of making contact with Joaquín and with the outside world, and the loss of men. We are now 22, with three injured, including myself, which decreases our mobility. We have had three clashes, including the taking of Samaipata. We have inflicted 7 dead and 10 wounded on the Army, figures which are unconfirmed because of the confusing reports. We have lost two men, with one man wounded.

The most important features are:

1) Total lack of contact continues.

2) We continue to feel the lack of peasant recruits, but there are some encouraging signs in the way peasants we already know have greeted us.

3) The legend of the guerrillas acquires continental dimensions: Onganía has sealed the frontiers, and Peru is taking precautions.

4) The attempt to make contact through Paulino failed.

5) The morale and combat experience of the guerrilla force increases with each battle. Only Camba and Chapaco are still weak.

6) The Army continues to reveal its incompetence, but there are units that seem more combative.

7) The political crisis in the government continues to

grow, but the USA is giving them small loans which are a great help by Bolivian standards and this mitigates general discontent.

The most urgent tasks are: to re-establish contacts, to recruit more combatants and to obtain medicines.

August 1967

1 August

A quiet day: Miguel and Camba started on the path but only advanced a little over a kilometre because of the difficult terrain and the vegetation. We killed a wild horse, which will give us meat for five to six days. We dug small trenches to set an ambush for the Army, should they come this way. The idea is to let them through if they come tomorrow or the day after and do not discover the camp. Then we'll fire on them afterwards.

h = 650m.

2 August

The path seems to have progressed well, thanks to Benigno and Pablo, who are continuing with it. It took them almost two hours from the end of the path to the camp. There is no news of us on the radio, after they announced that they had moved the body of an 'anti-social' person. My asthma hit me hard and I have used up the last anti-asthma injection. All I have now is tablets for about 10 days.

3 August

The path turned out to be a fiasco; Miguel and Urbano only took 57 minutes to return today; progress is very slow. There is no news. Pacho is recovering well, while I am worse; both day and night took their toll on me, and I see no temporary way out. I tried the intravenous Novocaine injection to no avail.

4 August

The men reached a canyon that turns in a south-west direction and may lead to streams that flow into the Río Grande. Tomorrow two pairs will go up to clear a path, and Miguel will follow our trail and explore what looks like abandoned farmland. My asthma improved somewhat.

5 August

Benigno, Camba, Urbano and León went out in pairs to make better progress, but they ended up at a stream that flows into the Rosita, and then struck out across country. Miguel went to explore the farm, but did not find it. We finished the horsemeat; tomorrow we will try to fish and the day after tomorrow we will kill another beast. Tomorrow we will advance up to the new watering place. My asthma was merciless. In spite of my reluctance to separate the men, I will have to send a group ahead. Benigno and Julio volunteered; I need to see if Ñato is willing to go as well.

6 August

We moved the camp; unfortunately it took not three hours but one to cover the path that has been cleared, which means that we are still far away. Benigno, Urbano, Camba and León went on clearing a track, while Miguel and Aniceto went out exploring the new stream until it flows into the Rosita. At night they had not returned, so we took precautions, the more so as I had heard something like a mortar shell in the distance. Inti, Chapaco and I said a few words about today's date, the anniversary of Bolivian independence.
h = 720m.

7 August

At 11.00 in the morning I had given Miguel and Aniceto up as lost; I ordered Benigno to advance with great caution to the mouth of the Rosita, to find out what direction they had taken – if in fact they had arrived that far. However, at 13.00 the lost men appeared. They had simply met difficulties along the road, and night had fallen before they had reached the Rosita. I was very worried and had a really hard time, thanks to Miguel. We remained on the same site, but the trail-cutters have found another stream. We will go there tomorrow. Anselmo, the old horse, died today. We now have only one left to carry all our kit. My asthma is unchanged, but the medicines are running out. Tomorrow I will decide whether to send a group to the Ñacahuasu.

Today is exactly nine months since the initiation of the guerrillas and my arrival. Of the initial six, two are dead, one has disappeared and two wounded, and me with my asthma which I don't know how to halt.

8 August

We walked for something like an hour's progress, which for me was more like two because the little mare was so tired. At one point I lacerated her neck with my knife and opened a wound. The new camp must be the last one with water before we reach the Rosita or the Río Grande. The trail-cutters are 40 minutes away from here (two to three kilometres). I have chosen a group of eight men for the following mission: they are to leave here tomorrow and walk all day; the following day Camba comes back with the news of what is there. The next day, Pablito and Darío return with that day's news; the five remaining men carry on as far as Vargas's house. From there Coco and Aniceto will return to tell us how things are. Benigno, Julio and Ñato go on to Ñacahuasu to get my medicines. They must take care and avoid ambushes. We shall follow them, and the meeting point will be: Vargas's house or further up, depending on our speed, or the stream that faces the cave at the Río Grande, or the Masicuri (Honorato) or the Ñacahuasu. It is reported that the Army has discovered a weapons cache at one of our camps.

At night I gathered everyone together and made the following speech: we face a difficult situation. Pacho is recovering, but I am a wreck and the episode with the little mare proves that at times I have lost my self-control. This will be corrected, but the situation is equally serious for us all, and those who are not able to cope must say so. It is one of those times when great decisions must be made; this type of struggle gives us the opportunity to become revolutionaries, but it also allows us to prove we are men. Those who are unable to reach either of these stages must say so and leave the struggle.

All the Cubans and some Bolivians said that they would carry on until the end. Eustaquio did too, but he criticised Muganga for putting his rucksack on the mule and for not carrying wood, which elicited an irate reply by the latter. Julio lashed out at Pacho for similar behaviour and another irate reply followed, this time from Pacho. I closed the debate by saying that we were discussing two different things: one was whether they were ready or not to carry on; the other was the minor squabbles or internal problems of the guerrillas, which diminished the importance of the main decision. I did not like Eustaquio's or Julio's stance, but neither did I like the replies from Moro or Pacho. To conclude, we must become more revolutionary and set an example.

9 August
The eight explorers left in the morning. The trail-cutters, Miguel, Urbano and León, progressed another 50 minutes further from the camp. An abscess on my heel was lanced, which allows me to put weight on my foot, although I am still in great pain and have a temperature. Pacho is doing very well.
h = 780m.

10 August

Antonio and Chapaco went to the rear to hunt and caught a *urina*, and a turkey hen. They explored the first camp without incident and brought back a load of oranges. I ate two and immediately got asthma, although not much. At 13.30 Camba, who was one of the eight explorers, arrived with the following news: yesterday they slept without finding water, and today they continued on until 9.00, still without finding any. Benigno has surveyed the site and will set off towards the Rosita to get water. Pablo and Darío will return if they find water.

A long speech by Fidel in which he attacks the traditional parties and above all the Venezuelans. It would appear that there has been a ferocious row behind the scenes. My foot was seen to again. I am getting better, but I am not really well. In any case, tomorrow we must leave and set up camp closer to the trail-cutters, who are only progressing 35 minutes a day.

11 August

The trail-cutters are making very slow progress. At 16.00 Pablo and Darío arrived with a note from Benigno, saying that he is near the Rosita, and he calculates it will take three more days to Vargas's house. Pablito left at 8.15 from the watering place where they spent the night, and at about 15.00 he ran into Miguel, which means there is a lot to cover before we get there. It appears that turkey is bad for my asthma, because it brought on an attack, so I gave my share to Pacho. We changed camps and set ourselves up beside a new stream, which disappears at midday and reappears at night. It rained, but it is not cold. A lot of *marigüís*, those small black gnats.

h = 740m.

12 August

A grey day. The trail-cutters made little progress. There was nothing new here, and not much food. Tomorrow we will slaughter another horse, and that must last us six days. My asthma has settled at a bearable level. Barrientos announced the decline of the guerrillas and threatened again to intervene in Cuba; he was as stupid as ever.

The radio announced an assault near Monteagudo, which resulted in one dead on our part: Antonio Fernández, from Tarata. The name is quite similar to the real name of Pedro, who is from Tarata.

13 August

Miguel, Urbano, León and Camba left to set up camp by the watering place discovered by Benigno and advance from there. They are carrying food for three days – that is, pieces of meat from Pacho's horse, which was slaughtered today. We have four animals left and everything seems to indicate that we will have to slaughter another one before we reach other supplies. If all has gone well, Coco and Aniceto will arrive here tomorrow. Arturo caught two turkey hens, which were apportioned to me as there is hardly any corn left. Chapaco is showing growing signs of instability. Pacho is recovering at a good pace, and my asthma has been on the increase since yesterday; I am now taking three tablets a day. My foot is almost healed.

14 August

Black day. It was grey in relation to our activities, and there were no incidents, but at night the radio bulletin gave the news that the Army has captured our cave, where our group was heading. The information was so precise that it is impossible to doubt it. Now I am condemned to suffer from asthma for who knows how long. They also took every type of document, and photographs. It is the hardest blow they have inflicted on us. Someone has talked. Who? That is the question.

15 August

Early I sent Pablito with a message to Miguel that he should send two men to look for Benigno – that is, if Coco and Aniceto had not come back. But he ran into them on the way and the three returned together. Miguel sent word that he would camp wherever they were when night fell and asked for some water to be sent. Darío was sent to warn him that we would in any case be setting off early tomorrow morning, but he ran into León, who was returning to tell us that the path had been cleared.

A radio station from Santa Cruz mentioned in passing that the Army had taken two prisoners from the Muyupampa group. There is no doubt now it is Joaquín's group and they must be pursuing him relentlessly, quite apart from the fact that the two prisoners have talked. It was cold, but I did not have a bad night; another abscess on the same foot needs lancing. Pacho is fit again.

Another clash in Chuyuyako was announced, without Army losses.

16 August

We walked effectively for three hours forty minutes, then rested for one, along a relatively good path. The mule threw me clear out of the saddle when a stick spiked it, but I was not hurt; my foot is getting better. Miguel, Urbano and Camba continued clearing the path and reached the Rosita. Today is the day when Benigno and his comrades should reach the cave. Planes flew over the area several times. It may be because they left some tracks near Vargas's, or because some troops are coming down the Rosita or advancing by the Río Grande. At night I warned the men about the danger of crossing the river and we made careful preparations for tomorrow.

h = 600m.

17 August

We set out early and arrived at the Rosita at 9.00. Coco thought he heard two shots there, so we set an ambush, but nothing happened. The rest of the way was slow because we continually mistook the track or lost our way. We reached the Río Grande at 16.30 and camped there. I intended to carry on by moonlight, but the men were very tired. We have horsemeat for two days, if we ration it, and for me there is *mote* for one day. It looks like we will have to slaughter another animal. The radio announced that documents and evidence from four caves at Ñacahuasu will be displayed, which means that they also found the Monkey cave. My asthma behaved rather well, considering.

h = 640m. (illogical, if we take into account that yesterday it was 600)

18 August

We started off earlier than usual, but we had to cross four fords, one of them rather deep, and cut trails at some points. In view of all this, we arrived at the stream at 14.00, and the men dropped down to rest, half-dead. There was no further activity. There are clouds of *niborigüises* in the area, and the nights continue to be cold. Inti informed me that Camba wants to leave; according to him, his physical condition won't allow him to go on, but he also sees no future in the struggle. Naturally, it is a typical case of cowardice and the remedy would be to let him go, but now he knows the route we shall take to try and join forces with Joaquín, so he cannot leave. I will talk to him and Chapaco tomorrow.

h = 680m.

19 August

Miguel, Coco, Inti and Aniceto went out to explore to try and find the best route to Vargas's house, where there seems to be an Army detachment, but there was nothing and it appears that we must continue on the old trail. Arturo and Chapaco went out to hunt and they shot a *urina*, and Arturo himself, while on sentry duty with Urbano, shot an *anta*, or tapir, which alerted the camp because seven shots were heard. The beast will give us meat for four days, the *urina* for one day and there is a reserve stock of beans and sardines, a total for six days. It seems that the white horse, next on the list, gets a reprieve. I talked to Camba and told him that he could not leave until our next stage, to be reunited with Joaquín, is defined. Chapaco said that he would not leave because that is cowardly, but that he wanted to be given some hope of being able to leave in six months to one year, which I gave him. He spoke about a series of unrelated things. He is not well.

The news reports are full of Debray, with no mention of the other defendants. No news of Benigno. He should be here by now.

20 August

The trail-cutters, Miguel and Urbano, and my 'public works' men, Willy and Darío, made so little progress that we decided to stay here one more day. Coco and Inti did not catch anything, but Chapaco caught a monkey and a *urina*. I ate *urina* and at midnight I got a serious attack of asthma. The Doctor is still in pain, apparently with lumbago, which affects his general health and turns him into an invalid. There is no news from Benigno, and from this moment on it is very worrying.

The radio announces the presence of guerrillas 85 kilometres from Sucre.

21 August

One more day at the same place, and yet another day without news of Benigno and his comrades. Five monkeys were caught: four by Eustaquio while hunting, and one by Moro when it wandered past him. The latter is still afflicted with lumbago and was given a Meperidine. My asthma is triggered by *urina*.

22 August

We finally left, but before that there was an alarm because a man was seen apparently escaping along the sandbank. It turned out to be Urbano, lost. I gave the Doctor a local anaesthetic so that he could ride the mare and, although he arrived in pain, he seems to be a little better. Pacho went on foot. We camped on the right bank and only a little trail-cutting is needed to open the way to Vargas's house. We have *anta* meat for tomorrow and the day after, and from tomorrow onwards we will not be able to hunt. There is no news of Benigno. It is 10 days since they were separated from Coco.

h = 580m.

23 August

The day was full of complications since we had to climb around a very dangerous cliff. The white horse refused to go on and they left him trapped in the mud, without even taking advantage of its bones. We reached a little hunter's hut where there were signs of habitation. There we lay in ambush and, not long after, two men fell into it. Their explanation was that they had set 10 traps and had gone to inspect them. According to them, the Army is positioned at Vargas's house, in Tatarenda, Caraguatarenda, Ipitá and Yumón. Two days ago there was a clash in Caraguatarenda, with one soldier wounded. It could be Benigno, trapped by hunger or surrounded. The men said that the Army would arrive to fish tomorrow; they come in groups of 15 to 20 men. We distributed *anta* and some fish, which were caught with a cartridge bag. I ate rice, which suited me; the Doctor is better. The postponement of Debray's trial until September was announced.

h = 580m.

24 August

Reveille was at 5.30 and we headed towards the ravine that we intended to follow. The Vanguard started the march, and had advanced only a few metres when three peasants appeared on the other side. Miguel and his men were summoned and we all lay in ambush. Eight soldiers appeared. The instructions were to let them cross the river by the ford, then fire at them when they were about to arrive on the other side. But they did not cross. All they did was come and go, passing near our rifles, without us firing at them. The civilians we had detained said that they were only hunters. Miguel and Urbano, with Camba and Darío and Hugo Guzmán, the hunter, set out to follow a path that turns to the west, but we do not know where it ends. We spent the day at the ambush. At nightfall the trail-cutters returned with the traps, bringing a condor and a rotten cat. We tucked into it all, together with the *anta*. We only have beans and whatever we can kill. Camba is in the lowest depths of moral degradation; he trembles at the mere mention of soldiers. The Doctor is still in pain and being treated with Talamonal. I am quite well, but ravenously hungry. The Army issued a despatch stating that they had captured another cave, and that two of their men were slightly wounded and that there were 'guerrilla losses'. Radio Havana gave the unconfirmed news of combat in Taperillas, with one wounded on the Army's side.

25 August

The day went by uneventfully. Reveille was at 5.00 and the trail-cutters left early. The Army, seven men, came to within a few steps of our position, but did not try to cross. Their shots seem to be signals to the hunters. We will attack them tomorrow if the opportunity arises. There was not enough progress on the path because Miguel sent Urbano with a query, and the latter got the message wrong, and by that time nothing could be done.

The radio reported combat at Monte Dorado, which seems to be in Joaquín's jurisdiction, as well as the presence of guerrillas three kilometres from Camiri.

26 August

Everything went wrong. The seven men came, but they spread out; five went downstream and as two were about to cross, Antonio, who had responsibility for the ambush, fired prematurely and missed, enabling the two men to escape at full speed to fetch reinforcements. The other five leaped off at full speed, and Inti and Coco fell on them from behind, but the soldiers took cover and repelled them. While I observed the chase, I realised that the bullets were coming from our own side and landing near us. I ran towards them and discovered that Eustaquio was firing at them, since Antonio had not told him what was going on. I was so furious that I lost control and treated Antonio very roughly.

We left at a slow and heavy pace because the Doctor cannot walk faster, while 20 or 30 Army men, having recovered, advanced from the opposite side. It was not worth confronting them. There may have been up to two wounded, at most. Coco and Inti distinguished themselves by their decisiveness.

Things went well until the Doctor became exhausted and began to hold us up badly. At 18.30 we stopped without having caught up with Miguel, who it turned out was only a few metres from us, and made contact with us. Moro remained in a ravine, unable to climb the last stretch, and we slept divided into three groups. There are no signs of pursuit.

h = 900m.

27 August

The day passed in a desperate search for a way out, the results of which are not yet clear. We are near the Río Grande, and we have already passed Yumao, but there are no new fords, according to our information, so we could go there and continue along Miguel's cliff, but the mules will not be able to make it. There is the possibility of crossing a small chain of mountains, and then continuing on to the Río Grande–Masicuri, but we shall only know if it is feasible tomorrow. We have crossed heights of 1,300 metres, which is about the maximum altitude for the area. We slept at 1,240 metres, feeling rather cold. I am very well, but the Doctor is rather ill. We are out of water, with only a little for him.

The good news, or the good event, was the return of Benigno, Ñato and Julio. Theirs was a long odyssey because there are soldiers at Vargas and Yumao and they almost clashed with them. Afterwards they followed some troops that climbed down the Saladillo and up the Ñacahuasu, and they found that the stream of the Congrí has three outlets made by the soldiers. The Bear Cave, which they reached on the 18th, is now an anti-guerrilla camp that has about 150 soldiers. They were almost caught there, but managed to return without being seen. They went to the grandfather's plot, where they found *jocos* – the only thing there is, since it has been totally abandoned – and they passed the soldiers again, and heard our fire. They stayed the night nearby, and followed our tracks until they caught up with us. According to Benigno, Ñato behaved very well, but Julio got lost twice and was a bit scared of the soldiers. Benigno believes that some of Joaquín's men had passed through only a few days ago.

28 August

A grey and somewhat distressing day. We quenched our thirst with *caracoré,** which is actually more like a distraction for one's throat. Miguel sent Pablito to look for water on his own, with one of the hunters and, worse still,

---

*A parasitic plant whose fruit has a liquid centre that is known to quench thirst.

with just a small revolver. At 16.30 they had not returned,
so I sent Coco and Aniceto to find him; they did not return
all night. The Rearguard remained in the hollow of the
ravine and we could not listen to the radio; it seems there is
a new message. Finally, we slaughtered the little mare, after
she had been with us for two harsh months; I did all I could
to save her, but the hunger was unbearable and, at least for
the moment, we only suffer from thirst. It looks as if we will
not reach water tomorrow, either.

The radio reported that a soldier was wounded in the
region of Tatarenda. The unanswered question for me is
this: if they inform of their losses so scrupulously, why
would they lie about ánything else? And if they are not
lying, who is causing the casualties, in such isolated places
as Caraguatarenda and Taperillas? Unless Joaquín's group is
divided into two, or there are new independent *focci*.*
h = 1,200m.

29 August

A heavy day and rather distressing. The trail-cutters made
little progress, and at one point they went the wrong way,
believing that they were going towards the Masicuri. We
camped at an altitude of 1,600 metres, in a relatively humid
place, where there is a little cane plant whose pulp is known
to quench thirst. Some comrades, Chapaco, Eustaquio and
Chino, are collapsing for lack of water. Tomorrow we will
have to make for the first water we see. The mule drivers are
bearing up quite well.

There was no big news on the radio, the most important
being Debray's trial, which is dragged out from one week to
the next.

---

*The theory of *foquismo* argues that anti-establishment attacks by a small band of
guerrillas – a *foco* – can win peasants over to the insurrections without political
preparation. *Foquismo* rejects the orthodox Marxist emphasis on the working classes,
and the need to take account of objective conditions before launching an insurrection.
Foquismo also rejects the Maoist emphasis on the need for prior political work among
the peasantry.

30 August

The situation was becoming desperate, with the trail-cutters passing out. Miguel and Darío were drinking their own urine and so was Chino. This had the horrible consequences of diarrhoea and stomach cramps. Urbano, Benigno and Julio descended into a canyon and found water. They advised me that the mules could not go down and I decided to stay behind with Ñato, but Inti came up again bringing us water, and the three of us stayed and ate the mare. The radio was left below so we had no news.

h = 1,200m.

31 August

In the morning Aniceto and León left to explore the canyon below, and came back at 16.00 with the news that there was a mule track from the water camp onwards: the bad stretch was before that, but I looked and saw that the animals can go through, so I gave Miguel orders to cut open a detour for us tomorrow at the last cliff, and to carry on clearing the path ahead. We will bring down the mules. There is a message from Manila, but it could not be recorded.

Analysis of the month

It was, without doubt, the worst month we have had so far in this war. The loss of all the caves, with their documents and medicines, was a terrible blow, mainly psychologically. The loss of two men towards the end of the month, and the subsequent march, on horsemeat alone, demoralised the men, and we had the first man to abandon our ranks, Camba. This would have been considered a net gain in other circumstances. The lack of contact with the outside world and with Joaquín, and the fact that captives from his group have talked, also demoralised the men. My sickness made several of them insecure and this was reflected in our only clash, when we should have inflicted heavy losses on the enemy and only succeeded in wounding one. Moreover, the difficult march over the hills, with no water, brought out some negative traits in the men.

The most important features are:

1) We continue without contact of any kind and with no reasonable hope of establishing any in the near future.

2) We still have not recruited any peasants, which is logical, if one takes into account what few dealings we have had with them recently.

3) There is a decline, I hope temporary, in combat morale.

4) The Army has not increased its effectiveness, nor its capacity to attack.

We are at a low point in our morale and in our revolutionary legend. The most urgent tasks continue to be the same as last month, i.e. to re-establish contacts, recruit more combatants, and get supplies of medicines and equipment.

We note that Inti and Coco are firmly and progressively emerging as revolutionary and military leaders.

September 1967

1 September

We led the mules down early, after a few incidents, which included the male's spectacular fall from the cliff face. The Doctor has not yet recovered, but I have, and I lead the mule, walking perfectly. The march took longer than we thought, and only at 18.15 did we realise that we had reached the stream by Honorato's house. Miguel went on at full speed, but only arrived at the road when it was completely dark. Benigno and Urbano advanced cautiously and did not notice anything abnormal, so they took the house, which was empty.

2 September

Early in the morning we withdrew to the farmland, leaving an ambush at the house, led by Miguel, with Coco, Pablo and Benigno. A sentry was posted on the other side. At 8.00 Coco came to tell us that a herdsman had passed by looking for Honorato. There were four of them, and Coco was ordered to let the other three go through. All this took some time because it took an hour between our position and the house. At 13.30 some shots were heard, and then we learned that a peasant was coming with a soldier and a horse. Chino, who was on sentry duty with Pombo and Eustaquio, shouted: 'A soldier.' He then cocked his rifle. The soldier shot at him and fled. Pombo fired and killed the horse. I erupted with fury as this was the height of incompetence. Poor Chino was crushed. We freed the four men who had gone by in the meantime, as well as our two prisoners, sending all of them upstream along the Masicuri. We bought a bullock from the herdsmen for 700 pesos and gave Hugo 100 pesos for his work, and 50 for some things we had commandeered from him. The dead horse turned out to be one that had been left at Honorato's house because it was lame. The herdsmen told us that Honorato's wife had complained about the Army, for the beating they had given her husband and because they had eaten everything she had. When the herdsmen passed, eight days ago, Honorato was in Vallegrande, recovering from a wildcat's bite. In any case, there had been someone in the house because a fire was burning when we arrived. Owing to Chino's mistake, I decided to leave that night in the same direction as the herdsmen and to try and reach the first house. I assumed that there had been only a few soldiers, and that they had withdrawn. But we left very late, and only crossed the ford at 3.45, without finding the house. We slept on a cattle track until daybreak.

The radio brought some ugly news about the annihilation of a group of 10 men, led by a Cuban called Joaquín, in the region of Camiri. However, the news came from the Voice of America, and the local stations have not said anything.

3 September

As befits a Sunday, there was a clash. At dawn we followed the Masicuri downstream to its mouth. We then went up the Río Grande for a little while. At 13.00 Inti, Coco, Benigno, Pablito, Julio and León set off to reach the house, if the Army is not there, and to purchase some supplies to make our life more bearable. The group first captured two hired hands, who said that the owner was not around and that there were no soldiers. They said that they could get hold of enough food supplies. Other reports: yesterday some soldiers galloped by without stopping at the house. Honorato passed two days ago on his way home, with two of his children. When our men reached the house of the landowner, they found that 40 soldiers had just arrived.

There was a confused skirmish in which our men killed at least one soldier, who had a dog with him. The soldiers reacted by surrounding our men, but later retreated, when they heard shouts. Not even a grain of rice could be salvaged. The plane flew over the area and fired a few small rockets, apparently over the Ñacahuasu. Other reports from the peasants: no guerrillas have been seen in the area, and the first information they had had was from the herdsmen who went by yesterday.

Once again the voice of the United States broadcast a report about clashes with the Army, and this time it named José Carrillo as the only survivor of a group of 10 men. As this Carrillo is Paco, one of the rejects, and the annihilation allegedly took place in Masicuri, it would seem that it is all one almighty fabrication.

h = 650m.

4 September

A group of eight men, led by Miguel, set an ambush on the road from Masicuri to Honorato's house until 13.00, but without incident. Meanwhile, Ñato and León brought back a cow, after strenuous efforts. Later we got two magnificent tame oxen. Urbano and Camba walked some 10 kilometres upstream; they had to cross four fords, one of which is rather deep. The bullock was killed and volunteers were sought to go and find food and information. Inti, Coco, Julio, Aniceto, Chapaco and Arturo were chosen, led by Inti. Pacho, Pombo, Antonio and Eustaquio also volunteered. Inti's instructions are: to reach the house at daybreak, observe any movements and get supplies if there are no soldiers. If there are any, surround it and carry on, try to capture one, and remember that the main thing is not to suffer losses. Use the utmost caution.

The radio broadcast the news of one death at Vado del Yeso in a new clash, near the spot where the group of 10 men was wiped out. This makes the report about Joaquín seem like a lie. But on the other hand, they gave the details of Negro, the Peruvian doctor who died at Palmarito, whose body was taken to Camiri. Pelado helped identify him. Apparently this is a real death; the others could be fictitious deaths or refer to some of the rejects. In any case, there is something unusual about the reports saying they are now being taken to Masicuri and Camiri.

5 September

The day went by uneventfully, awaiting results. At 4.30 the group returned with a mule and some goods. At the house of Morón, the landowner, there were some soldiers, who were on the point of discovering our men, because they had dogs. Apparently they work by night. Our men surrounded the house and then went up to Montaños's place, cutting through the woods. There was nobody there, but they found maize and brought back a quintal, one hundred kilos, of it. At approximately 12.00 they crossed the river and came across two houses on the other side. From one, everybody ran away and a mule was requisitioned. There was little co-operation from the other, and we had to resort to threats. The reports they gave us were that up to now they had never seen any guerrillas, and only at Pérez's house had there been a group (us), and that was before carnival. Our men returned during the day and waited until night to sneak past Morón's house. Everything was going fine, but Arturo got lost and lay down to sleep on the path. Two hours were wasted looking for him. They have left some tracks that could be traced, unless the cattle erase them. Besides, they dropped some things along the way. The men's mood changed at once.

The radio says that the dead guerrillas could not be identified, but there may be developments at any moment. The whole communiqué has been decoded. It says that OLAS*

*The Conference of the Organisation of American Solidarity (OLAS), which took place in Havana between 31 July and 10 August and was attended by leaders of revolutionary and national liberation movements from the Americas. Fidel Castro gave the closing speech.

was a triumph, but the Bolivian delegation was shit. Aldo
Flores of the Communist Party of Bolivia pretended that he
was the representative of the National Liberation Army of
Bolivia and had to be contradicted. They have asked for one
of Kolle's men to go for discussions. Lozano's house was
raided and he has gone underground: he thinks there could
be an exchange for Debray. That is all; obviously they have
not received our last message.

6 September
Benigno's birthday.

The day of Benigno's birthday looked promising: at dawn
we made cornmeal with what had just been brought and
drank some *maté* with sugar. Then Miguel, in charge of
eight men, set up an ambush, while León went to get
another bullock to take with us. As it was a little late, after
10.00, and he did not return, I sent Urbano to tell them to lift
the ambush by 12.00. A few minutes later we heard a shot,
then a short burst of fire and a shot sounded in our direction.
As we were taking up our positions, Urbano arrived at full
speed: he had run into a patrol that had dogs with them. I
was in despair as nine of my men were on the other side and
I did not know their exact position. We improved the path so
that we could take it almost to the river bank. Moro, Pombo
and Camba were sent with Coco. I thought I would transfer
the rucksacks and make contact with the Rearguard if
possible, until they could rejoin the group. On the other
hand, we could fall into an ambush. However, Miguel
rejoined us with all his men, cutting through the woods.

The explanation of the events: Miguel advanced, without
leaving a sentry on our little path, and his men devoted their
efforts to collecting the cattle. León heard a dog bark and
Miguel, in doubt, decided to retreat. At that moment shots
were heard. They realised that a patrol had passed between
them and the woods and was already ahead of them, so they
cut their way back through the woods.

We withdrew calmly, with the three mules and the three head of cattle. After crossing four fords, two of them difficult, we pitched camp about seven kilometres from the previous one and slaughtered the cow. We ate sumptuously. The Rearguard told us that they had heard sustained gunfire in the direction of the camp, a lot of it from machine guns. h = 640m.

7 September

Short march. We crossed only one ford and then ran into difficulties because of a cliff. Miguel decided to camp and wait. Tomorrow we will explore thoroughly. The situation is as follows: the Air Force is not looking for us here, despite reaching our camp. The radio even reports that I am the leader of the group. The question is: are they afraid? Not very likely. Do they consider it impossible to reach up here? In view of what we have been through, which they know about, I don't think so. Do they want to let us advance, and wait for us at some strategic point? It is possible. Do they believe that we shall have to get supplies in the area of Masicuri? That is also possible. The Doctor is much better, but I had a relapse and spent a sleepless night.

The radio speaks of the valuable information José Carrillo (Paco) has supplied. He should be taught a lesson.

Debray responded to Paco's accusations, saying that he sometimes went hunting and that is why he was seen with a rifle. Radio La Cruz del Sur announced the discovery of the body of the guerrilla fighter Tania, on the banks of the Río Grande. This report does not ring true, as the news about Negro does. The body was taken to Santa Cruz, according to this radio station, although Radio Altiplano does not report it.

I talked to Julio; he is fine, but feels acutely the lack of contact and recruitment of more men. h = 720m.

8 September

Quiet day. Two eight-men ambushes were set, from morning until night, under Antonio and Pombo. The animals ate well in a cane-field, and the mule is recovering from its injuries. Aniceto and Chapaco went to explore upstream and came back with the news that the path was a relatively good one for the animals. Coco and Camba crossed the river with the water up to their chests, then climbed a hill up ahead, but did not gather anything new. I sent Miguel with Aniceto, and after a lengthier exploration it seems that, according to Miguel, it will be very difficult to get through with the animals. For tomorrow we will stay on this side, since there is always the possibility that the animals might get through the water without their loads.

The radio reported that Barrientos had attended the funeral of Tania the guerrilla, who was given a 'Christian burial'. He later went to Puerto Mauricio, where Honorato's house is. He has made an offer to those Bolivians who have been deceived, those who did not get what they had been promised. He is asking them to present themselves at Army posts with their hands above their heads, and no punitive measures will be taken against them. A small plane bombed the area near Honorato's house, as if making a show for Barrientos.

A Budapest newspaper has published a critique of Che Guevara, as a pathetic and apparently irresponsible figure. They salute the Marxist stance of the Chilean Communist Party for taking a practical attitude in the face of reality. How I should like to be in power, just to unmask the cowards and lackeys of every description and rub their snouts in their own filth.

9 September

Miguel and Ñato went to explore, and returned with the news that it is possible for the animals to get through but they must swim across. For the men there are fords. There is quite a large stream on the left bank and we will camp there. We continued setting ambushes with eight men, under Antonio and Pombo, without incident. I spoke to Aniceto; he seems very firm, but he thinks some of the Bolivians are weakening. He complained of the lack of political work by Coco and Inti. We finished off the cow. There are only the four leg bones left for a broth in the morning.

The only news on the radio is the postponement of Debray's trial until 17 September, at the earliest.

10 *September*

Bad day. It began under good auspices, but then the animals put up a struggle because the path was so bad, and finally the male would not walk any further and we had to leave it on the other bank. The decision was taken by Coco because the waters were rising violently. However, four weapons were left behind on the other side, including Moro's and three anti-tank shells for Benigno's. I crossed the river swimming with the mule but I lost my boots during the crossing and am now wearing sandals, something that does not amuse me. Ñato made a bundle of his clothes and weapons, wrapping them all in an oilskin cloth. He jumped in where the current was strongest, losing everything during the crossing. The other mule got bogged down and then plunged in to cross by itself, but had to be brought back, because there was no passage. When León attempted the crossing again, he and the mule almost drowned since it started to rain heavily as well. In the end we all reached the stream, which was our objective. The Doctor was in very bad shape and later complained of neuralgia in his limbs throughout the night. Our next plan was to send the animals across once more, swimming to the other bank, but the floods have foiled this plan, at least until the water goes down. In addition, planes and helicopters are flying over the area. I don't like the helicopters at all; they may be setting ambushes along the river. Tomorrow we will explore upriver and upstream, to try to determine exactly where we are.

I was forgetting to highlight an event: today, after a little more than six months, I took a bath. This constitutes a record that some of the others are already approaching.

h = 789m.; walked = 3–5 kilometres

11 September

Quiet day. Some went to explore up the river and others upstream. Those who went to the river came back in the evening with the news that we can probably cross when the waters drop a little more, and that there are beaches where the animals can walk. Benigno and Julio went to explore the stream, but they did it only superficially and by 12.00 they were back. Ñato and Coco went, supported by the Rearguard, to collect the things that had been left behind. They crossed with the male mule and left behind only a sack containing casings of machine-gun bullets.

There was an unpleasant incident. Chino came to tell me that Ñato had roasted and eaten a whole cut of meat in front of him. I was furious with Chino because it was up to him to prevent it, but after investigating further matters became more complicated, because it was not possible to find out whether Chino had authorised the action or not. He asked to be replaced and I put Pombo in charge once more. For Chino it was a bitter pill to swallow.

In the morning the radio relayed the news that Barrientos claims that I have been dead for some time and that everything else was propaganda. In the evening he offered 50,000 pesos (4,200 US dollars) for information leading to my capture, dead or alive. It seems the Armed Forces gave him a [illegible]. They have probably been dropping leaflets over the region with my description. Reque Terán* says that

*Colonel Luis A. Reque Terán of the Bolivian Army.

Barrientos's offer is for psychological purposes, for the tenacity of the guerrillas is well known and the Army is preparing for a long war.

I talked at length with Pablito. Like the rest of them, he is concerned over the lack of contacts, and he thinks that our main task is to re-establish our links with the city. But he was firm and decisive, 'Homeland or Death' until the end.

12 September

The day began with a tragicomic episode. At 6.00, the time for reveille, Eustaquio came to warn us that there were people advancing along the stream. He called us to arms and everyone was mobilised. Antonio saw them, and when I asked him how many, he raised his hand, showing five fingers. In the end it turned out to be a hallucination. This is dangerous for the morale of the men because they immediately started to talk about psychosis. I had a chat with Antonio afterwards, and it is evident he is not normal; he could not contain the tears, but he denied that he is upset and said that it is only the lack of sleep that is affecting him. He has been on assistant duties for six days, because he fell asleep on sentry duty and then denied it. Chapaco disobeyed an order and was punished by three days as camp assistant. In the evening he asked me if he could join the Vanguard because he does not get on with Antonio. I refused. Inti, León and Eustaquio left to explore the stream, to see if we can get across and reach a large mountain range we can see in the distance. Coco, Aniceto and Julio went upriver to try and explore the fords, and see how we should take the animals, if we go that way.

It seems that Barrientos's offer has caused a furore: in any case, a mad journalist thought that 4,200 US dollars was too little money, in view of the menace that I am. Radio Havana reported that OLAS had received a message of support from the National Liberation Army of Bolivia. A miracle of telepathy!

13 September

The explorers returned: Inti and his group had climbed upstream all day. They slept at quite a high altitude and it was rather cold. The stream apparently originates in a mountain range in front of us and runs west. The animals cannot make the crossing. Coco and his comrades tried unsuccessfully to cross the river. They crossed 11 cliffs before reaching the canyon of what must be the La Pesca river. There are signs of life, burned farmland and an ox. The animals need to cross to the other side, unless we construct a raft and go together, which is what we will try to do.

I talked to Darío about the problem of his departure, if that is what he wants. At first he said that leaving would be very dangerous, so I warned him that it is no safe haven here, and that if he decides to stay, it is once and for all. He said he would, and that he would correct the error of his ways. We shall see.

The only news on the radio was that a shot had been fired into the air in front of Debray Senior. The son had all his papers for the preparation of his defence confiscated, on the pretext that they don't want his defence to be turned into a political pamphlet.

14 September

Exhausting day. At 7.00 Miguel left with all the Vanguard plus Ñato. His instructions were to walk as far as possible along this side of the river, and build a raft when it becomes too difficult to cross over. Antonio stayed behind, lying in ambush with all the Rearguard. We left a couple of M-1s in a little cave that Ñato and Willi know. At 15.30, in view of the lack of news, we began to march.

It was not possible to ride a mule, and I, with the beginning of an asthma attack, had to leave the animal to León and continue on foot. The Rearguard had orders to start walking at 15.00, unless there was a counter-order. At approximately that time, Pablito arrived with the news that the leading ox had reached the crossing for the animals, and that the raft was being built one kilometre further up. I waited for the animals to arrive, which they did only at 18.15, after some men had gone to help them. At that time the two mules crossed (the ox had crossed earlier) and we continued to march slowly up to where the raft was. We found that there were still 12 men on this side; only 10 had crossed. We spent the night in two groups and ate the last ration of half-rotten ox.

h = 720m.; walked 2–3 kilometres

15 September
We covered a little more ground: five to six kilometres. But we did not reach the La Pesca river, because we had to cross with the animals twice, and one of the mules refused to go across. We still need to cross once more, and we'll see if the mules can make it through.

The radio brought the news of the detention of Loyola. The photos must be to blame. The bull we still had died, at the hands of the executioner, of course.

h = 780m.

16 September
The whole day was spent building a raft and crossing the river. We only marched 500 metres, the distance to the camp, where there is a small stream. The crossing went without problems on a good raft, which was pulled by ropes from both banks. Later on, when we left them on their own, Antonio and Chapaco had another argument and Antonio gave Chapaco six days' punishment for insulting him. I stood by his decision, although I am not sure that it is fair. At night there was another incident because Eustaquio denounced Ñato for eating an extra meal. It turned out to be some fat on the hide. Yet another miserable situation because of food. The Doctor told me of another little problem over his illness, and what the others think about it,

based on comments made by Julio. It all seems unimportant.
h = 820m.

17 September
Pablito's birthday.

Day at the surgery: I extracted teeth from Arturo and
Chapaco. Miguel explored as far as the river and Benigno to
the path. The news is that the mules can go up, but first they
will have to swim, crossing and recrossing the river. In
honour of Pablito, we prepared some rice for him. It is his
22nd birthday, and he is the youngest of the guerrilla force.

The radio only brought news of the postponement of the
trial and a protest over Loyola's detention.

18 September
The march began at 7.00, but Miguel soon arrived with the
news that he had seen three peasants beyond the next bend.
He did not know if they had seen us. We gave the order to
detain them. Chapaco staged the inevitable row, accusing
Arturo of stealing 15 bullets from his magazine. It bodes ill.
The only good thing is that his quarrels are with the Cubans;
the rest of the Bolivians ignore him. The mules went all the
way without swimming, but the black mule fell and hurt
itself while crossing a gully, rolling down for about 50
metres. We apprehended four peasants with their little
donkeys, who were going to Piraypandi, a river that is about
a league upstream from here. They said that Aladino
Gutiérrez and his men were on the bank of the Río Grande,
hunting and fishing. Benigno showed the utmost carelessness, letting himself be seen and then allowing the man, his
wife and another peasant to leave. When I found out, I blew
my top and called his behaviour an act of treason, which
reduced Benigno to tears. All the peasants have been warned
that tomorrow they leave with us for Zitano, the settlement
where they live, some six to eight leagues from here.
Aladino and his wife are quite sly and it was difficult to get

them to sell us food. Now the radio brings the news of two suicide attempts by Loyola, who 'fears the guerrillas' reprisals', and the arrest of several teachers, who if not involved, are at least sympathetic to us. It seems they seized many things from Loyola's house, but that is not strange if it was a result of the photos from the cave.

At night the small plane and the Mustang flew over the area in a suspicious way.

h = 800m.

19 September

We did not leave very early because the peasants could not find their animals. In the end, after I had given them a good talking to, we left with the caravan of prisoners. We walked slowly with Moro, and when we got to the river we were given the news that three more prisoners had been taken. The Vanguard had just left and thought they would reach a farm where there was sugarcane, two leagues away. These seemed very long, as long as the first two leagues. Around 21.00 at night, we reached the farm, which is only a cane-field. The Rearguard arrived well after 21.00.

I had a conversation with Inti about some weaknesses of his over food and he replied, really upset, that it was true. He said he would make a public self-criticism when we were alone, but he denied some of the accusations. We reached heights of 1,404 metres and are now at 1,000. From here to Los Sitanos is a three-hour march, maybe four, according to the pessimists. At last we ate pork, and the sugar-eaters were able to fill themselves up with *chankaka*, a brown sugar cake.

The radio continued to report on the Loyola case; the teachers have gone on strike; the secondary students where Higueras, one of the arrested men, was teaching, are on hunger strike; and the oil workers are on strike over the setting up of the oil company.

A sign of the times: I have run out of ink.

20 September

I decided to leave at 15.00 to arrive at the Los Sitanos settlement at dusk. They told us it would take about three hours, but several mishaps held us up until 17.00, and total darkness caught us on the hill. In spite of lighting a lamp, we only reached Aladino Gutiérrez's house at 23.00. There was not much in the way of supplies, just some cigarettes and a few trifles, but no clothes. We took a short nap and started the march towards Alto Seco at 3.00. They say it is four leagues away. We took the magistrate's telephone, but it has not worked for years, and the line is down anyway. The magistrate's name is Vargas and he has not had the post for long.

The radio reported nothing important. We reached heights of 1,800 metres, and Los Sitanos is at 1,400 metres.

We walked some two leagues to the settlement.

21 September

We set out at 3.00 under a bright moon, along the route we had been shown beforehand, and we walked until approximately 9.00, without meeting a soul and crossing heights of up to 2,040 metres, the highest ever. At this time we ran into a couple of herdsmen who showed us the way to Alto Seco, with two leagues still to go. All that part of the night and the morning we had walked only two leagues. When we reached the first houses, at the bottom of the hill, we bought some provisions and went to the mayor's house to cook. Later we passed a hydraulic corn mill on the banks of the Piraymiri, 1,400 metres in height. The people are really afraid of us and tried to hide. We have lost a lot of time with our lack of mobility. We walked the two leagues to Alto Seco between 12.35 and 17.00.

22 September

When we, the main body of men, arrived at Alto Seco, we found out that the magistrate had apparently left to report our presence in the vicinity. As a reprisal, we took all his groceries. Alto Seco is a village of about 50 houses, at an altitude of 1,900 metres. The people greeted us with a well-seasoned mixture of fear and curiosity. The supply mechanism began to operate and very soon we had accumulated a respectable amount of foodstuffs at our camp, which was in an abandoned house near the watering hole. The truck that should have arrived from Vallegrande did not come, which seems to confirm the tale that the magistrate had gone to warn them. However, I was forced to put up with the wailing of his wife, who, in the name of God and her children, demanded payment, which I refused to give. At night Inti gave a talk in the school building (1st and 2nd Grades) to a group of amazed and silent peasants, explaining the scope of our revolution. The teacher was the only one to interrupt and asked if we fought in the villages. He is a mixture of cunning peasant and literate man, with the ingenuity of a child. He asked a lot of questions about socialism. A big lad offered to be our guide, but warned us against the teacher, who they say is as cunning as a fox. We left at 1.30 for Santa Elena, where we arrived at 10.00.

Barrientos and Ovando gave a press conference, during which they aired all the data from the documents and declared Joaquín's group liquidated.

h = 1,300m.

23 September
The place was a beautiful orange grove, which still had a considerable amount of fruit. We spent the day resting and sleeping, although we had to change guard frequently. At 1.00 we got up, and left at 2.00 for Loma Larga, where we arrived at dawn. We passed altitudes of 1,800 metres. The men are loaded down and marching is slow. I got indigestion from Benigno's cooking.

24 September

We reached the settlement called Loma Larga. I had a liver upset and arrived vomiting. The men were exhausted by these marches that produce no results. I decided to spend the night at the junction of the road to Pujío and we killed a pig sold to us by Sóstenos Vargas, the only peasant still in his house. The rest ran away when they saw us.

h = 1,400m.

25 September

We arrived at Pujío early, but there were people there who had spotted us the previous day, which means we are preceded by Radio Bemba.* Pujío is a small settlement, located on a hill and the population ran away when they saw us. But then they began to approach us and treated us well. At dawn a policeman, who had come to arrest a debtor from Serrano, in the department of Chuquisaca, had left. We are at a point where three departments converge. Travelling with the mules is now dangerous, but I am trying to make it as easy as possible for the Doctor as he is very weak. The peasants say they do not know of any Army presence in the area. We walked in short stretches until we reached Tranca Mayo, where we slept by the road, since Miguel did not take the precautions I asked. The magistrate of La Higuera is in the area and we have given the sentries the order to detain him.

Inti and I talked to Camba and he agreed to accompany us until we sight La Higuera, a point situated near Pucará, and from there he will try to leave towards Santa Cruz.

h = 1,800m.

26 September

Defeat. At dawn we arrived at Picacho, where there was a fiesta. It is the highest point we have reached, 2,280 metres.

---

*Radio Bemba: a Cuban expression meaning information originating from a rumour, or word of mouth.

The peasants treated us very well and we carried on without too many fears, despite Ovando's assurances that I will be captured at any moment. When we arrived at La Higuera everything changed. All the men had disappeared and there were only a few women left. Coco went to the house of the telegraph operator, where there is a telephone, and came back with a cable dated the 22nd in which the magistrate warned the sub-prefect of Vallegrande that they had reports of a guerrilla presence in the area. Any news was to be sent to Vallegrande, which will pay the costs. The telegraphist had run away, but the wife assured us that they had not spoken today because at the next village, Jagüey, everybody is on holiday.

At 13.00 the Vanguard left to try and get to Jagüey, and to reach a decision about the mules and the Doctor once they are there. Not long afterwards I was talking to the only man left in the village, who was very scared, when a coca merchant arrived saying that he had come from Vallegrande and Pucará and had not seen anything. He was also very nervous, but said that was because of our presence here, and I let them both go, in spite of the lies they had told us. When I started for the top of the hill, at 13.30 approximately, the shots that came from all along the ridge meant that our men had fallen into an ambush. I organised a defence in the village, in order to wait for the survivors, and found an exit by a path that leads to the Río Grande. A few moments later Benigno arrived, wounded, followed by Aniceto and Pablito, whose foot is in a bad state. Miguel, Coco and Julio had fallen and Camba disappeared, leaving his rucksack behind. The Rearguard advanced rapidly along the path and I followed, still leading the two mules. The men at the rear were still under fire and Inti lost contact. After waiting for him for half an hour in a small ambush, under fire from the hill above, we decided to leave him, but not much later he caught up with us. We then saw that León had disappeared, and Inti told us he had seen his rucksack in the canyon that

he had come through. We saw a man walking rapidly along
the canyon and concluded that it was him. To throw the
soldiers off our tracks, we released the mules into the
canyon, and continued into another small canyon, which we
later discovered had brackish water. We slept until 24.00
because it was impossible to advance.

27 September

At 4.00 we resumed the march, trying to find a place to
ascend. This we managed to do by 7.00, but it was on the
side opposite where we wanted to be. In front there was a
bare hill, which looked harmless. We climbed a bit higher,
to a sparse little wood, seeking protection from the Air
Force, and there we discovered that the hill had a path.
However, nobody went past all day. In the evening a peasant
and a soldier climbed halfway up the hill and spent a while
there without seeing us. Aniceto had just finished exploring
and saw a large group of soldiers at a nearby house. That
would have been the easiest path for us, but it was now
blocked off. In the morning we saw a column climbing up a
nearby hill. Their equipment shone in the sun, and then at
midday, we heard isolated shots and some bursts of
machine-gun fire. Later we heard shouts of: 'There he is';
'Come out of there'; 'Are you coming out or not?',
accompanied by shots. We do not know the fate of the man,
who we presume may have been Camba. We left at dusk, to
try and get down to the water by a different route, and
remained in a thicket a little denser than the previous one.
We had to look for water in the canyon itself because a cliff
prevented us from doing so here.

The radio reported the news that we had clashed with the
Galindo Company, leaving three dead, who would be taken
to Vallegrande for identification. It seems they have not
captured Camba and León. This time our losses have been
very great. The loss of Coco is the worst to bear, but Miguel
and Julio were magnificent fighters and the human value of

the three is incalculable. Even León was showing promise.
h = 1,400m.

28 September

A day of anguish, and for a moment it seemed it could be our last. At dawn we fetched water, and almost at once Inti and Willi went out to explore another possible route into the canyon. But they returned straight away because a track crosses the hill in front and a peasant on horseback was travelling along it. At 10.00 some 46 soldiers went past us with their rucksacks on and took for ever to go on. At 12.00 another group appeared, this time 77 men, and to make matters worse a shot was heard, and the soldiers took up their positions. The officer ordered them down into the ravine, which might have been ours, but in the end they spoke by radio and he seemed to be satisfied with what he heard and restarted the march. Our shelter had no cover against an attack from above and, if detected, the possibility of escape was remote. Later a soldier who was lagging behind went by with an exhausted dog, which he had to drag behind him, and later still, a peasant guided another young soldier who had fallen behind. The peasant came back after a while and there was no more movement, but the anxiety when we heard the shot had been great. All the soldiers went by carrying their rucksacks, which gave the impression they were withdrawing. We saw no fires at the house after dark, nor did we hear the salutes they usually fire in the evening. Tomorrow we will spend the day exploring the area of the settlement. A light rain got us wet, but I don't think it was enough to erase our tracks.

The radio reported on Coco's identification, and brought confusing news about Julio. Miguel has been mixed up with Antonio – they mentioned his position in Manila. To begin with, they gave the news of my death, but then retracted it.

29 September

Another tense day. The explorers, Inti and Aniceto, left early to watch the house throughout the day. From early on, there was traffic on the road, and by mid-morning there were soldiers travelling in both directions without rucksacks, as well as others who came up with unloaded donkeys and went back loaded. Inti arrived at 18.15 and said that the 16 soldiers who went down to the farm had not been seen again, and that the donkeys seem to have been loaded there. In view of this report, it was difficult to decide to go on that path, the easiest and more logical one, since the soldiers are probably lying in ambush there, and in any case there are dogs in the house that would give away our presence. Two groups will go out exploring tomorrow: one to the same place, and one to try and walk up the ridge for as long as possible, to see if there is an exit that way, probably crossing the road that the soldiers take.

The radio gave no news.

30 September

Another day full of tension. Radio Balmaceda of Chile announced that highly placed Army sources stated that they have cornered Che Guevara in a canyon in the jungle. The local stations are silent. They seem to be certain of our presence in the area. Perhaps we have been betrayed. Not long afterwards the soldiers started to move from one place to the next. At 12.00 some 40 soldiers went by in separate columns, with their weapons at the ready. They halted at the little house, where they camped and established a nervous watch. Aniceto and Pacho reported this. Inti and Willy came back with the news that the Río Grande is some two kilometres away, in a direct line. There are three houses further up the canyon and we can camp in spots where we would not be seen from anywhere. We looked for water and at 22.00 we started a difficult nocturnal march, delayed by Chino, who cannot walk well in the dark.

Benigno is very well, but the Doctor has not fully recovered.

Analysis of the month

It should have been a month of recuperation and it almost was, but the ambush in which Miguel, Coco and Julio fell ruined everything and has left us in a dangerous position. We also lost León. Losing Camba was a net gain.

We had several minor skirmishes in which we killed a horse; we killed one soldier and wounded another; and Urbano exchanged fire with a patrol; and the fateful ambush at La Higuera. We have given up the mules and I think we will not use that sort of animal for some time, unless I succumb again to an asthmatic attack.

On the other hand, there may be truth in some of the news about the deaths of the other group, which must be given up as lost. It is possible that a small group could still be wandering, avoiding contact with the Army, as the reports of the death of all seven together could be false, or at least an exaggeration.

The features are the same as last month, except that the Army is becoming more effective in action, and the peasant mass is not helping us at all and is turning into informers.

The most important task is to slip away and find more suitable terrain; then revive our contacts, in spite of the fact that the whole structure in La Paz has been shattered,* as there we have also been dealt hard blows. The morale of the rest of the men remains quite high and I only have my doubts about Willy, who may try to take advantage of some clash to escape on his own, if we don't have a word with him.

---

* This refers to the fact that Hugo Lozano's house was raided and he had gone underground on 5 September, as well as to Loyola's detention on 15 September. Loyola's house was also raided and compromising photographs of Loyola in the guerrilla camp had been found.

October 1967

1 October

This first day of the month went by without incident. At dawn we arrived at a sparsely wooded area where we camped, placing sentries at the various points of approach. The 40 soldiers moved away from us through the canyon that we were planning to take, firing a few shots. At 14.00 the last shots were heard. There seems to be no one in the little houses, although Urbano saw five soldiers who were not following any trail. I decided to remain here one more day, since the place is all right and has a guaranteed exit route, as it overlooks almost all the movements of enemy troops. Pacho, with Ñato, Darío and Eustaquio, went to find water and returned at 21.00. Chapaco cooked fritters and we distributed some *charqui*, which quelled our hunger pangs.

There was no news.

h = 1,600m.

2 October

Antonio's birthday.

The day went by without any sign of soldiers, but some small goats herded by sheepdogs passed our positions and the dogs barked. We decided we would try to leave by skirting beside one of the farms closest to the canyons, and we started our descent at 18.00, so that we had ample time to arrive and cook before making the crossing. Ñato got lost, but he insisted that we carry on. When we decided to make our way back, we too got lost, and stopped for the night at the top of the ridge, where we were unable to cook and were very thirsty. The radio brought us the explanation of the deployment of soldiers on the 30th. According to news broadcast by La Cruz del Sur, the Army announced that they had had an encounter at the Abra del Quiñol with a small group of ours, without any casualties on either side, although they claimed to have found traces of blood after our escape. The group consisted of six men, according to the same source.

3 October

A long and unnecessarily intense day: as we were moving to get to our base camp, Urbano arrived with the news that he had heard some passing peasants remark, 'Those are the ones who we heard talking last night', while we were on our way. It is evident that the report was inaccurate but I decided to treat it as if it were true and, without quenching our thirst, we climbed back to a ridge that overlooked the soldiers' path.

The rest of the day passed by absolutely calmly and at nightfall we all went down and made coffee, which tasted heavenly, in spite of the brackish water and the greasiness of the pot in which it was made. Then we prepared cornmeal to eat then and there, and rice with *anta* meat to carry with us. At 3.00 we started to walk, after we had explored the area, and we crossed the farmland easily and arrived at the ravine we had chosen, which has no water and which shows signs of having been searched by the soldiers.

The radio brought us the news of two prisoners: Antonio Domínguez Flores (León) and Orlando Jiménez Bazán (Camba), who admits to fighting against the Army. León stated that he surrendered, trusting in the president's word. Both have spoken at length of Fernando (Che) and his illness, and everything else, let alone all that they may have said that is not being made public. Thus ends the story of two heroic guerrillas.

An interview with Debray was broadcast, very brave

when he was confronted with a student who had been an *agent provocateur.*
h = 1,360m.

4 October
After a rest in the ravine, we followed it downhill for half an hour and, finding another one that joined it, we climbed that and then rested until 15.00 to escape the sun. Then we resumed the march for over half an hour; the scouting party was there, having reached the end of the small canyons and not found any water. At 18.00 we left the ravine and followed a cattle track until 19.30, by which time we could not see at all, so we stopped until 3.00. The radio announced that the General Staff of the Fourth Division had moved its advance party from Lagunillas to Padilla, in order to have the Serrano region better covered – since it is assumed that is where the guerrillas will try to flee. They added that if I am captured by the Fourth Division I will be tried in Camiri and if by the Eighth in Santa Cruz.
h = 1,650m.

5 October
When we resumed the march, we walked with some difficulty until 5.15, at which point we left a cattle track and entered a small and sparsely wooded area, but its vegetation is sufficiently high to conceal us from prying eyes. Benigno and Pacho went on several expeditions scouting for water, and circled the nearest house without finding any; there is probably a little well next to it. When they had finished their exploration they saw six soldiers arrive at the house, who were apparently just passing by. We left at nightfall, the men exhausted from lack of water, with Eustaquio making a scene and crying for a mouthful of water. After a very bad track, which held us up many times, at dawn we arrived at a little wood where we could hear dogs barking close by. You can see a high, barren ridge nearby.

We treated Benigno, whose wound is oozing a little pus, and I gave the Doctor an injection. As a result of the treatment, Benigno complained of pain in the night.

The radio announced that our two Cambas had been taken to Camiri, to act as witnesses in Debray's trial.

h = 2,000m.

6 October

The explorations revealed that we were very close to a house and there was water in a ravine further away. We headed there and spent the day cooking under a large ledge that served as a roof. Nonetheless I felt uneasy all day because we had passed populated places in broad daylight, and we are now in a hollow. Since preparing the meal took longer than expected, we decided to leave at dawn and make for a nearby tributary. Once there, we shall carry out a more exhaustive exploration to establish our future direction.

La Cruz del Sur broadcast an interview with the Cambas. Orlando was a little less vile. A Chilean radio station broadcast news that was censored here, which indicated that there are 1,800 soldiers searching for us in the area.

h = 1,750m.

7 October

Today we mark the 11th month of our guerrilla inauguration. An almost bucolic day, without complications – that is, until 12.30 when an old woman herding her goats entered the canyon where we had camped, and we had to take her prisoner. The woman has not given us any reliable news about the soldiers, answering every question by saying that she does not know and that it was a long time since she was here. She could only give information about the roads: as a result of her report, we conclude that we are approximately one league from Higueras, another from Jagüey and around two from Pucará. At 17.30 Inti, Aniceto and Pablito went to the old woman's house: she has one bedridden daughter and one who is a sort of dwarf. She was given 50 pesos and told that she must not say a word, without much faith that she will keep her promises. All 17 of us left under a small moon. The march was very tiring and we left many traces in the canyon where we had been. There were no houses nearby, just some potato fields irrigated by ditches from the same stream. At 2.00 we stopped to rest, for it was by now useless to continue to advance. Chino becomes a real burden when we need to march by night.

The Army issued a strange report about the presence of some 250 men at Serrano to prevent the escape of the men who are surrounded, 37 in total. They say we are sheltering in between the rivers Acero and Oro. The news seems to be deliberately misleading.

h = 2,000m.

The Guerrilla Force

Vanguard

Miguel
Manuel Hernández Osorio
Cuban

Benigno
Dariel Alarcón Ramírez
Cuban

Pacho/Pachungo
Alberto Fernández Montes de Oca
Cuban

Loro/Bigotes/Jorge
Jorge Vázquez Viaña
Bolivian

Aniceto
Aniceto Reinaga Gordillo
Bolivian

Camba
Orlando Jiménez Bazán
Bolivian

Coco
Roberto Peredo Leigue
Bolivian

Darío
David Adriazola Veizaga
Bolivian

Julio
Mario Gutiérrez Ardaya
Bolivian

Pablo/Pablito
Francisco Huanca Flores
Bolivian

Raúl
Raúl Quispaya Choque
Bolivian

Main Force

Ramón/Fernando/Che
Ernesto Guevara de la Serna
Argentine-Cuban

Alejandro
Gustavo Machín Hoed de Beche
Cuban

Rolando/San Luis
Eliseo Reyes Rodríguez
Cuban

Inti
Guido Álvaro Peredo Leigue
Bolivian

Pombo
Harry Villegas Tamayo
Cuban

Ñato
Julio Luis Méndez Korne
Bolivian

Tuma/Tumaini
Carlos Coello
Cuban

Urbano
Leonardo Tamayo Núñez
Cuban

Moro/Muganga/Doctor/Morogoro
Octavio de la Concepción de la Pedraja
Cuban

Negro/Doctor
Restituto José Cabrera Flores
Peruvian

Papi/Ricardo/Chinchu
José María Martínez Tamayo
Cuban

Arturo
René Martínez Tamayo
Cuban

Eustaquio
Lucio Edilberto Galván Hidalgo
Peruvian

Moisés Guevara
Moisés Guevara Rodríguez
Bolivian

Willy/Wily/Willi/Wyly
Simón Cuba Sarabia
Bolivian

Chapaco/Luis
Jaime Arana Campero
Bolivian

Antonio/Olo
Orlando Pantoja Tamayo
Cuban

León/Antonio
Antonio Domínguez Flores
Bolivian

Chino
Juan Pablo Chang Navarro
Peruvian

Serapio/Serafín
Serapio Aquino Tudela
Bolivian

Rearguard

Joaquín/Vilo
Juan Vitalio Acuña Núñez
Cuban

Braulio
Israel Reyes Zayas
Cuban

Rubio/Félix
Jesús Suárez Gayol
Cuban

Marcos/Pinares
Antonio Sánchez Díaz
Cuban

Pedro/Pan Divino
Antonio Jiménez Tardío
Bolivian

Ernesto/Doctor
Freddy Maymura Hurtado
Bolivian

Apolinar/Polo/Apolinario
Apolinar Aquino Quispe
Bolivian

Walter
Walter Arancibia Ayala
Bolivian

Víctor
Casildo Condorí Vargas
Bolivian

Tania
Haydée Tamara Bunke Bider
Argentine/German

The following four guerrillas had been expelled from the force but were attached to Joaquín's group until it became possible for them to leave the area:

Pepe
Julio Velazco Montana
Bolivian

Paco
José Castillo Chávez
Bolivian

Eusebio
Eusebio Tapia Aruni
Bolivian

Chingolo
Hugo Choque Silva
Bolivian

The following were not members of the guerrilla force but were attached to Joaquín's group until it became possible for them to leave the area:

Pelado/Mauricio/Carlos
Ciro Roberto Bustos
Argentine

Dantón
Jules Régis Debray
French

The following two guerrillas drowned in the Río Grande:

Benjamín
Benjamín Coronado Córdoba
Bolivian

Carlos
Lorgio Vaca Marchetti
Bolivian

The following guerrilla was taken prisoner by the Army:

Salustio
Salustio Choque Choque
Bolivian

The following two guerrillas were deserters:

Pastor
Pastor Barrera Quintana
Bolivian

Vicente
Vicente Rocabado Terrazas
Bolivian

Biographical Notes

Guerrilla fighters are in bold type, listed alphabetically by their *nom de guerre*.

Alejandro: Machín Hoed de Beche, Gustavo (1937–67). Cuban guerrilla, initially with the Main Force, then with Joaquín's Group. Fought with Che Guevara's column in the decisive battle of Santa Clara during the Cuban Revolution and was made a *comandante*. Fell at Puerto Mauricio on 31 August 1967.

Almeida, Juan (1927–). A *comandante* in the Rebel Army during the Cuban Revolution. Held various important posts after the triumph of the Revolution. Member of the Central Committee and Political Bureau of the Communist Party of Cuba.

Aniceto: Reinaga Gordillo, Aniceto (1940–67). Bolivian guerrilla (Main Force). Studied in Cuba. Member of the Executive Committee of the Communist Youth. Fell at Quebrada del Yuro on 8 October 1967.

Antonio/Olo: Pantoja Tamayo, Orlando (1933–67). Cuban guerrilla (Main Force). Member of the 26 July Movement. Was a captain in Che Guevara's column in the Rebel Army during the Cuban Revolution. Fell at Quebrada del Yuro on

8 October 1967.

Antonio: see also León.

Apolinar/Apolinario/Polo: Aquino Quispe, Apolinar (1935–67). Bolivian guerrilla (Rearguard). One of the three members of the Communist Party of Bolivia who were at the farm when Che Guevara arrived in November 1966. He asked to join the guerrillas. Fell at Puerto Mauricio, on 31 August 1967.

Argañaraz, Ciro. Owner of the farm El Pincal, next to the one used by the guerrillas as their first camp at Ñacahuasu.

Arturo: Martinez Tamayo, René (1941–67). Cuban guerrilla (Main Force). Brother of José María Martinez Tamayo (Ricardo in Bolivia). Served in the Cuban Air Force. Radio operator for the Main Force. Fell at Quebrada del Yuro on 8 October 1967.

Bakunin, Mikhail (1814–76). Russian anarchist who opposed Marx and Engels in the Communist International. He believed that Communism was an essential step towards anarchism.

Barrientos Ortuño, René (1919–69). Bolivian Air Force general. Vice-president of the country during the second presidency of Víctor Paz Estenssoro. Became president by means of a *coup d'état* (1966–9). He died in a helicopter crash while in office.

Benigno: Alarcón Ramirez, Dariel (1939–). Cuban guerrilla (Vanguard). Survivor. A peasant of the Sierra Maestra, joined the Rebel Army and fought with Che Guevara in Cuba. Accompanied Che Guevara to China, Europe, the USSR and Algeria and went with him to the Congo. Returned to Cuba in 1968 and went back to Bolivia to join the Teoponte guerrillas under Inti Peredo, until Inti was killed in La Paz in 1969. In 1973 he served in Guinea-Bissau and in 1978 in Nicaragua. Back in Cuba, in 1983 he went to university to study history. In 1996 he left Cuba for France, never to return.

Benjamín: Coronado Córdoba, Benjamín (1941–67). Bolivian guerrilla (Vanguard). Drowned in the Río Grande on 26 February 1967.

Bigotes: see Loro.

Bolívar, Simón (1783–1830). Venezuelan general and statesman who liberated seven countries of South America from Spanish rule.

Braulio: Reyes Zayas, Israel (1933–67). Cuban guerrilla (Rearguard). Was a labourer in the Sierra Maestra until he joined Raúl Castro's column and became his escort and was later promoted to first lieutenant. Fought with Che Guevara in the Congo. Fell in combat at Puerto Mauricio on 31 August 1967.

Bravo, Douglas (1933–). Venezuelan. Member of the Central Committee of the FALN (National Liberation Armed Forces of Venezuela). Fought against the dictatorship of Marcos Pérez Jiménez, opposed the suspension of armed struggle and was expelled from the party.

Bustos, Ciro Roberto (Mauricio, Pelado, Carlos). Argentine. Painter and journalist who had raised funds for the 1963–4 guerrilla movement led by Jorge Ricardo Masetti in northern Argentina. Invited to Bolivia by Che Guevara to discuss international support activities. Taken prisoner on 20 April at Muyupampa with Régis Debray and George Andrew

Roth. Tried and sentenced to 30 years' imprisonment, but was released in 1970. Lives in Sweden.

Calixto: Béjar Rivera, Héctor. In 1963 Peruvian leader of the National Liberation Army of Peru. In 1966 he was arrested and incarcerated at San Quintín.

Calvimonte. Member of the urban support group of the guerrillas.

Camba: Jiménez Bazán, Orlando. Bolivian guerrilla (Vanguard). Member of the Communist Party of Bolivia. Worked at the guerrillas' farm in Caranaví until he joined the group at Ñacahuasu. He deserted and was captured by the Army. Tried and sentenced to 10 years in prison, released in 1970.

Carlos: Vaca Marchetti, Lorgio (1934–67). Bolivian guerrilla (Rearguard). Studied in Cuba. Member of the Bolivian Communist Youth. Drowned on 16 March 1967 in the Río Grande.

Carlos: see Bustos, Ciro Roberto.

Castro, Fidel (1926–). Leader of the Cuban Revolution. Had previously led the failed attack on the Moncada Barracks in 1953. Founded the 26 July Movement, sailed from Mexico to Cuba with 80 men on board the yatch *Granma*, commanded the Rebel Army during the Cuban Revolution. Was prime minister (1959–76), president of the Council of State and Council of Ministers since 1976, commander-in-chief of the Armed Forces, first secretary of the Communist Party.

Castro, Raúl (1931–). *Comandante* of the Rebel Army during the Cuban Revolution. Brother of Fidel Castro. Vice-president of the Council of State and Council of Ministers, second secretary of the Communist Party of Cuba.

Chapaco/Luis: Arana Campero, Jaime (1938–67). Bolivian guerrilla (Main Force). A leader of the Revolutionary Nationalist Movement (MNR). Studied in Cuba. Was a member of the Bolivian Communist Youth. Fell in combat on 12 October 1967 in Cajones.

Che: see Ramón.

Chinchu: see Ricardo.

Chingolo: Choque Silva, Hugo. Bolivian guerrilla. Member of Moisés Guevara's group. Was attached to Joaquín's column. Deserted in July 1967 and was captured. Led the Army to the guerrillas' supply caves.

Chino: Chang Navarro, Juan Pablo (1930–67). Peruvian guerrilla (Main Force). Was active in Peru against the military dictatorship. Spent time in jail and in exile. Member of the Communist Party of Peru. Participated in the guerrilla movement organised by the Ejército de Liberación Nacional del Perú in 1963. After it was crushed, he spent two years living clandestinely in Bolivia. Captured at Quebrada del Yuro and assassinated at La Higuera on 9 October 1967.

Coco: Peredo Leigue, Roberto (1938–67). Bolivian guerrilla (Vanguard). Brother of Inti Peredo. Member of the Communist Party of Bolivia. In 1963–4 assisted guerrilla movements in Peru and Argentina. Imprisoned several times for his political activities. Fell at Quebrada de Batán, near La Higuera, on 26 September 1967.

Codovila, Victorio (1894–1970). Argentine. First secretary of the Communist Party of Argentina (1941–63). President of the Communist Party (1963–70).

Daniel: Barrera Quintana, Pastor. Bolivian guerrilla, a member of Moisés Guevara's group. Deserted and became an informer.

Danton: see Debray, Jules Régis.

Darío: Adriazola Veizaga, David (1939–69). Bolivian guerrilla (Vanguard). Miner from Oruro. Member of Moisés Guevara's group. Survived the guerrilla struggle. Lived clandestinely and sought to resume armed struggle. Assassinated in La Paz on 31 December 1969.

Debray, Jules Régis (Danton, Debré, Frenchman) (1940–). French journalist, author of *Révolution dans la Révolution?* Taught philosophy at the University of Havana. Invited to the guerrilla camp to discuss support activities in Europe. Was captured by the Army in Muyupampa with Ciro Roberto Bustos and tried in Camiri. Sentenced to 30 years in prison. Released in 1970. Held a number of official posts in the 1980s in the government of François Mitterrand.

Doctor/Ernesto: Maymura Hurtado, Freddy (1941–67). Bolivian guerrilla (Main Force). Member of the Bolivian Communist Youth. Studied medicine in Cuba. Survived the ambush of Puerto Mauricio, was captured and assassinated on 31 August 1967.

Estanislao: see Monje, Mario.

Eusebio: Tapia Aruni, Eusebio. Bolivian guerrilla. Expelled from the guerrillas, he was attached to Joaquín's group and deserted. He was captured by the Army and imprisoned until 1970.

Eustaquio: Galván Hidalgo, Lucio Edilberto (1937–67). Peruvian guerrilla (Main Force). Radio technician. Participated in the guerrilla movement of the Ejército de Liberación Nacional del Perú. He was a member of Chino's group. Fell at the Mizque river, in Cajones on 12 October 1967.

Félix: see Rubio.

Fernando: see Ramón.

Frenchman: see Debray, Jules Régis.

Galindo Grandchamps, Eduardo. Known as 'Champitas', he led the Galindo Company, an anti-guerrilla company of the Regimiento Manchego 12 de Infantería (part of the 8th Army Division). He was ultimately a general, and in 2001 published *Crónicas de un Soldado*, giving vivid details of the search for Che Guevara's guerrilla band and their many clashes, from the point of view of the Bolivian Army.

Gelman, Juan. Member of the Communist Party of Argentina.

Guevara, Moisés: see Moisés.

Guzmán Lara, Loyola. Bolivian. In charge of finances for the guerrilla organisation, and leader of the urban support group. Member of the Bolivian Communist Youth. Expelled from its Executive Committee because of her support of the guerrillas. Arrested in 1967, released in 1970. Lives in Bolivia and heads the organisation of relatives of the 'disappeared'.

Honorato: see Rojas, Honorato.

Hugo: see Lozano, Hugo.

Humberto: see Ramírez, Humberto.

Inti: Peredo Leigue, Guido Álvaro (1937–69). Bolivian guerrilla (Main Force). Member of the Communist Party of Bolivia since the age of 14. Gave logistic support to the guerrilla movement in northern Argentina in 1963. Was jailed several times for his political activities. Survived the guerrilla struggle. Wrote *My Campaign with Che*. Attempted to relaunch the Ejército de Liberación Nacional de Bolivia. Assassinated on 9 September 1969 in La Paz.

Iván: Montero, Renán. Member of the underground guerrilla support group in La Paz.

Joaquín/Vilo: Acuña Nuñez, Juan Vitalio (1925–67). Cuban guerrilla (leader of the Rearguard). A peasant from the Sierra Maestra, he initially fought in Che Guevara's column during the Cuban Revolution. Was promoted to *comandante* and given his own column. Member of the Central Committee of the Communist Party of Cuba. Fell in combat at Puerto Mauricio, 31 August 1967.

Jorge: see Loro.

Jozami, Eduardo. Ex-militant from the Communist Party of Argentina. Journalist and lawyer.

Julio: Gutiérrez Ardaya, Mario (1939–67). Bolivian guerrilla (Vanguard). Studied medicine in Cuba. Leader of the student movement in Bolivia. Member of the Bolivian Communist Youth. Fell at Quebrada de Batán, near La Higuera, on 26 September 1967.

Kolle: Kolle Cueto, Jorge. Leader of the Communist Party of

Bolivia. Replaced Mario Monje as First Secretary in December 1967 and held the post until 1985.

Lagunillero: Chávez, Mario. Bolivian. Member of the Communist Party of Bolivia. Collaborated with the guerrillas.

Lechín Oquendo, Juan. Bolivian. At the time, leader of the COB (Central Obrera Boliviana, Trade Union Federation). Organised the Revolutionary Party of the National Left in 1964.

León/Antonio: Domínguez Flores, Antonio. Bolivian guerrilla (Main Force). Was one of the three members of the Communist Party of Bolivia who were at the farm in Ñacahuasu when Che Guevara arrived in November. Later joined as a combatant. Deserted, was captured and gave information to the Army. Released from jail in 1970.

Leoni, Raúl (1905–72). President of Venezuela (1964–9).

Loro/Bigotes: Vázquez Viaña, Jorge (1939–67). Bolivian guerrilla (Vanguard). Disappeared 22 April 1967. Was captured, tortured and assassinated at the hospital in Choreti, then thrown into the jungle from a helicopter.

Loyola: see Guzmán, Loyola.

Lozano, Hugo. Bolivian doctor, and radio operator of the guerrillas' urban network.

Luis: see Chapaco.

Maceo y Grajales, Antonio (1845–96). Cuban general, second in command of the Cuban Army of Independence. Was one of the outstanding guerrillas in nineteenth-century Latin

America. Fought against Spanish colonial rule. Captured and killed on 7 December 1896 as he attempted to rejoin the Army under Máximo Gómez.

Manuel: see Miguel.

Marcos, Pinares: Sánchez Díaz, Antonio (1927–67). Cuban guerrilla (Rearguard). Originally a bricklayer, he became a *comandante* of the Rebel Army in Cuba. Member of the Central Committee of the Communist Party of Cuba. Fell on 2 June 1967, ambushed by a Bolivian Army patrol at Peñon Colorado, Buena Vista.

Martí, José (1853–95). Cuban poet, writer, political thinker and activist, hero of several of his country's attempts at independence from Spain and the USA. He died in battle in Dos Ríos, eastern Cuba.

Masetti: Masetti, Jorge Ricardo (1929–64). Argentine. The first Latin American journalist to interview Fidel Castro in the Sierra Maestra. Founder and first director of the news agency Prensa Latina. Close friend of Che Guevara. Led the insurrection in northern Argentina. Fell in combat on 21 April 1964 in the mountains of Salta, Argentina. His *nom de guerre* was Comandante Segundo.

Mauricio: see Bustos, Ciro Roberto.

Maymura: see Ernesto.

Megía. Member of the guerrilla urban support network.

Mella, Julio Antonio (1903–29). One of the founders of the Cuban Communist Party in 1925. Assassinated in Mexico.

Merci. Codename of a person sent from Cuba to work

with the underground guerrilla support organisation in La Paz.

Miguel/Manuel: Hernández Osorio, Manuel (1931–67). Cuban guerrilla (Head of the Vanguard). One of the founders of the 26 July Movement. Fought with Che Guevara in the Rebel Army of Cuba and was made a captain. Held various posts in the Armed Forces. Fell at Quebrada de Batán on 26 September 1967.

Mito. Member of the guerrilla urban support group.

Moisés: Guevara Rodríguez, Moisés (1939–67). Bolivian guerrilla (Rearguard). Born at the Huanuni Mining Camp in Oruro, he became a leader of the Miners' Union. Member of the Communist Party of Bolivia. Arrested for his political activities. Left with Oscar Zamora when the party split but his group was later expelled. Joined Che Guevara with 12 members of his group. Fell at Puerto Mauricio on 31 August 1967.

Monje Molina, Mario: Estanislao, Mario. General secretary of the Communist Party of Bolivia until December 1967. Later a leading member of its Central Committee. Lives in Moscow.

Moro/Morogoro/Muganga: de la Concepción de la Pedraja, Octavio (1935–67). Cuban guerrilla (Main Force). A veteran of the Cuban Revolution, surgeon and combatant with the Rebel Army. Held several medical posts in Cuba. Fought with Che Guevara in the Congo. Died in combat on 12 October 1967 at Cajones, on the Mizque river.

Morogoro: see Moro.

Muganga: see Moro.

Ñato: Méndez Korne, Julio Luis (1937–67). Bolivian guerrilla (Main Force). Member of the Communist Party of Bolivia. In 1963 he helped a group of Peruvian guerrillas cross into Bolivia through the mountains. One of the five survivors of the battle of Quebrada del Yuro, he was killed on 15 November 1967 at Mataral.

Negro: Cabrera Flores, Restituto José (1931–67). Peruvian guerrilla (Rearguard). Survived the ambush at Puerto Mauricio, was captured and killed on 4 September 1967 at Palmarito river.

Oliver, María Rosa (1898–1977). Argentine writer. Friend of the Guevara family. Vice-president and advisor to the board of the World Peace Council, an international peace organisation. Travelled extensively (China, USSR, Europe, USA) on lecture tours as well as to peace congresses, in spite of being confined to a wheelchair since the age of 10.

Olo: see Antonio.

Onganía, Juan Carlos (1914–95). General. *De facto* president of Argentina from 1966 to 1970, who ousted President Arturo Illia in a military coup.

Orlando: Rocabado Terrazas, Vicente. Bolivian guerrilla. Member of Moisés Guevara's group. Deserted, was captured by the Army and turned informer.

Ovando Candía, Alfredo (1918–82). Commander-in-chief of the Bolivian Armed Forces (1966–9). Overthrew Víctor Paz Estenssoro and became *de facto* President of Bolivia 1965–6, and from 1969 until 1970 when he in turn was overthrown.

Pablito/Pablo: Huanca Flores, Francisco (1945–67). Bolivian guerrilla (Vanguard). Had been a member of the Communist Party of Bolivia. Member of Moisés Guevara's group. The youngest member of the guerrilla force. Led four survivors of the battle at Quebrada del Yuro, but fell on 12 October 1967 at Cajones, near the Mizque river.

Pacho/Pachungo: Fernández Montes de Oca, Alberto (1935–67). Cuban guerrilla (Vanguard). Was a captain in the Rebel Army and served with Che Guevara's column. After the Revolution, he held several administrative posts in Cuba and was head of the State Mining Enterprise. Captured at Quebrada del Yuro, he died of his wounds on 8 October 1967.

Pachungo: see Pacho.

Paco: Castillo Chávez, José. Bolivian guerrilla. Member of Moisés Guevara's group. Expelled from the guerrilla force and captured at Vado del Yeso while attached to Joaquín's column in August 1967. Released in 1970.

Pan Divino: see Pedro.

Papi: see Ricardo.

Pareja Fernández, Walter. Doctor. Militant from the Communist Party of Bolivia. Head of the guerrilla urban network.

Paulino: Baigorria, Paulino. Bolivian peasant from Abapó. Messenger for the guerrillas, accompanied them for days in June and asked to join. Detained at Comarapa, held incommunicado and tortured.

Paz Estenssoro, Víctor (1907–2001). Three times President of Bolivia (1952–6, 1960–4, 1985–9).

Pedro/Pan Divino: Jiménez Tardío, Antonio (1941–67). Bolivian guerrilla (Rearguard). Member of the national leadership of the Bolivian Communist Youth. Studied in Cuba. Expelled from the Executive Committee of the Communist Youth for joining the guerrillas. Fell at Iñao, near Monteagudo, on 9 August 1967.

Pelado: see Bustos, Ciro Roberto.

Pepe: Velasco Montaño, Julio. Bolivian guerrilla. Member of Moisés Guevara's group. Expelled from the guerrilla force. Deserted while accompanying Joaquín's group. Captured and assassinated by the Army.

Peredo, Coco: see Coco.

Peredo, Inti: see Inti.

Pinares: see Marcos.

Polo: see Apolinar.

Pombo: Villegas Tamayo, Harry (1940–). Cuban guerrilla (Main Force). Captain with the Cuban Rebel Army. Was Che Guevara's personal escort in Cuba and the Congo. Survivor of the battle of Quebrada del Yuro, he escaped to Chile. Reached Cuba in 1968 with Benigno and Urbano. Served three tours of duty in Angola. Brigadier-general of the Cuban Army.

Ramírez, Humberto. A leading member of the Communist Party of Bolivia. In 1987 he became its general secretary.

Ramón/Fernando/Che: Ernesto Guevara de la Serna. (1928–67). Argentine-Cuban. Guerrilla leader (Main Force). *Comandante* of the Rebel Army during the Cuban

Revolution. His victory at Santa Clara marked the end of the struggle as it prompted the dictator Fulgencio Batista to leave for Miami. Went to the Congo at the head of a guerrilla group in 1965 to join forces with Laurent Kabila. When that campaign failed he returned to Cuba secretly to train for Bolivia. Arrived at the camp in Ñacahuasu in November 1966. Wounded at Quebrada del Yuro. Assassinated at La Higuera on 9 October 1967.

Raúl: Quispaya Choque, Raúl (1939–67). Bolivian guerrilla (Vanguard). Tailor. Member of Moisés Guevara's group. Fell in combat on 30 July 1967 on the banks of the Rosita river.

Remberto: Villa, Remberto. Owner of the farm at Ñacahuasu who sold it to Coco. Subsequently arrested by the Army as a guerrilla collaborator.

Renán: See Iván.

Reyes, Simón/Simón Rodríguez. Leader of the Communist Party of Bolivia and the mine workers union. General secretary of the Communist Party (1985–7).

Rhea Clavijo, Humberto. Bolivian member of the guerrilla urban support group in charge of the supply of medical equipment for the guerrillas.

Ricardo/Papi/Chinchu: Martínez Tamayo, José María (1936–67). Cuban guerrilla (Main Force). Brother of René Martínez Tamayo. Founder member of the 26 July Movement. Joined the insurrection in northern Argentina under Comandante Segundo (Jorge Ricardo Masetti) who had been sent there by Che Guevara. After the failure of the Argentine insurrection he went with Che Guevara to the Congo and then returned to Bolivia to prepare the ground for the Bolivian campaign. Wounded in combat on 30 July 1967 on the banks of the Rosita river, he died later.

Rodolfo: see Saldaña, Rodolfo.

Rodríguez, Simón: see Reyes, Simón.

Rojas, Honorato. Bolivian peasant. Che Guevara met him on 10 February and cured his sick children. Yet he led Joaquín's group to an ambush in Puerto Mauricio, for which the Army rewarded him. He was executed by the Ejército de Liberación Nacional de Bolivia in 1969.

Rolando, Capitán San Luis: Reyes Rodríguez, Eliseo (1940–67). Cuban guerrilla (Main Force). Served with the Rebel Army in Che Guevara's column during the Cuban Revolution. Was head of the military police at the La Cabaña garrison after the triumph of the Revolution. Was a captain in the Cuban Armed Forces, and participated in operations against counter-revolutionaries. Elected to the Central Committee of the Communist Party. Fell in combat on 25 April 1967 at El Mesón.

Roth, George Andrew. Anglo-Chilean journalist. Probably a CIA agent. Arrested with Debray and Bustos in Muyupampa in April and released in July 1967. Disappeared from the scene and was never heard of again.

Rubio/Félix: Suárez Gayol, Jesús (1936–67). Cuban guerrilla (Rearguard). Member of the 26 July Movement. Joined Che Guevara's Rebel Army column at Las Villas, and was promoted to lieutenant. Held various posts in the Army and government. Was vice-minister for the sugar industry. Fell in combat at Iripiti on 10 April 1967.

Russell, (Lord) Bertrand Arthur William (1872–1970). English philosopher and mathematician. Wrote *The*

Principles of Mathematics, *Mathematical Philosophy*, *Analysis of the Mind* and many other seminal works. Actively participated in the World Peace Movement. Opposed the American invasion of Vietnam. Awarded the Nobel Prize for Literature in 1950.

Saldaña, Rodolfo (1932–2000). Member of the Communist Party of Bolivia. Provided logistical support to Masetti's failed guerrilla campaign in northern Argentina in 1963–4 and was the leader of the urban support network in Bolivia in 1966–7. Helped organise the escape of the five guerrilla survivors after the end of the struggle. Was arrested in 1970 and, on his release, left for Cuba. Returned to Bolivia from 1983 until 1990, when he went back to Cuba. Author of *Fertile Ground*, a book about Che Guevara in Bolivia.

Salustio: Choque Choque, Salustio. Bolivian guerrilla. Member of Moisés Guevara's group. Captured by the Army in March 1967.

Sánchez: Dagnino Pacheco, Julio. Peruvian revolutionary and member of the urban support group in La Paz.

San Luis: see Rolando.

Sartre, Jean-Paul (1905–80). French writer and philosopher. Member of the French Resistance during the Second World War and of the World Council for Peace. Opposed the US war in Vietnam. Was awarded the Nobel Prize for Literature in 1964.

Segundo: see Masetti.

Serafín: see Serapio.

Serapio/Serafín: Aquino Tudela, Serapio (1941–67). Bolivian guerrilla (Rearguard). One of the three workers from the Communist Party of Bolivia who were at the farm when Che Guevara arrived, and later joined as a guerrilla. Fell at the Ikira river on 9 July 1967, after alerting his comrades of an Army ambush.

Siles Salinas, Adolfo (1925–). Vice-president of Bolivia (1966–9). President (1969).

Stamponi Corinaldesi, Luis Faustino (1935–76). Argentine revolutionary. Member of the Socialist Party. He lived in Bolivia after 1969 and participated in the peasants' and miners' struggles. Founded the Revolutionary Party of the Workers of Bolivia. In 1976 he was detained in the mines of Llallagua, tortured and assassinated and his body was 'disappeared' somewhere between Bolivia and Argentina.

Sucre, Antonio José de (1795–1830). General. Venezuelan soldier-patriot who was Bolívar's lieutenant on several campaigns against the Spanish. First president of Bolivia (1826–8).

Tania: Bunke Bider, Haydée Tamara (1937–67). Argentine-German guerrilla (Rearguard). Born in Argentina of German parents, she lived in East Germany and later in Cuba. Member of the Communist Party. Worked as a translator. Trained for clandestine work. Went to Bolivia in 1964 to prepare the ground for the guerrilla movement. When her cover was blown she remained with the guerrilla force and became a combatant. Fell at Puerto Mauricio on 31 August 1967.

Tuma/Tumaini: Coello, Carlos (1940–67). Cuban guerrilla (Main Force). An agricultural worker. Member of the 26 July Movement. Joined the Rebel Army and fought with Che

Guevara in Cuba and then in the Congo. Was his bodyguard and accompanied him abroad when Che Guevara was minister for industry. Fell in combat at Piray on 26 June 1967.

Tumaini: see Tuma.

Urbano: Tamayo Nuñez, Urbano (1941–). Cuban guerrilla (Main Force). Peasant from the Sierra Maestra. Served in the Rebel Army with Che Guevara's column. After the triumph of the Revolution he was Che Guevara's adjutant and travelled with him abroad. Survived the battle of Quebrada del Yuro. Reached Cuba in 1968. Later went on internationalist missions to Angola and Nicaragua. Lives in Cuba.

Vallegrandino, Tomás Rosales. Bolivian. Detained, tortured and hanged in the jail at Camiri.

Víctor: Condorí Vargas, Casildo (1941–67). Bolivian guerrilla (Rearguard). Baker and driver. Killed in action on 2 June 1967 at Peñon Colorado, Bella Vista.

Vilo: see Joaquín.

Walter: Arancibia Ayala, Walter (1941–67). Bolivian guerrilla (Rearguard). National leader of the Bolivian Communist Youth. Studied in Cuba. Fell at Puerto Mauricio on 31 August 1967.

Willi/Willy/Wyly: Cuba Sarabia, Simón (1932–67). Bolivian guerrilla (Main Force). Miner from Oruro and leader of the miners' union in Huanuni. Member of the Communist Party of Bolivia. Member of Moisés Guevara's group. Captured with Che Guevara at Quebrada del Yuro and assassinated at La Higuera on 9 October 1967.

Zamora, Oscar (1934–). Leader of the group that split from the Communist Party of Bolivia in 1965, which had Maoist political orientation. Refused to support Che Guevara's guerrillas in 1966–7.

Chronology

1928
14 June: Ernesto Guevara de la Serna is born in the port city of Rosario, Province of Santa Fe, Argentina, to an upper middle-class family of Spanish and Irish origin. He will be the eldest of five children. Ernesto spends the first 18 months of his life in Puerto Caraguatay, in the northern province of Misiones, where his parents have a *maté* plantation. He lives in contact with the wild tropical nature of the region.

1930
When he is two years old, Ernesto is diagnosed as suffering from asthma – a condition that will be with him all his life.

1933
The Guevaras move to Córdoba in search of a healthier climate for their asthmatic son. Ernesto attends primary school irregularly due to his asthma. His mother teaches him the school syllabus at home, as well as French, in which he will be fluent all his life.

1939
The Second World War breaks out in Europe. Argentina declares its neutrality. During the war Argentina sold iron to the Axis and beef to Britain, thus emerging from the conflict a rich and prosperous nation.

1945

General Juan Domingo Perón becomes President of Argentina with a six-year mandate.

Argentina declares war on Germany and Japan one month before the German capitulation. The USA drops atomic bombs on Hiroshima and Nagasaki.

1946

The Guevaras establish themselves in Buenos Aires. Ernesto enrols in the Medical Faculty of the University of Buenos Aires.

1950

Ernesto fits his bicycle with a small motor and goes on a trip to the provinces of north-west Argentina during the winter holidays. He covers 4,700 kilometres.

1951

Ernesto travels twice on board Argentine merchant ships from the southern port of Comodoro Rivadavia to Brazil, Venezuela and Trinidad as a male nurse.

In Bolivia, a right-wing military junta annuls the result of the elections and takes over power. Bolivian miners launch a strike as well as street protests.

1952

Ernesto goes on a trip through Latin America with his friend Alberto Granado. Visits Chile, Peru, Colombia, Venezuela and Miami. They work in a leper colony in Peru.

General Juan Domingo Perón is re-elected in Argentina.

Fulgencio Batista carries out a *coup d'état* in Cuba.

In Bolivia, there is a revolutionary upsurge that arms the people's militias (mainly peasants and miners), which replace the armed forces. Although the tin mines are nationalised, trade unions are legalised, land reform is initiated and the indigenous majority is enfranchised, the political system is not changed and continues to fail to represent vast sectors of the population, suffering constant upheaval and coups throughout the years.

1953
Ernesto receives his medical degree from the University of Buenos Aires.

He is conscripted for national military service but declared physically unfit for active duty and released.

He leaves Buenos Aires by train and goes on his second trip through Latin America.

Visits Bolivia, where he observes the impact of the 1952 revolution.

Travels to Guatemala where Jacobo Arbenz is the constitutionally elected president.

26 July: Fidel Castro leads an attack on the Moncada Barracks in Santiago de Cuba. The attack fails; Castro and other survivors are captured and imprisoned.

1954
January–June: In Guatemala Guevara does odd jobs, studies Marx and meets several Cuban revolutionaries, who are veterans of the attack on the Moncada Barracks. Witnesses the invasion of Guatemala by CIA-backed forces and the downfall of President Arbenz, who refuses to arm the population. Takes refuge in the Argentine Embassy.

21 September: Guevara leaves Guatemala and arrives in Mexico City where he works as a doctor at the Central Hospital.

1955
In Mexico Guevara meets Fidel Castro who has been released from prison in Cuba.

Marries Peruvian economist Hilda Gadea and his first daughter Hilda Beatriz is born.

Trains as a guerrilla with Castro and his men who are preparing to return to Cuba to launch a guerrilla war.

He is nicknamed Che by his Cuban friends, an expression then used throughout Latin America to refer to the people of Argentina.

In Argentina General Juan Domingo Perón is ousted from power by a military coup.

1956
Gamal Abdel Nasser of the United Arab Republic (Egypt) nationalises the British and French-owned Suez Canal despite the opposition of combined Israeli, British and French forces.

25 November: Guevara leaves from the Mexican port of Tuxpan for Cuba on board the *Granma* with Fidel Castro and 80 Cuban guerrillas and arrives at Las Coloradas in Oriente Province.

5 December: The rebels are surprised by government troops at Alegría de Pío and dispersed. Guevara is wounded.

20 December: Guevara and his group manage to reunite with Fidel Castro and his men. Most of the invading force have been captured and killed. Castro's guerrillas number two dozen.

1957
January–May: First Rebel Army victories at La Plata, Arroyo del Infierno, Palma Mocha and El Uvero.

July: Guevara is promoted to *comandante* and put in charge of the Columna Cuatro, to disguise the fact that there are only two.

Arturo Frondizi wins the presidential elections in Argentina and takes over from the military junta.

1958
24 May: In Cuba Batista launches a military offensive against the Rebel Army in the Sierra Maestra.

July: Rebel Army victory at El Jigüe.

16 October: Guevara and his column arrive at the Escambray Mountains to consolidate the rebel forces.

December: Guevara captures strategic locations in the Province of Las Villas in central Cuba.

28 December: The Rebel forces commence the decisive battle for Santa Clara, the capital of Las Villas.

1959

1 January: Santa Clara falls to the Rebel Army column under Guevara. Fulgencio Batista flees to Miami.

2 January: Guevara enters Havana at the head of his troops and claims it for the Revolution. He establishes himself at La Cabaña fortress and presides over the summary trials of the enemies of the Revolution.

9 February: Guevara is made a Cuban citizen in recognition for his contribution to the Revolution.

26 July: Fidel Castro becomes prime minister.

2 June: Guevara and Hilda Gadea have divorced amicably and Guevara marries Aleida March, his assistant during the military campaign. They will have two sons and two daughters.

Guevara goes on a fifteen-day visit to Nasser's United Arab Republic and the Suez Canal. The purpose of the trip is to study the UAR's methods of land reform.

Visits India and holds talks with Pandit Nehru.

Visits Burma, Thailand, Japan, Indonesia, Ceylon, Pakistan, Yugoslavia, Sudan, Italy, Spain and Morocco, meeting heads of state while acting as roving ambassador for the Cuban Revolution. He signs several commercial, technical and cultural agreements.

Guevara is appointed director of industries for the National Institute of Agrarian Reform.

Guevara is appointed governor of the National Bank of Cuba and takes up the study of higher mathematics for the next three years.

1960

First declaration of Havana: Fidel Castro refers to 'Our America, the America that Bolívar, Hidalgo, Juárez, San Martín, O'Higgins, Tiradentes, Sucre and Martí wished to see free'.

Guevara publishes his book *Guerrilla Warfare – A Method* which will become the handbook for guerrilla movements all over the world.

President Eisenhower orders the CIA to begin the preparation of Cuban exiles to invade the island.

Cuba and the Soviet Union establish diplomatic relations.

The Revolutionary Government nationalises the refineries of Texaco, Shell and Esso as a result of their refusal to refine oil from the USSR.

President Eisenhower reduces by 700,000 tons the amount of sugar the US will purchase from Cuba.

The USSR announces that it will purchase the Cuban sugar the USA refuses to buy.

Castro nationalises major US companies and foreign banks in Cuba as well as 382 large Cuban industries.

USA declares partial embargo against trading with Cuba.

In response to the US partial trade embargo, Guevara makes his first visit to the socialist countries at the head of a Cuban delegation: he visits the USSR, the German Democratic Republic, Czechoslovakia, China and the People's Democratic Republic of Korea.

1961

In January, Patrice Lumumba, the first prime minister of the Republic of Congo, newly independent from Belgium, is deposed in a US-backed coup and assassinated.

USA breaks diplomatic relations with Cuba.

Guevara is appointed minister for industries.

President Kennedy abolishes Cuba's sugar quota.

1,500 exiled Cubans invade the Bay of Pigs and are routed by Cuban troops led by Fidel Castro. Guevara commands the troops at Pinar del Río. The invaders surrender at Playa Girón.

Guevara attends the Economic Summit of the Organisation of American States in Punta del Este, Uruguay, as head of the Cuban delegation and denounces the US Alliance for Progress. He then crosses over to Argentina secretly for a private visit to President Arturo Frondizi.

Guevara visits Brazil and is decorated by President Janio Quadros.

Cuba completes first year of nation-wide literacy campaign.

1962

Algeria installs a revolutionary government, having won its independence from France after a long and bloody liberation struggle.

29 March: In Argentina the military oust President Arturo Frondizi and install his vice-president in his place when they discover that he has met with Che Guevara in his presidential residence in the outskirts of Buenos Aires.

The Organisation of American States votes to expel Cuba.

President Kennedy orders total embargo on trade with Cuba.

27 August–7 September: Guevara visits the USSR for the second time at the head of an economic delegation.

President Kennedy imposes naval blockade on Cuba and threatens the USSR with nuclear war as a result of Cuba's acquisition of missiles with nuclear warheads capable of attacking the USA. Soviet premier Khrushchev agrees to remove missiles from Cuba in exchange for Kennedy's pledge not to invade Cuba.

1963

The Chinese Communist Party split Communist ideology, and gradually the world Communist parties divide between 'Moscovites' and 'Pekinistas'.

In May an attempt to establish a guerrilla movement in Peru to fight against the US-backed military dictatorship fails and its leader Javier Heraud is killed.

Guevara attends the ceremonies commemorating the first

anniversary of Algerian independence and sets down the basis for good relations with President Ahmed Ben Bella. Attends International Seminar on Planning in Algiers.

In Cuba the Second Agrarian Reform law is drafted.

Guevara publishes his *Reminiscences of the Cuban Revolutionary War.*

Dr Arturo Illia wins the elections in Argentina.

1964

In Brazil a US-backed military coup overthrows the government of João Goulart and a period of bloodletting and struggle begins.

Colombia sees the formation of two subversive groups, the Revolutionary Armed Forces of Columbia (FARC) and the National Liberation Army (ELN). The armed struggle between the FARC and the ELN against the government of Colombia and later the right-wing paramilitaries will last over 40 years.

The insurrection started by Jorge Ricardo Masetti in Salta, northern Argentina – an initiative which had the blessing of Che Guevara and the support of both Cubans and Bolivians – is routed and Masetti is killed in combat.

Guevara travels to Geneva to speak before the UNCTAD conference.

Travels to Algeria via Prague to meet up with President Ben Bella and returns to Havana.

Visits the Soviet Union for the celebration of the 47th anniversary of the October Revolution. Meets Ho Chi Minh. Addresses the UN General Assembly in New York.

Travels to Algeria via Canada and Ireland, to meet with President Ben Bella. During a three-month trip, he visits President Modibo Keita of Mali and then travels to Dahomey. Cuba and Bolivia break off diplomatic relations.

1965

Guevara visits President Massemba-Debat in Congo-

Brazzaville and President Sekou-Touré in Guinea. He has several meetings with President Nkrumah of Ghana in Accra.

Travels to Algeria. Makes a stop-over in Paris and travels to Tanzania on an official visit.

Travels to Egypt to meet President Nasser and returns to Algiers for the Second Seminar of the Organisation of Afro-Asian Solidarity.

Returns to Egypt and spends time with President Nasser.

14 March: Returns to Cuba and disappears from public life to train secretly for the Congo.

April: Departs from Cuba at the head of a group of Cuban guerrillas for an internationalist mission in the Congo, which is to join forces with Laurent Kabila. He leaves his letter of resignation with Fidel Castro.

In June the Revolutionary Government of Ben Bella of Algeria is overthrown in a military coup.

1 October: The Communist Party of Cuba is officially launched.

3 October: Fidel Castro reads Guevara's farewell letter.

December: After the failure of the Congo campaign Guevara returns to Cuba secretly.

23,000 US troops invade Santo Domingo, in the Dominican Republic, in support of dictator Rafael Leonidas Trujillo.

Peru sees the formation of *focos* that sustain action for six months under saturation bombing with napalm and high explosives. The ELN of Peru, under Héctor Bejar, then begins action in La Convención, which ends in defeat in December.

1966

Since 1961 in Venezuela groups of students and even dissident Army officers have begun to form *focos* to prepare for armed struggle but by 1966 the armed offensive, led by Douglas Bravo, has failed as the Communist Party abandoned the guerrillas operating in the mountains.

3–14 January: The Tricontinental Conference of Solidarity of the Peoples of Asia, Africa and Latin America is held in Havana and Cuba commits itself to support continental revolution.

July: In secret, Guevara selects and trains a guerrilla group for the mission in Bolivia in Pinar del Río province.

4 November: Guevara arrives in Bolivia in disguise and with a false Uruguayan passport to start the insurgency.

7 November: He arrives at the site of his Bolivian camp at Ñacahuasu where he is joined by 17 Cubans and several Bolivian recruits.

In Argentina, General Juan Carlos Onganía puts an end to the democratic government of Dr Arturo Illia, in a bloodless coup.

1967

23 March: First successful guerrilla military action against Bolivian Army column.

16 April: Guevara's message to the Tricontinental, in which he calls for 'two, three, many Vietnams', is published.

31 July–10 August: The Organisation of Latin American Solidarity (OLAS) holds its conference in Havana. Guevara is made honorary chairman in his absence.

May–October: Massive force of Bolivian and US troops close in on Guevara's guerrillas who suffer heavy losses.

8 October: Guevara is wounded, captured and shot on 9 October.

18 October: Castro confirms that Guevara is dead and declares three days of official mourning. He delivers the memorial speech in the Plaza de la Revolución before a crowd of thousands.

1997

The remains of Ernesto Che Guevara, and his comrades in arms Carlos Coello (Tuma), Alberto Fernández Montes de Oca (Pacho), René Martínez Tamayo (Arturo), Orlando

Pantoja Tamayo (Antonio) Simón Cuba Sarabia (Willi) and
Juan Pablo Chang Navarro (Chino) are dug up in Bolivia and
flown to Cuba.

Guevara and his comrades are buried with full military
honours in the city of Santa Clara, in the province of Las
Villas, where Guevara won the decisive battle of the Cuban
Revolution.

1998

The remains of the following comrades in arms of Ernesto
Che Guevara are found in Bolivia and flown to Cuba to be
buried in Santa Clara with full military honours: Haydée
Tamara Bunke Bider (Tania), Octavio de la Concepción y de
la Pedraja (Moro), Manuel Hernández Osorio (Miguel),
Francisco Huanca Flores (Pablito), Edilberto Lucio Galván
(Eustaquio), Julio Luis Mendez Korne (Ñato), Roberto Peredo
Leigue (Coco), Aniceto Reinaga Gordillo (Aniceto), Mario
Gutiérrez Ardaya (Julio) and Jaime Arana Campero (Chapaco).

1999

The remains of the following comrades in arms of Ernesto
Che Guevara are found in Bolivia and flown to Cuba to be
buried in Santa Clara with full military honours: Juan Vitalio
Acuña (Joaquín), Gustavo Machín Hoed de Beche (Alejandro),
Israel Reyes Zayas (Braulio), Walter Arancibia Ayala (Walter),
Freddy Maymura Hurtado (Ernesto), Moisés Guevara
Rodríguez (Moisés) and Apolinar Aquino Quispe (Polo).

2000

The remains of the following comrades in arms of Ernesto
Che Guevara are found in Bolivia and flown to Cuba to be
buried in Santa Clara with full military honours: Antonio
Sánchez Díaz (Marcos), José María Martínez Tamayo
(Ricardo), Eliseo Reyes Rodríguez (Rolando), Casildo
Condorí Vargas (Víctor), Serapio Aquino Tudela (Serapio)
and Restituto José Cabrera (Negro).